I0793200

IMAGES
of America

JAMAICA

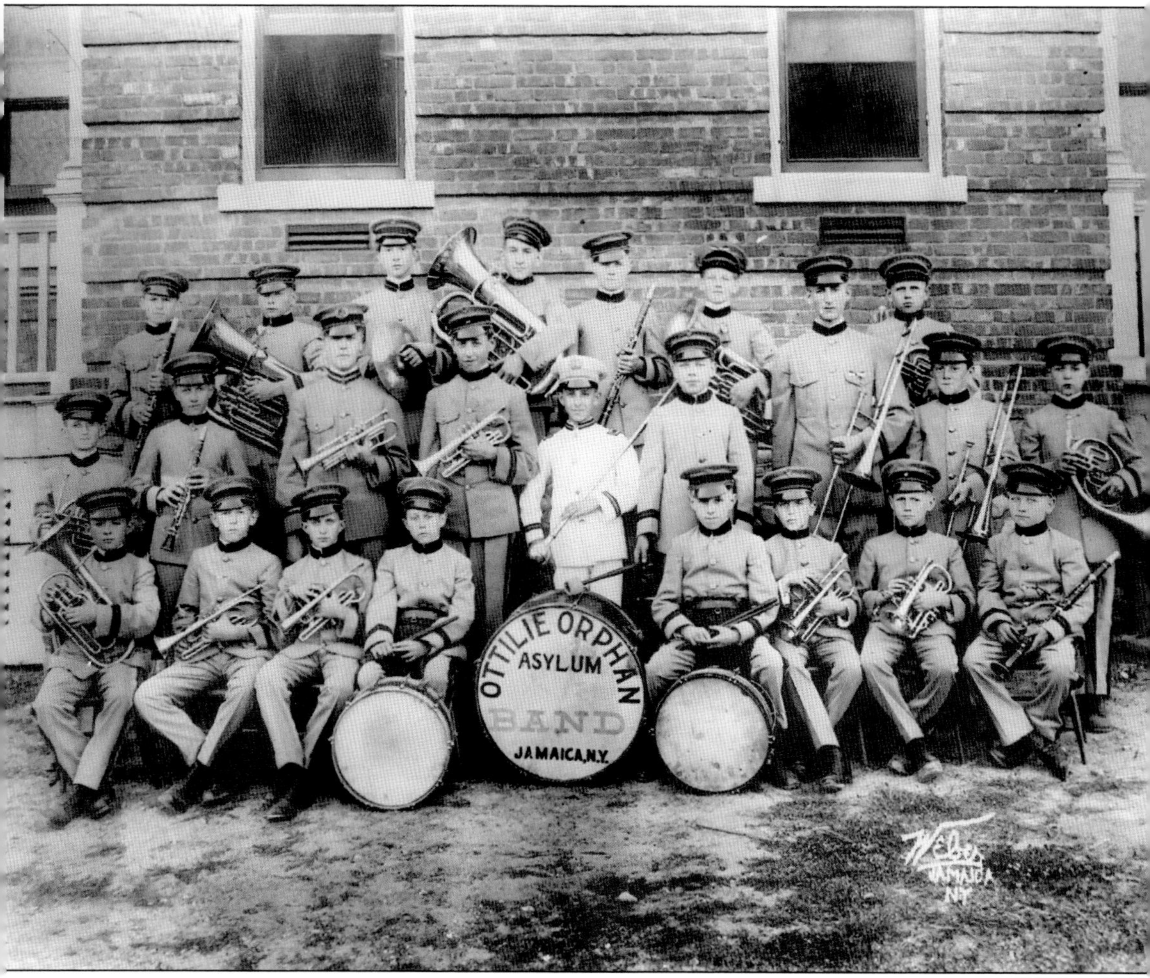

This 1906 photograph of the Ottilie Orphan Asylum Band of Jamaica is by noted Queens photographer Frederick Weber. (Archives at Queens Library, Frederick Weber Photographs.)

On the Cover: This May 1915 photograph was taken by well-known photographer Frederick Weber. The view is of Jamaica Avenue, looking south on Washington Street (160th Street). (Archives at Queens Library, Frederick Weber Photographs.)

IMAGES
of America

JAMAICA

Carl Ballenas with the Aquinas Honor Society of
the Immaculate Conception School

ARCADIA
PUBLISHING

ISBN 978-0-7385-7426-4

Published by Arcadia Publishing
Charleston, South Carolina

Printed in the United States of America

Library of Congress Control Number: 2010934815

For all general information, please contact Arcadia Publishing:
Telephone 843-853-2070
Fax 843-853-0044
E-mail sales@arcadiapublishing.com
For customer service and orders:
Toll-Free 1-888-313-2665

Visit us on the Internet at www.arcadiapublishing.com

We dedicate this book to Dr. and Mrs. Lawrence Waterhouse and family and the Alive in Hope Foundation, both instrumental in nurturing Immaculate Conception School and the Aquinas Honor Society. (Photographer Pearl Gabel.)

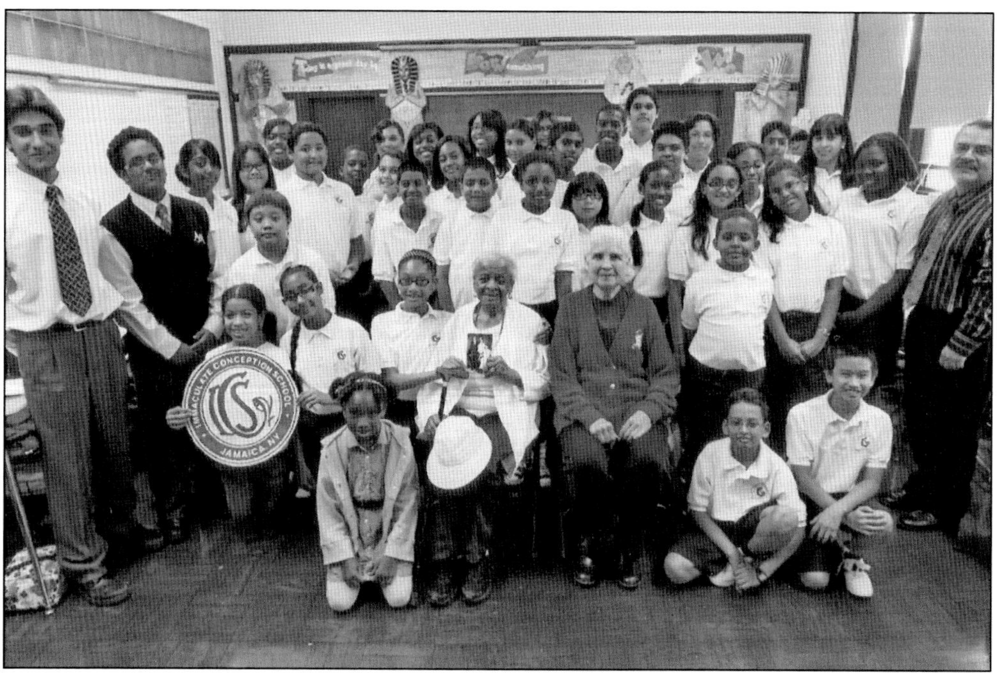

Contents

ACKNOWLEDGMENTS

The authors are Carl Ballenas, Varun Arjoonsingh, Brandon Arjun, Kirkland Arjun, Tobi Ayeni, Alyssa Balkarran, Amrit Singh Bhatti, Valerie Bresier, Sarika Tori Dasraj, Neela Dookhie, Tahina Felisca, Dominique Gay, Gabrielle Hollant, Amanda Lallemand, Lia Lewis, Amne Madi, Krystal Madrinan, Nandita Mathura, Cliff Mayard, Alexis McNeill, Patrick Menchaca, Derek Netto, Jessica Netto, Tarnjot Parhar, Bri'Elle Price, Abigail Rafael, Kimberly Ramcharitar, Nalisha Rampersaud, Jean-Philippe Rancy, Tarah-Anne Rancy, Sarah E. Rodriguez, Jewel Sabordo, Jexel Sabordo, Alex Samaroo, Orlando Santiago, Tracy Singh, Kemraj Sobhai, Aniyah Smith, Gaurav T. Srivastava, Nicholas Strickland, Mat Tupas, and Julio Ulloa Jr.

We have encountered individuals and institutions that have offered their invaluable services, such as the families of the authors, the Immaculate Conception School faculty and staff, Judith Todman and Eric Huber of the Long Island Room, Joseph Coen of the RC Diocese of Brooklyn Archives, Tim Garcia, William Krooss, Bonnie Dixon and the Maple Grove Cemetery Association, Kate Ludlum, Carol Scherick, St. John's University Archives, Carlisle Towery and the Greater Jamaica Development Corporation, Sejan Yun, Ron Marzlak, Helene and Bob Stonehill, Nanette Deakin Spector, Gladys Ripley, Martha Taylor, Susie J. Tanenbaum, Tashanie Narain, Philippe Woolley and family, Enyi Lu, Kem Gray, Lucy Ballenas, Dr. Carlos Ballenas, the Dr. Edgar Ballenas family, and the Dr. Nancy Baxter Ballenas family. A special note of gratitude to MTB. Photographs in this book belong to the private collection of the author, unless otherwise noted.

Introduction

Imagine being a New York City elementary school student and having the opportunity to research, write, and publish a book documenting the history of your community. This is exactly what the members of the Aquinas Honor Society at the Immaculate Conception School in Jamaica Estates have done—twice.

With the expert guidance of teacher and historian Carl Ballenas, these academically gifted students produced Images of America: *Jamaica Estates*, Arcadia Publishing. I am proud to have been among the first to acquire a copy of that remarkable book. It was so well received, and the students had accumulated so much research that they were inspired to write a second volume about the mother village of Jamaica. It is my honor to provide the Introduction to Images of America: *Jamaica*.

This volume offers astounding facts dating back thousands of years to the last great glacial period, when melting glaciers shaped the topography of what we now call Queens. It acquaints readers with 13 tribes of indigenous people who settled along a trail that eventually became Jamaica Avenue. Jamaica's historical legacy goes back 350 years and includes the arrival of Dutch and British settlers, the participation of the Jamaica minutemen in the Revolutionary War, and a visit from Pres. George Washington that is described in his personal diary. References cover the King Manor House along with other treasured historic sites and reveal how Jamaica became the industrious commercial area and the bustling transportation hub that we know today. This information is accompanied by 200 vintage and rare photographs, many of which have never before been seen by the public.

Being an educator by training, I am certain that the students involved in this extraordinary project have gained a set of critical skills and developed a sense of community that will strengthen them for the rest of their lives. Not surprisingly, these members of the Aquinas Honor Society are involved in many other community service projects as well. They were awarded foundation grants to erect the first historical plaque in Jamaica Estates, replaced a bronze bust of Jacob Riis that had gone missing for almost 50 years, and created a stained-glass memorial window to mark the events of September 11, 2001. In years to come, I expect to see these students emerging as the thoughtful and confident leaders of our borough and city.

As your borough president, I consider it a unique privilege to represent Queens, the most multiethnic county in the United States, and quite possibly in the world. Jamaica is a vibrant part of this diversity, and Images of America: *Jamaica* assures us that its future potential is great. To the students of the Immaculate Conception School in Jamaica Estates: you have succeeded in uncovering the rich history of your community, capturing the spirit of a bygone era, and demonstrating the promise of your generation. On behalf of the 2.3 million residents of Queens, I applaud you, and I thank you.

—Helen M. Marshall
Queens Borough President

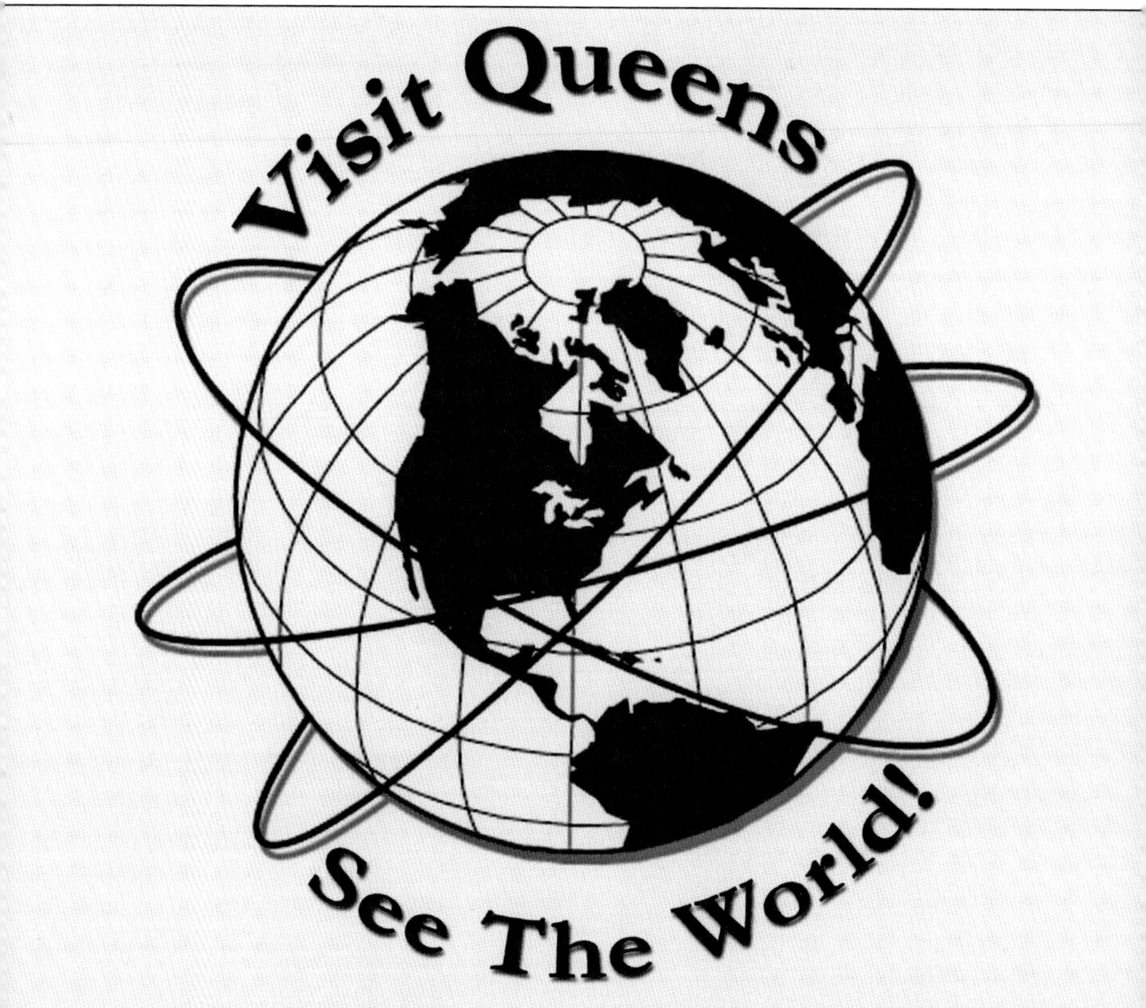

Pictured is one of the Queens borough president's logos. According to the New York City comptroller, "Well-known for its diverse population—some 138 languages are spoken in the Borough of Queens." (From the office of Borough Pres. Helen M. Marshall; Dominick Totino Photography.)

One

From the Beginning

Influenced by the Past

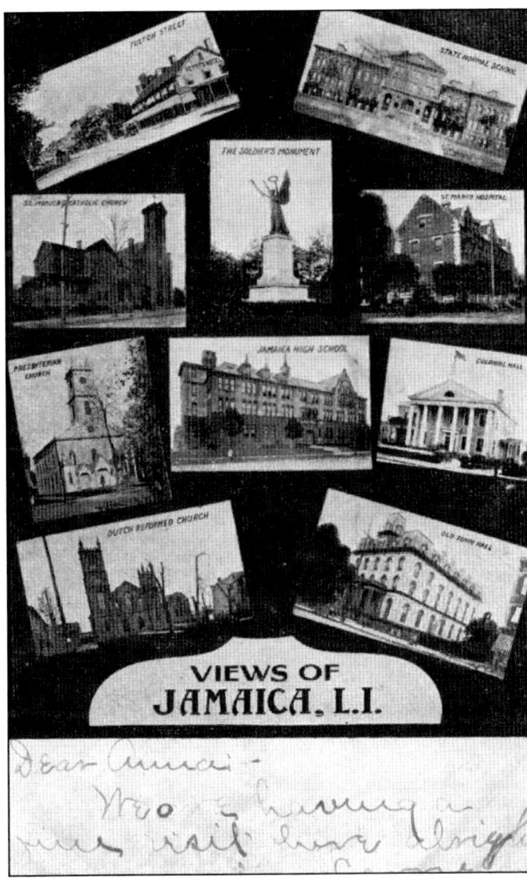

Jamaica is rich in history and known as the heart of the borough of Queens. It is a hub of commerce, transportation, education, religion, history, public services, and cultural resources with a treasure trove of designated landmarks: King Manor, Grace Church, St. Monica's Church, Dutch Reformed Church, Valencia Theater, Sidewalk Clock, La Casina, J. Kurtz Building, The Register, Jamaica Savings Bank, Jamaica High School, and Prospect Cemetery.

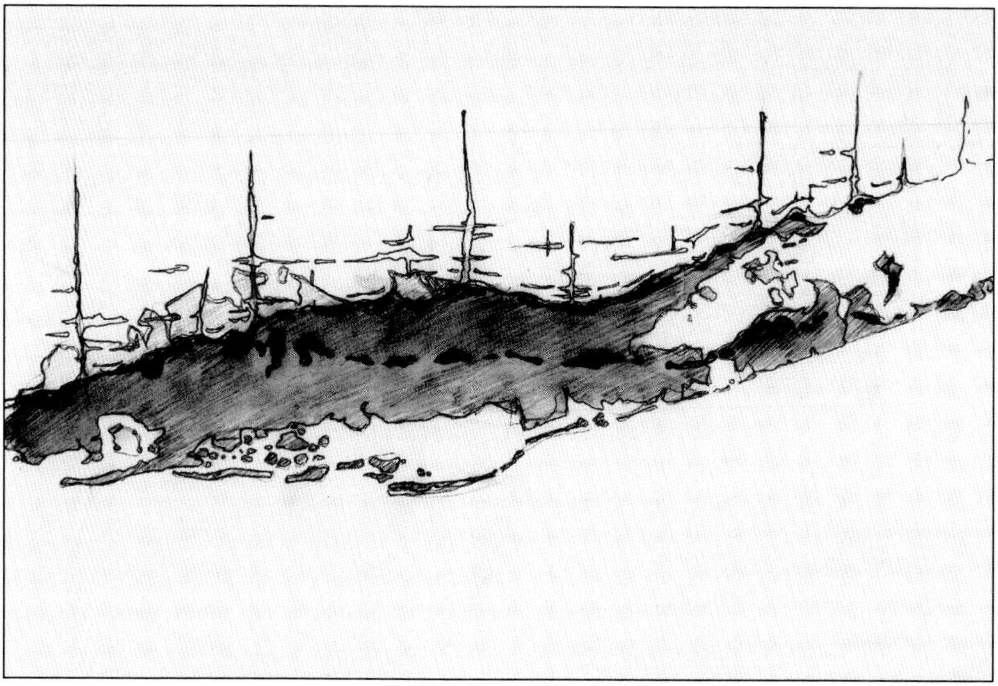

The period of glacial advance 18,000 years ago saw mile-high glaciers that—picking up soil, rocks, and boulders—created the backbone of Long Island. When glaciers stopped advancing and melted, the materials trapped were deposited at the glacier's edge and formed the hilly terminal moraine. The washout of water leveled the land all the way to Jamaica Bay. Jamaica is located at the foot of the moraine. (Artwork by Robert Baxter.)

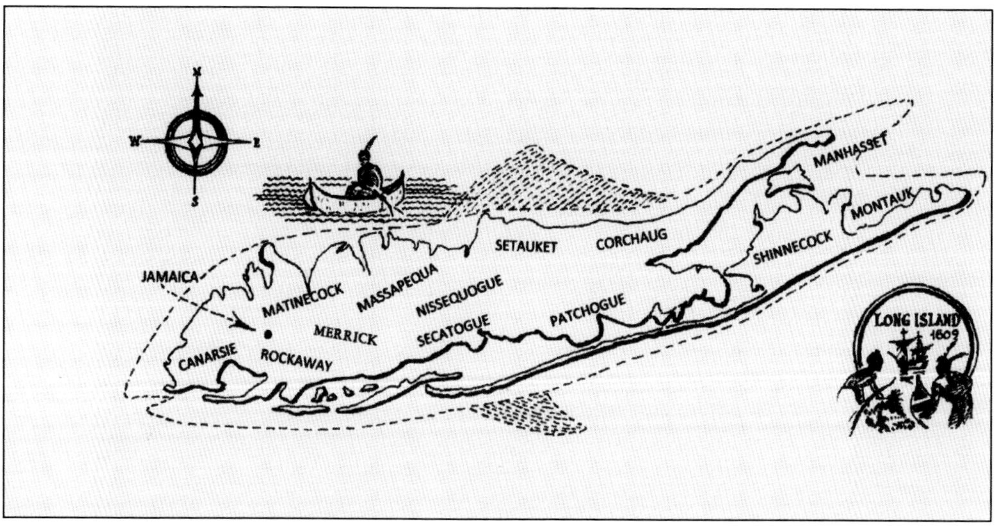

Tribes of indigenous people living on Long Island, which had the shape of a fish, called it *Paumanok*, meaning "the island that pays tribute." Powerful tribes in the surrounding areas forced the relatively peaceful Long Islanders to give tributes to avoid attacks. The people lived as hunters and fishermen, but some were farmers raising beans and corn. Animals found there included deer, bear, raccoon, turkey, quail, partridge, beaver, and duck.

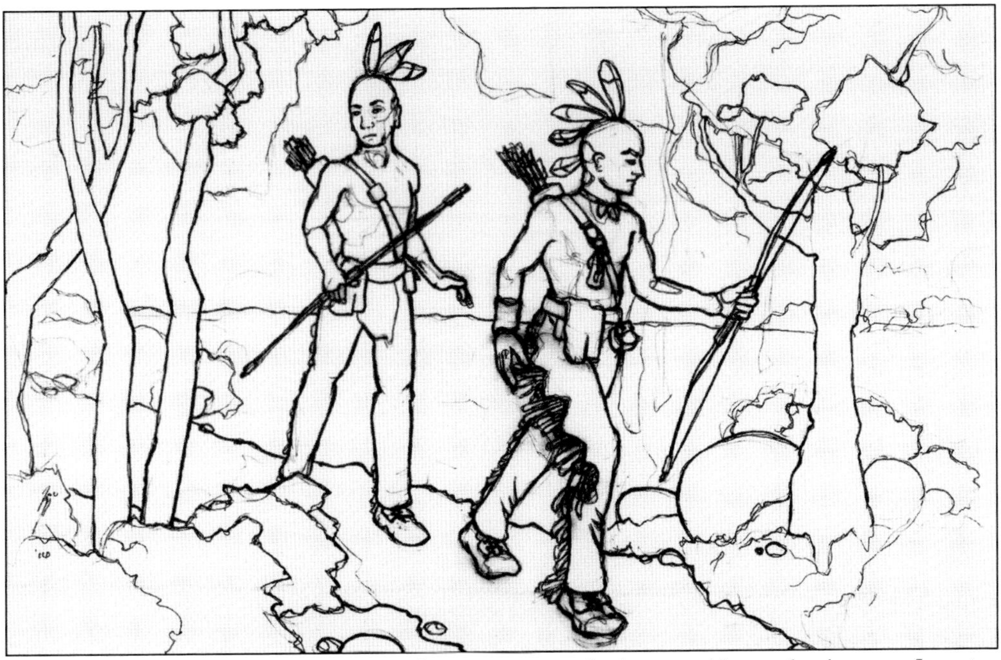

Indigenous people on Long Island used an ancient path that would one day become Jamaica Avenue. Native Americans from as far away as the Ohio River and Great Lakes used the trail to trade skins and furs for wampum, polished oblong shells strung on leather strings to form necklaces and belts. George Washington noted in his diary on April 20, 1790, "Jamaica Road is more sandy and appears to have less strength, but still good and productive." (Artwork by Robert Baxter.)

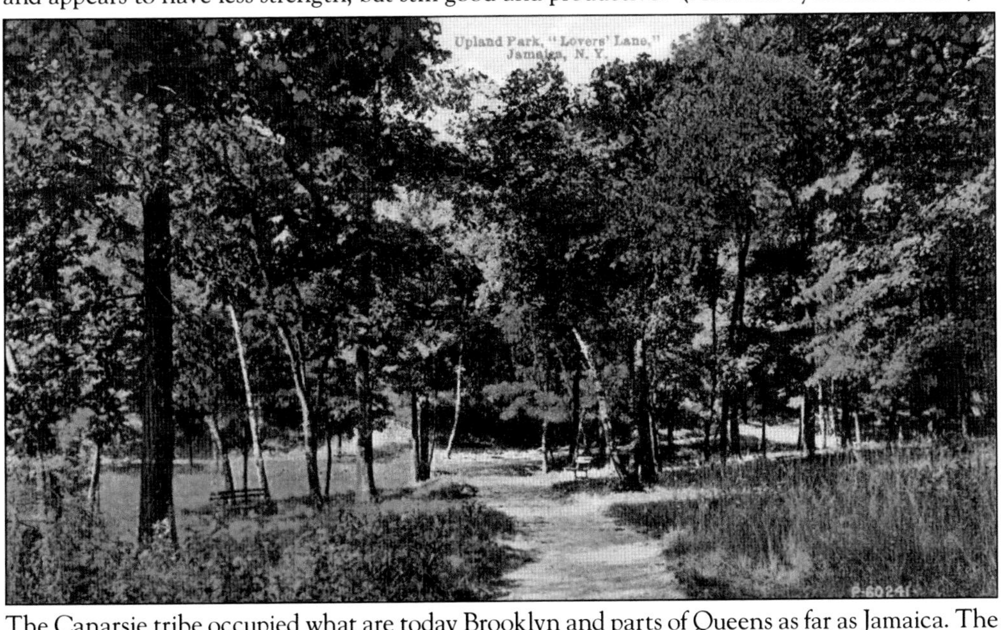

The Canarsie tribe occupied what are today Brooklyn and parts of Queens as far as Jamaica. The Rockaway tribe occupied what would become Hempstead, Rockaway, and parts of Jamaica and Elmhurst. The Native Americans of the island were often tall, muscular, and agile, with straight hair and a reddish-brown complexion. Their language was Algonquin. Transportation was by foot or in canoes along the waters.

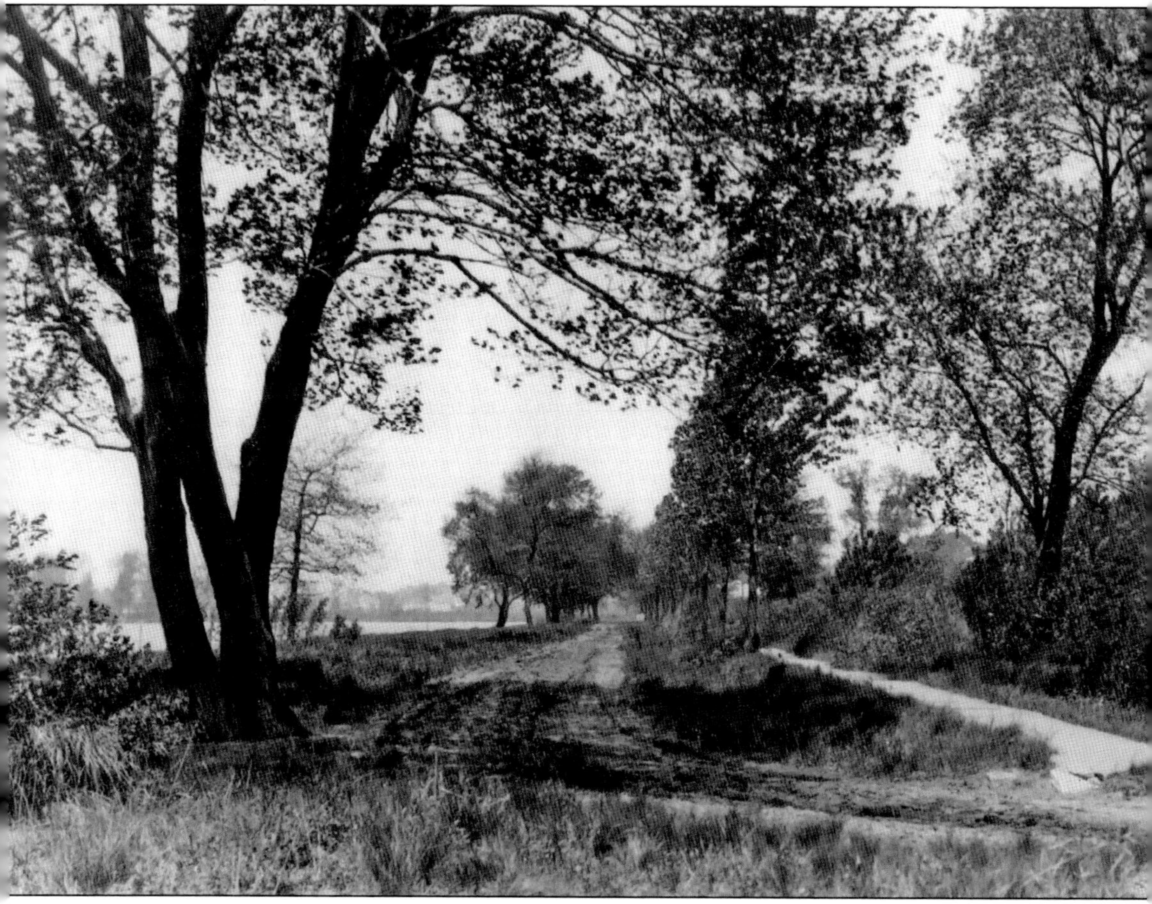

In colonial times, settlers from Connecticut came to Long Island to establish a colony. They stayed in the town of Hempstead until they paid the Native Americans two guns, a coat, and some gunpowder for a tract of land "beginning at a great swamp (Beaver Pond) on ye west side and running westward to a river." This area was located north of today's Baisley Pond (pictured). This purchase was recorded in the oldest known town document, a deed with the Native Americans, dated September 13, 1655. The following petitioned Gov. Peter Stuyvesant for permission to settle this Dutch land: Robert Jackson, Nicholas Tanner, Nathaniel Denton, Richard Everitt, Rodger Linas, Daniel Denton, John Eazar, Abraham Smith, Thomas Ireland, Thomas Carle, Edward Sprag, John Rhoades, Andrew Messenger, and Samuel Matthews. Stuyvesant replied, "The Directors and Council . . . do consent that the petitioners may begin a new town according to their plan between the land called by us Canaresse and the town of Heemsteede. Done at Fort Aamsterdam, in New Netherland, March 21st 1656. PETER STUYVESANT." Thus, the town of Jamaica was founded. (Q Gardens Gallery.)

In 1656, the settlers started their community near Beaver Pond, just south of what is present-day Jamaica Avenue and Parsons Boulevard. In 1660, Governor Stuyvesant, illustrated here, gave the settlers a more formal and extensive patent in which the town was incorporated with the Dutch name Rusdorp, which means "quiet village." It never caught on among the early inhabitants who referred to their town as either Canorasset or Crawford.

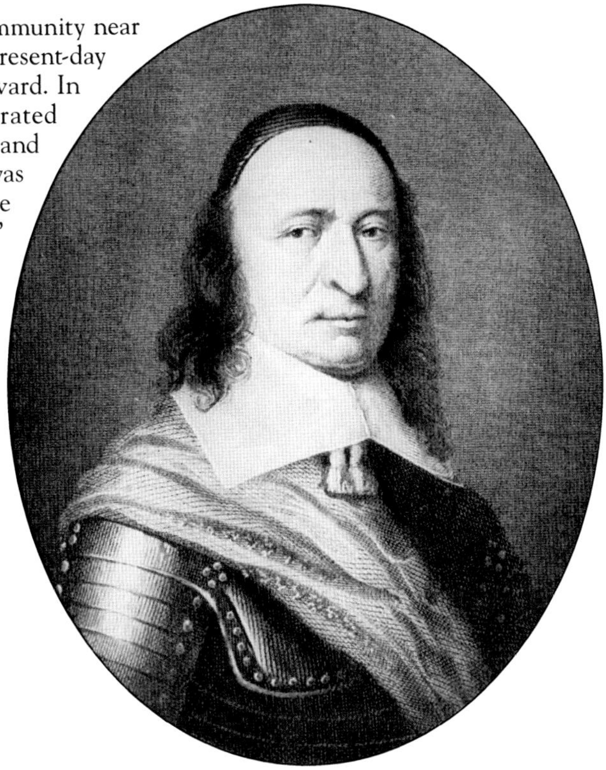

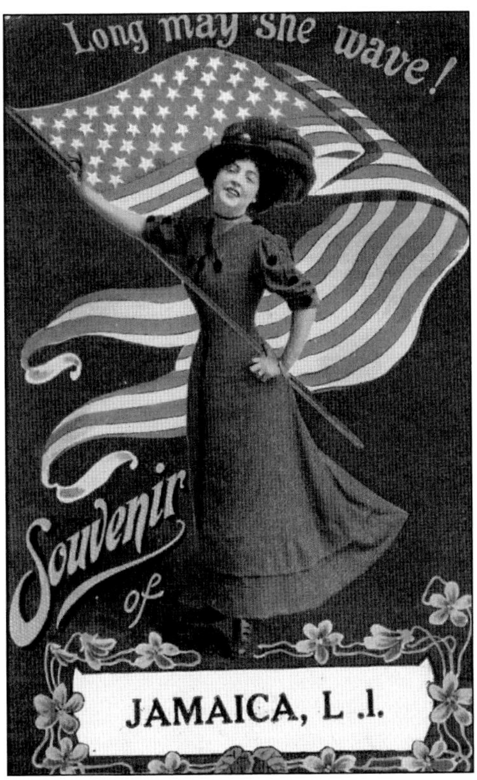

When New Amsterdam was conquered by the English in 1664, it became known as New York. The name of the Long Island settlement was changed to Jamaica. It was originally spelled Jameco, Jemeco, or, as it appears in town records, Yemacah, from a word used by the early indigenous people to describe the location as a "place of the beavers," which abounded on the land.

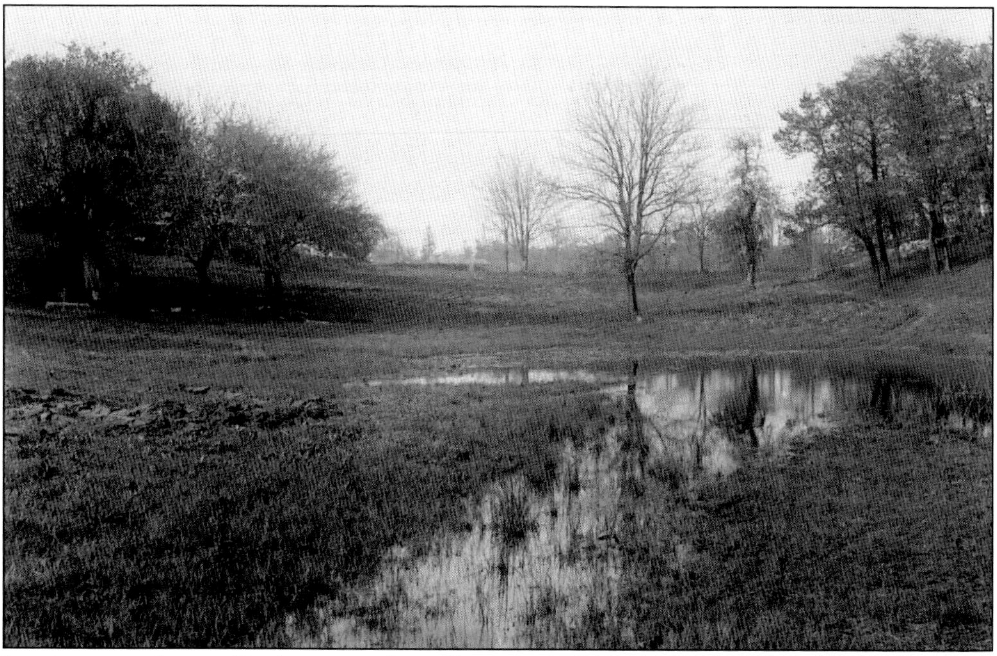

Jamaica was a cluster of log houses in the wilderness, roofed with thatches from the marshes. Most had two rooms below and lofts above for sleeping, as well as a lean-to kitchen. Food was mostly venison and fish, and dinner was often boiled Indian pudding, corn mixed with beans, and a slice of salted venison with boiled cabbages, baked or boiled pumpkin, and cider or home-brewed beer. (Archives at Queens Library, George Winans Collection.)

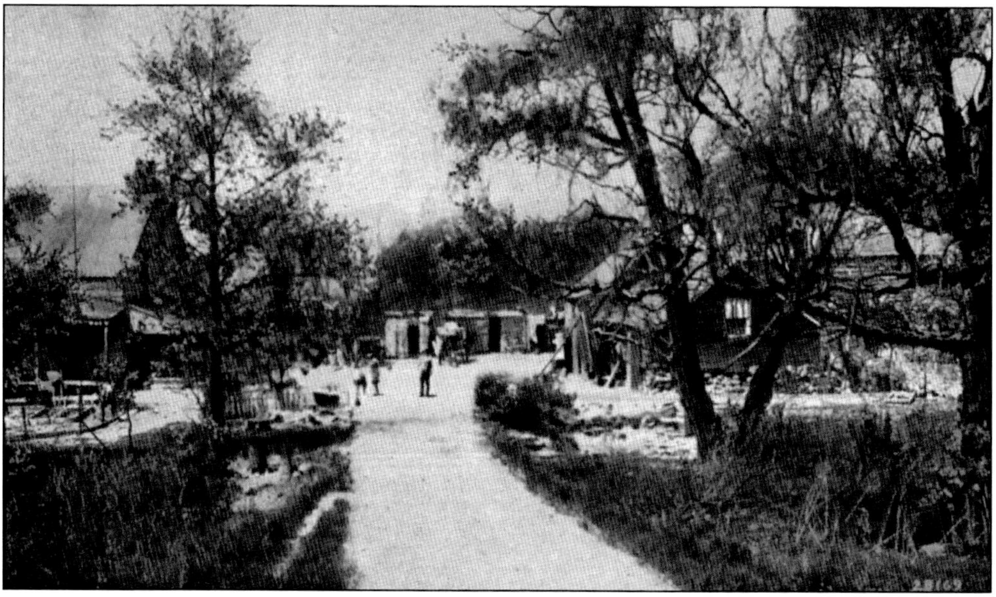

The early pioneers arose before dawn, breakfasted, had family worship, and went early into the fields. Agricultural implements included a musket for use against a possible wolf or bear, or in the event of a deer being discovered during their labors. The duties of the women were more demanding. Whether they were sick or well, the baking, cooking, washing, ironing, and clothes making and mending had to be done.

In the earliest cemetery document, the town agreed in 1668 with John Wascot to fence the burying place, 10 rods square with a sufficient five-rail fence, and promised him £4 in payment for his pains and labor. It is the oldest family burial ground in Queens and one of the oldest in New York City. Revolutionary War soldiers are buried here, along with many famous colonial families.

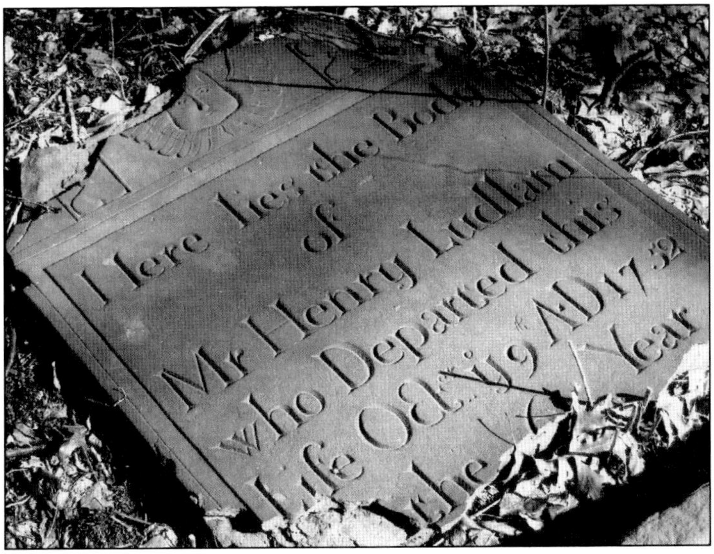

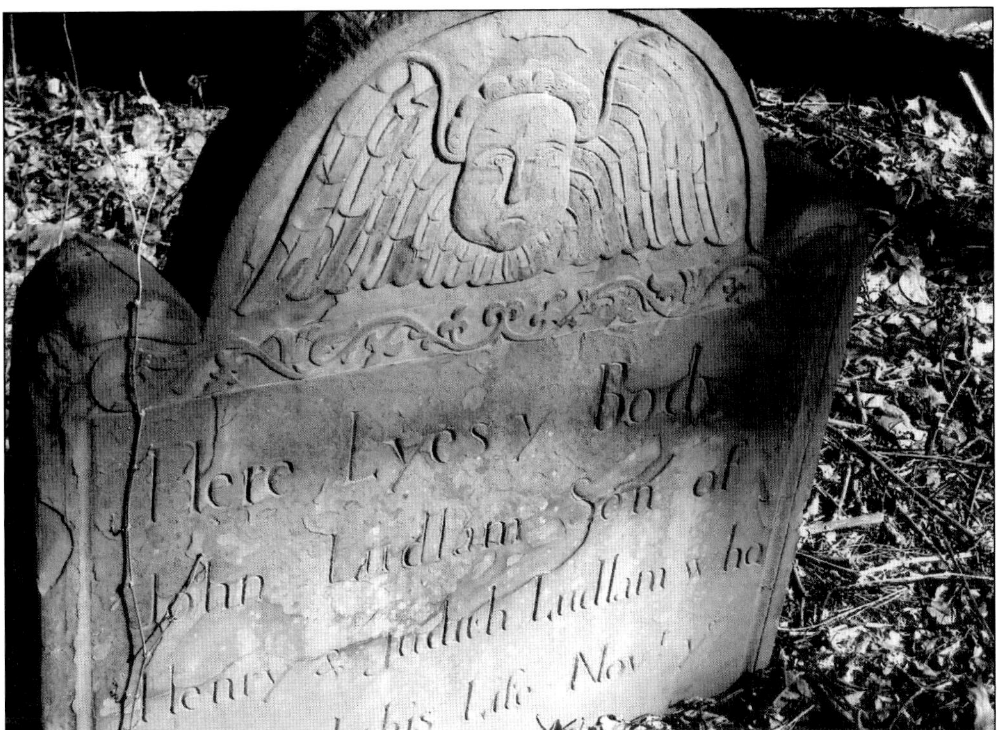

According to the *History of Queens County, 1683–1882*, "The cemetery was incorporated in 1879 under the name Prospect Cemetery, with Judge John Armstrong as president, John H. Brinkerhoff treasurer and Starr Edwards superintendent. Early tombstones were called field stones and had initials and year of death scratched on it. Walks and burial lots have been laid out, flowers planted and the grounds (about eight acres) beautified."

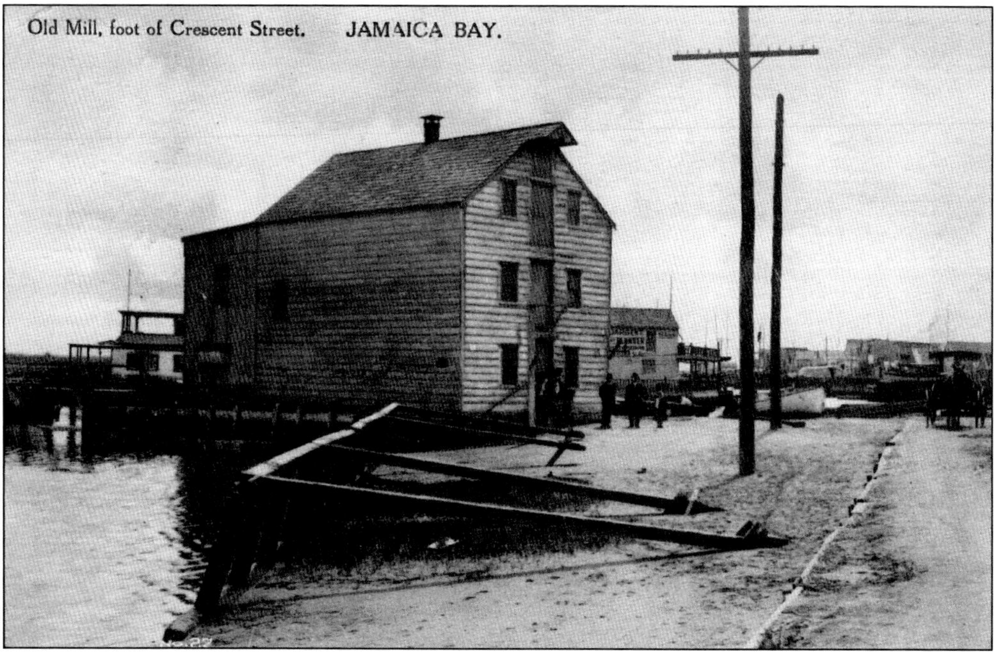

According to the town records of January 20, 1670, "The town of Jamaica agrees to build a dam for a mill, to be erected by Benjamin Coe. He is to grind the town's corn before strangers and they are to bring the corn on such days as he should designate." This photograph shows an old wooden mill that once stood at Crescent Street, Jamaica Bay.

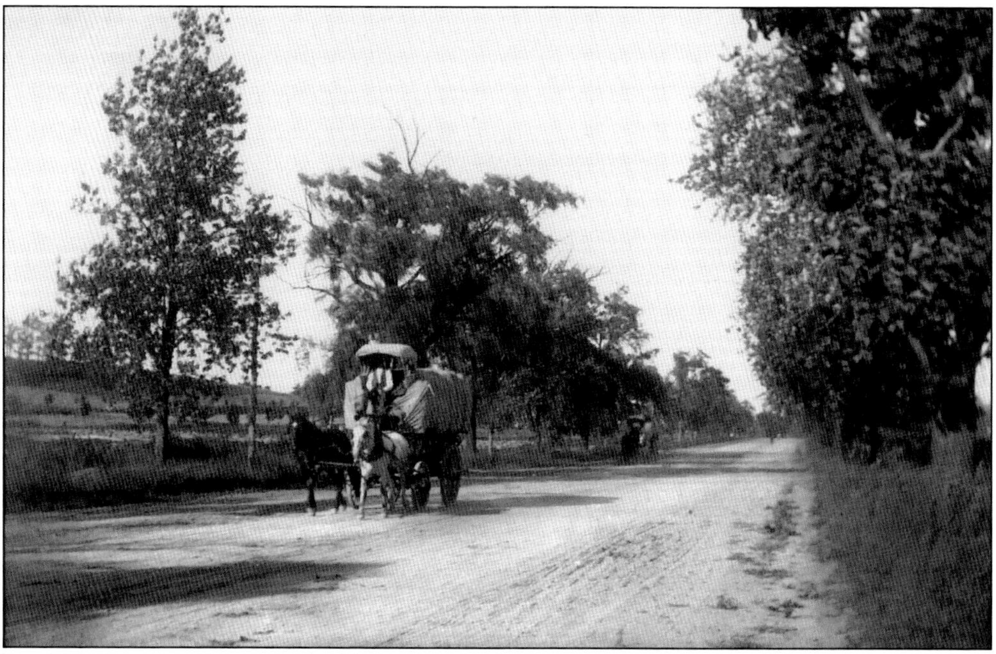

By 1776, the town of Jamaica had become a trading post for farmers and their produce. For over a century, their horse-drawn carts plodded along Jamaica Avenue. In this photograph dated 1904, farmers are shown going to market along Hillside Avenue near Flushing Avenue (Parsons Boulevard). (Archives at Queens Library, George Winans Collection.)

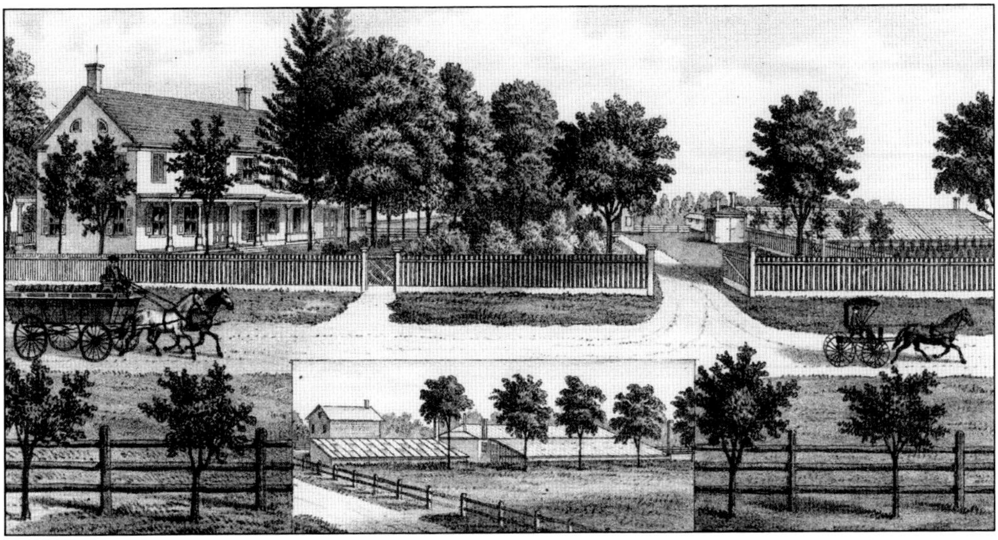

Slavery prevailed in many Long Island towns. The following are articles printed in local newspapers: "Andrus, a negro slave of Captain Wm. Lawrence, was whipped 39 stripes, and branded on the forehead with a hot iron, for theft and larceny of some linen etc., at Jamaica" (1672) and "A mulatto fellow, Isaac, aged 24, as having run away from John Betts, of Jamaica" (1749).

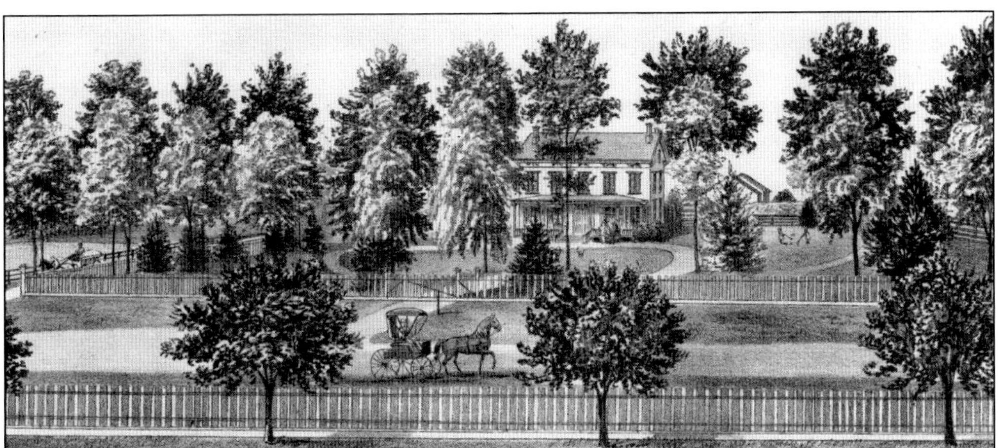

On September 19, 1893, the *Long Island Democrat* wrote, "A peculiarity of the colored population of Queens County is its avoidance of new villages. All the old villages such as Flushing, Jamaica, Westbury etc. contain many colored citizens, while new villages have scarcely any. Why? Would they rather cling to the old traditions which cluster around the villages which were settled long before the revolution? Evidently they do not care for places without a history." These engravings show two Jamaica farms.

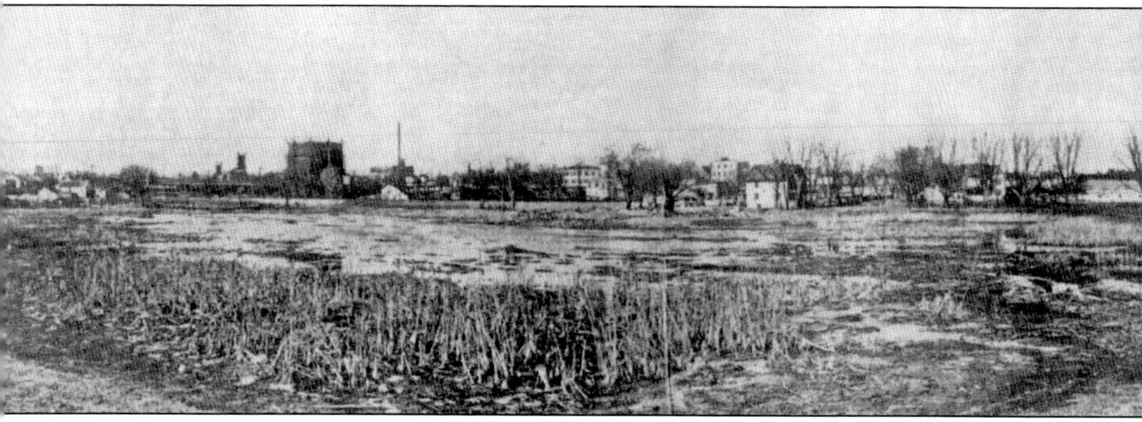

Beaver Pond, a natural pond, attracted the first settlers to establish their village here in 1656. Baisley Creek flowed from Beaver Pond south to Baisley Pond and continued farther, eventually emptying into Jamaica Bay. The Village Green was located near the pond. According to the *Queens County of Olden Times* (1865), "On November 2, 1784, William Guthrie and Joseph Alexander were hanged at Beaver Pond, for robbery and burglary" and "October 8, 1794—The Beaver Pond Races took place on Tuesday. Six horses ran for the Purse of 100 Pounds. Polydore, of New York, took the first and second heat and purse. On Wednesday, a purse of 50 Pounds was run for by seven horses, and taken by Young Messenger, from New Jersey, over Gold Toes, of New York. On Thursday, a purse of 47 Pounds 10 Shillings, was run for by six horse, and taken by Red Bird. There were between two and three thousand spectators and no accident happened." Later called Remsen's Pond, after its last owner, it was drained in 1906 and covered over, and streets were cut through.

Two

People, Places, and Events
Marking a Place in Time

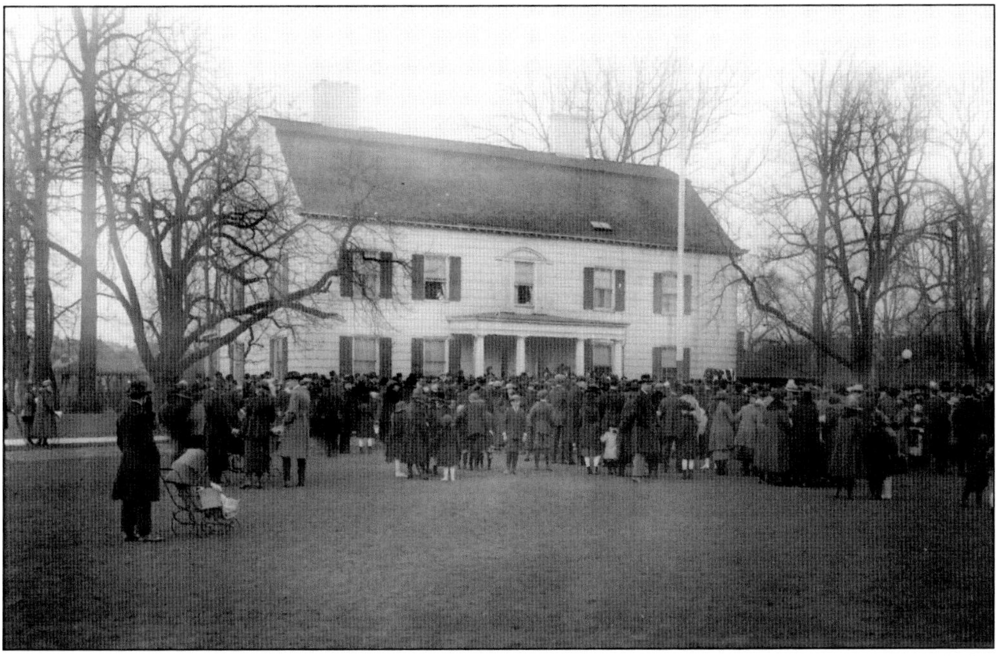

Crowds celebrate at the King Manor in 1921. Patriotic celebrations played an important role for generations. According to *Queens in Olden Times* on July 4, 1791, "At day-break, the bells of the churches in Jamaica rang. Thirteen platoons of Light Infantry announced the joyous day. At noon they proceeded to the Presbyterian church, where an eloquent oration was delivered by the Rev. Mr. Faitoute." (Archives at Queens Library, Frederick Weber Photographs.)

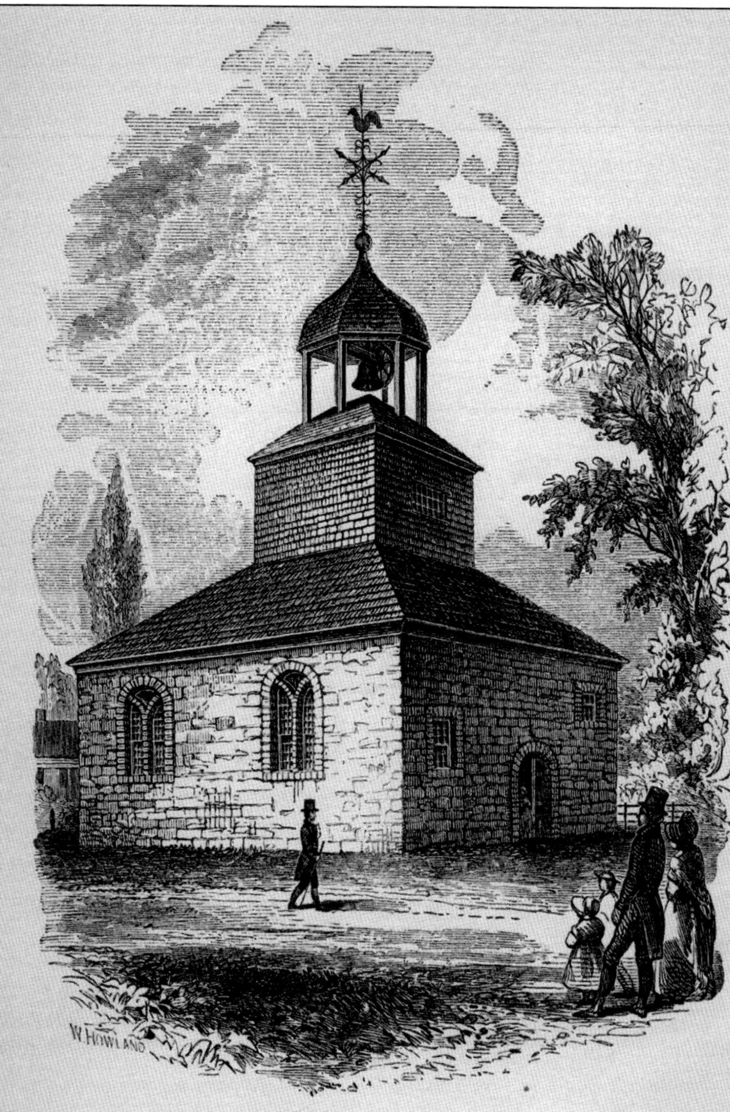

The "Old Stone Church," finished in 1699.

The first settlers to Jamaica were mostly Presbyterians, and church affairs were considered and transacted at town meetings. In 1661, according to the *History of Queens County, 1683–1882*, "some of the inhabitants petitioned Governor Stuyvesant to send a Dutch minister from New Amsterdam to preach and baptize. Reverend Samuel Drisius came to Jamaica on Saturday, January 8th. He preached two sermons and baptized eight children and two women. In 1662 the town voted to erect a minister's house, the following year they built a 20 feet square building to serve as church and town hall. In 1690 a new house, 60 by 30 feet, was built, and was succeed in 1699 by a stone building 40 feet square represented in this woodcut." It stood on Jamaica Avenue, at the head of Union Hall Street (162nd Street)—which once was known as Meeting House Lane—and had three doors and aisles to correspond. The pulpit, surmounted by a sounding board, stood on the north side, facing the gallery. The structure also served as a courthouse. Razed in 1813, it had been host to Presbyterian, Episcopalian, and Dutch preachers.

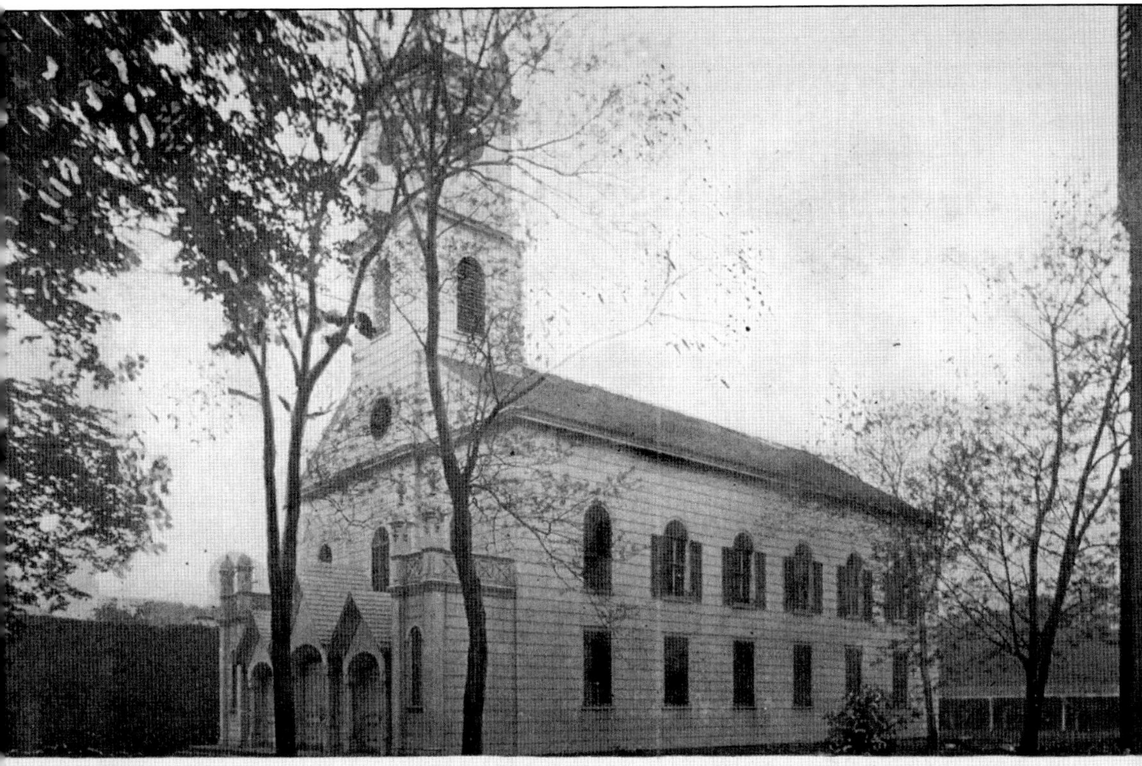

T PRESBYTERIAN CHURCH, OLDEST IN U. S. A. HISTORY DATES BACK TO 1662, JAMAICA, L. I.

The First Presbyterian Church of Jamaica was founded in 1662 and later used the stone church built in 1699 for services. In 1664, the colony changed hands from Dutch to English rule. Lord Cornbury became the New York governor in 1702 and had the Presbyterians removed from the stone church, declaring that it had been built by public tax and, therefore, belonged to the established Church of England, the Episcopalians. Pastor Hubbard was forever forbidden to preach again in the church. The Presbyterians then held services in a barn and later erected a building at the east end of the village. After many attempts, a lawsuit was presented in 1728, and the stone church was returned to them. It was torn down in 1813, and the stones were used for the foundation of the new Presbyterian church (pictured here), which once had a graceful spire that rose 102 feet. It was strained by the gale of 1821, which compromised the framework of the building, and the spire was shortened by 27 feet.

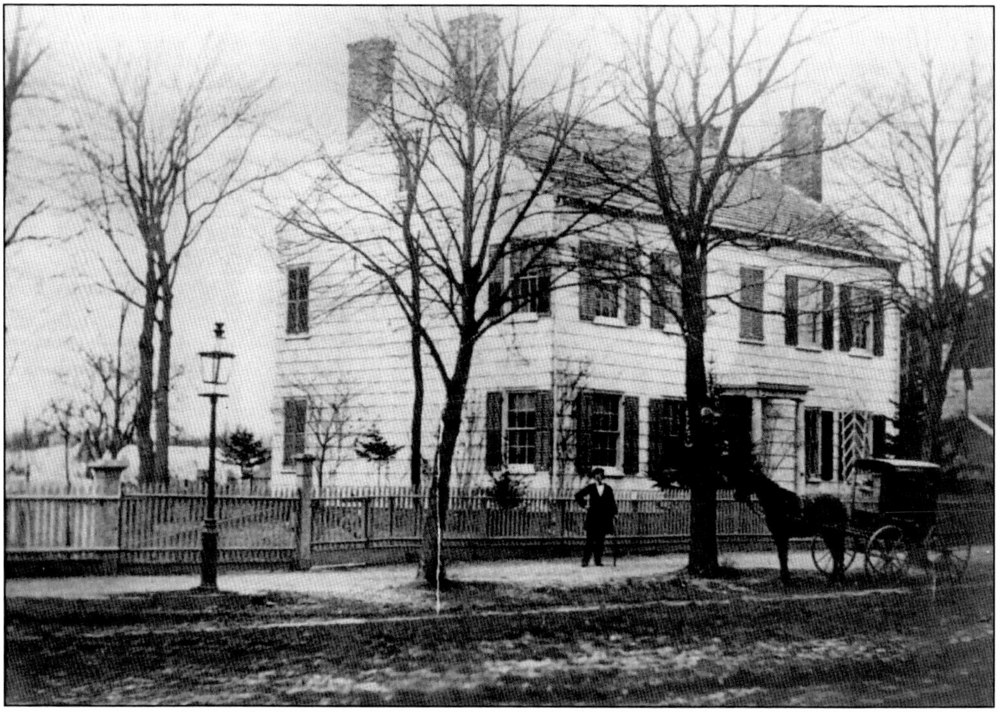

The Jamaica Presbyterian Church has a record of continuous activity from 1662 to the present. The church building dedicated in 1814 stood on the north side of Jamaica Avenue and Clinton Avenue (164th Street). When the village became part of a great metropolis, the noise of the automobile, trolleys, and elevated train caused the church and the parsonage (pictured above in 1866) to be moved farther back in 1920. (Archives at Queens Library, George Winans Collection.)

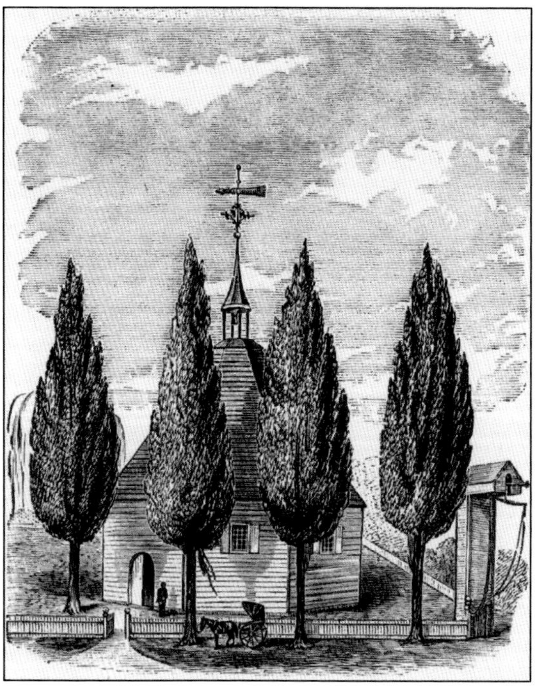

The First Dutch Reformed Church of Jamaica was established in 1702. The congregation first used the 1699 stone church. On June 15, 1716, a wooden octagonal building was erected and opened on Jamaica Avenue near 162nd Street. Its eight sides had a steep roof with a cupola and a bell cast in Amsterdam. In front of the church stood an old-fashioned hay scale.

The octagonal church building of the Dutch Reformed group stood for 117 years until a growing congregation rendered it necessary to erect a newer, larger building. On July 4, 1833, a Georgian church was dedicated at 153rd Street and Jamaica Avenue. A parsonage was built in 1853 at Jamaica Avenue and 149th Street. On November 19, 1857, a fire destroyed this church building.

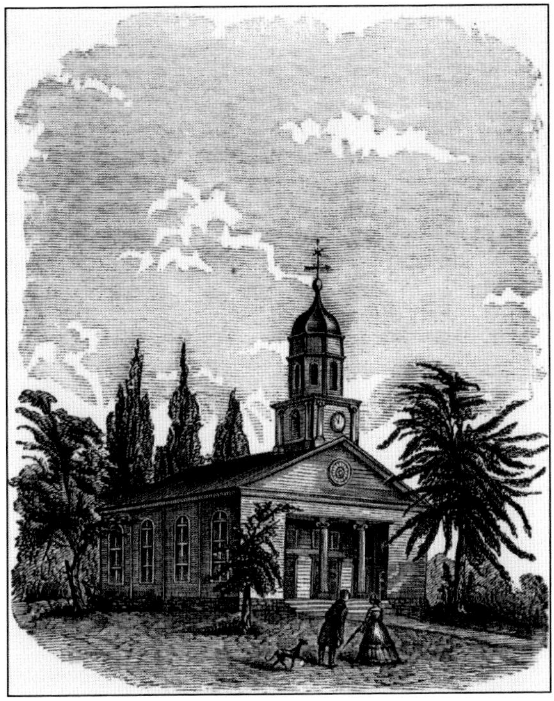

The cornerstone for a new building was laid at the same site. Designed and constructed by Sidney Young and master mason Anders Peterson in the Romanesque Revival style, it opened on October 6, 1859. By the 1980s, the congregation moved to a new building at Ninetieth Avenue and 159th Street. The old church was made a landmark and is now the Jamaica Performing Arts Center. (Archives at Queens Library, Frederick Weber Photographs.)

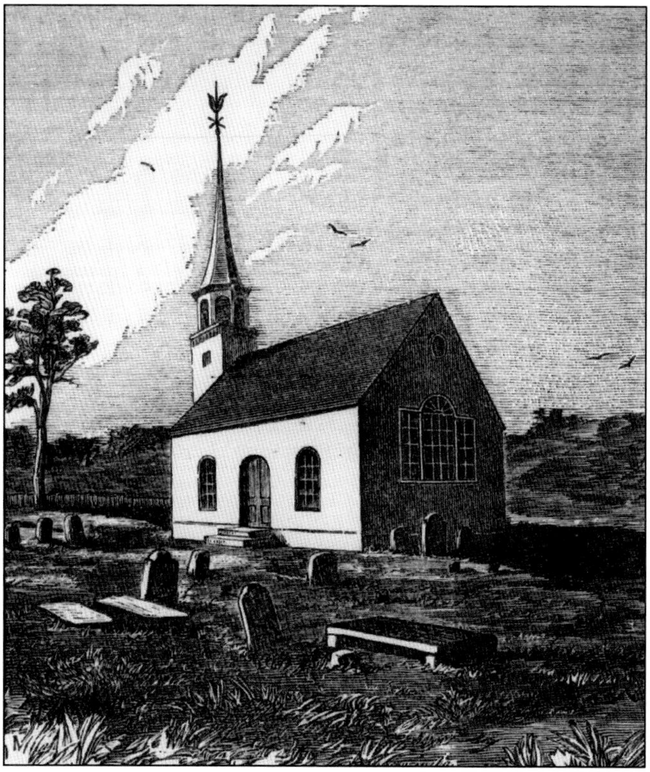

Grace Episcopal Church was established in 1702 and used the 1699 stone church for services. On April 5, 1734, a new church building was opened on Jamaica Avenue, west of Parsons Boulevard, along with a parish cemetery. According to the *Origin and History of Grace Church* by Horatio Ladd (1914), "There was no bell, but decent and comely vestments were furnished by the wife of NY Governor Cosby, 'a great friend and patroness.' "

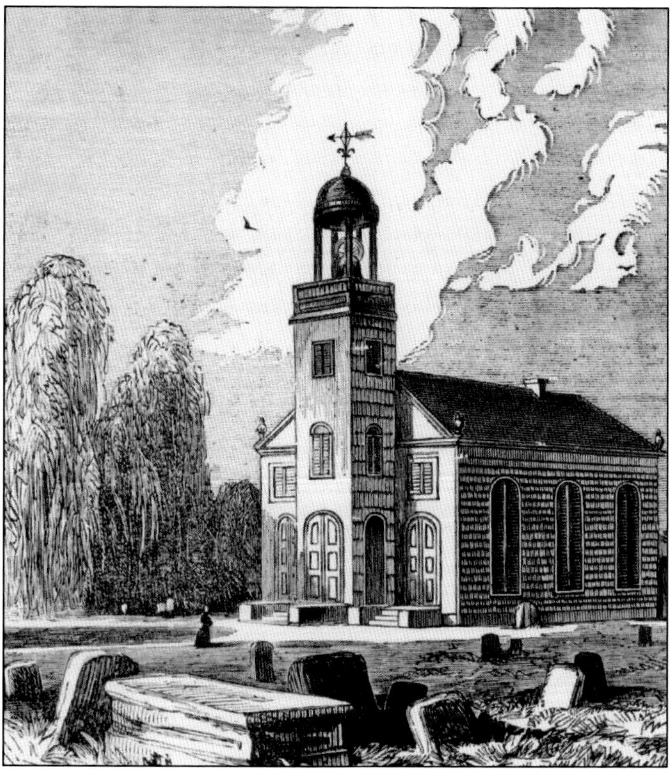

Grace church became too small, and in 1820, the building was repaired and enlarged, with 14 feet added to the west end and a new steeple erected. It was consecrated on July 15, 1822. A fire that broke out in the early morning hours of New Year's Day, 1861, destroyed the building. Lost in the flames were two tablets given as a gift by Queen Anne that contained the Ten Commandments, Apostles' Creed, and Lord's Prayer.

Replacing the church, Dudley Fields designed a new early English Gothic–style church built of New Jersey sandstone, with Anders Petersen as the masonry contractor. The new sanctuary opened on September 23, 1862. The Rufus King family gave generously to the church for many years, donating a baptismal font, organ, Oxford Bible, bishop's chair, and more land for the cemetery. (Archives at Queens Library, George Winans Collection.)

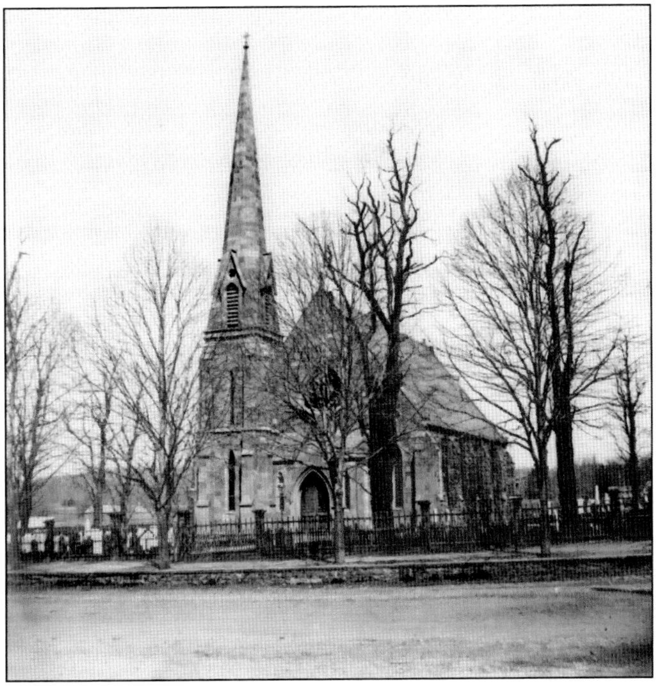

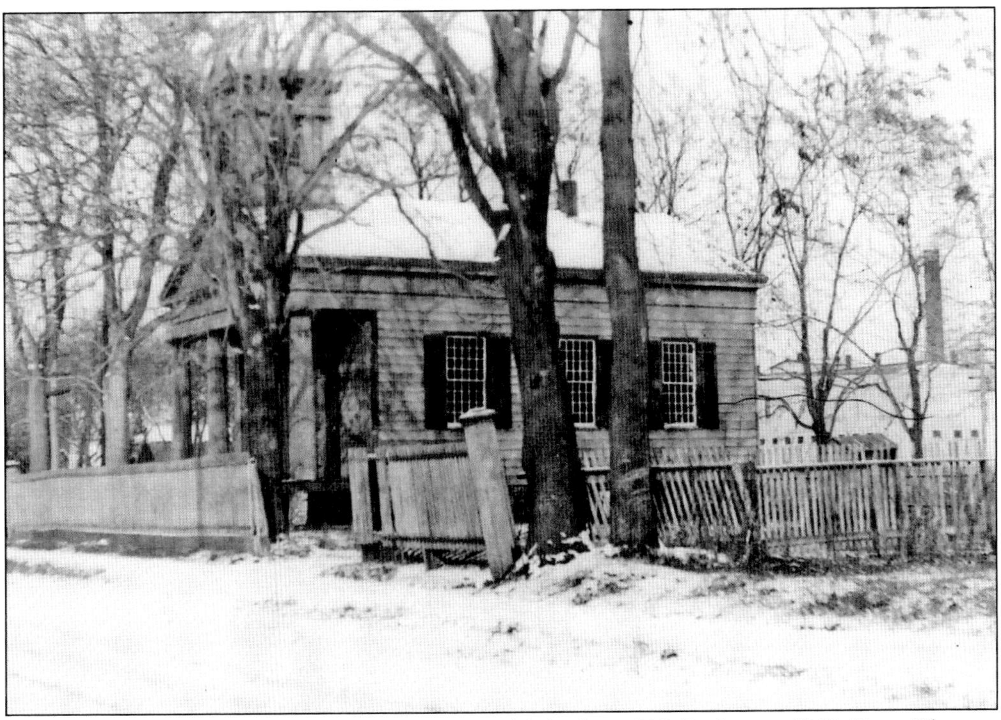

The First Methodist Church of Jamaica was established in 1807. Earlier, in 1767, Capt. Thomas Webb preached the first Methodist sermon in Jamaica, followed by the organization of a preaching circuit until 1807. In 1811, the Methodists built a church on Division Street, opposite the King Manor, with separate entrances for men and women. In 1847, a new church (pictured) was built at Jamaica and New York (now Guy Brewer) Avenues. (Bob Stonehill Collection.)

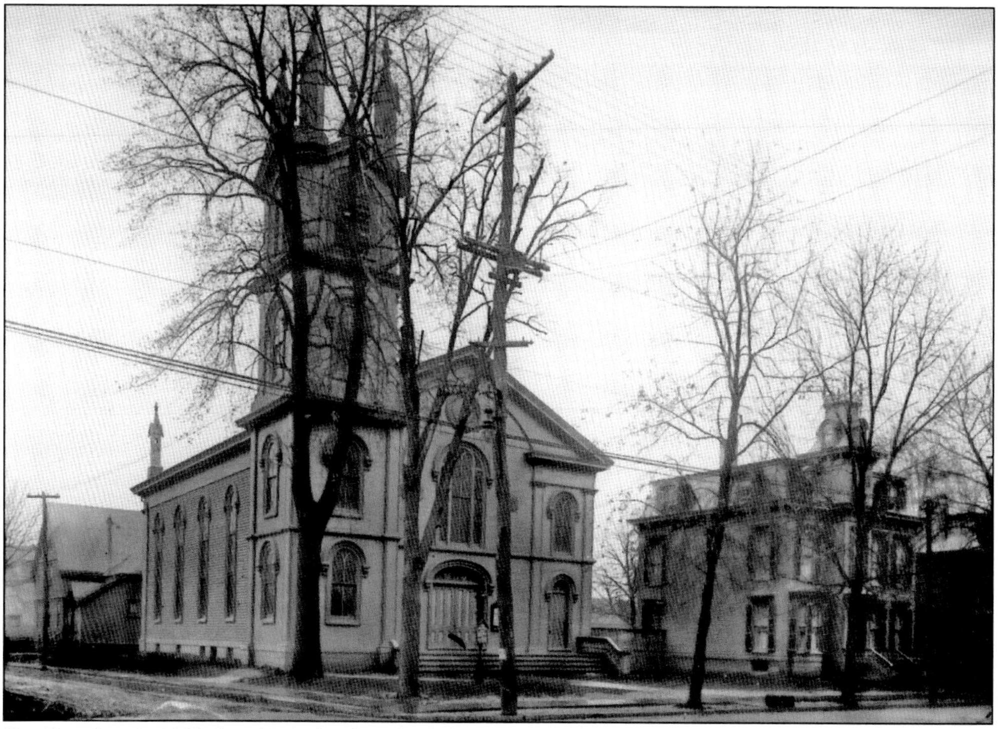

On October 9, 1873, local Methodists laid the cornerstone for their third church building at the corner of Jamaica Avenue and Puntine Street (165th Street). It was dedicated on October 1, 1874, with a parsonage built in that same year. In the rear of the church, there was a Sunday school and lecture room. (Archives at Queens Library, Frederick Weber Photographs.)

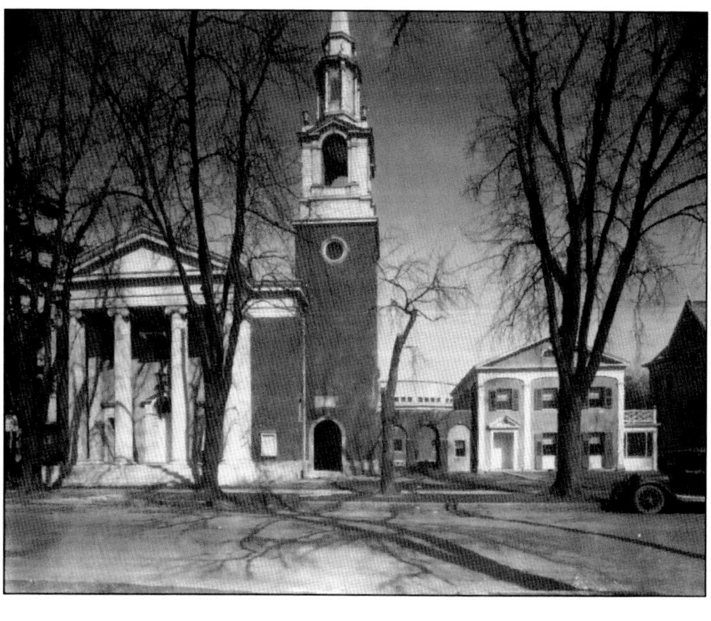

In 1920, the Methodists moved due to growth and noisy competition from the elevated train. In 1922, they built their fourth church (pictured) north of Jamaica Avenue on Clinton Avenue (164th Street). When the church membership dwindled, the congregation moved a fifth time to a new church at Highland Avenue and 164th Street and dedicated it on December 11, 1949. (Archives at Queens Library, Frederick Weber Photographs.)

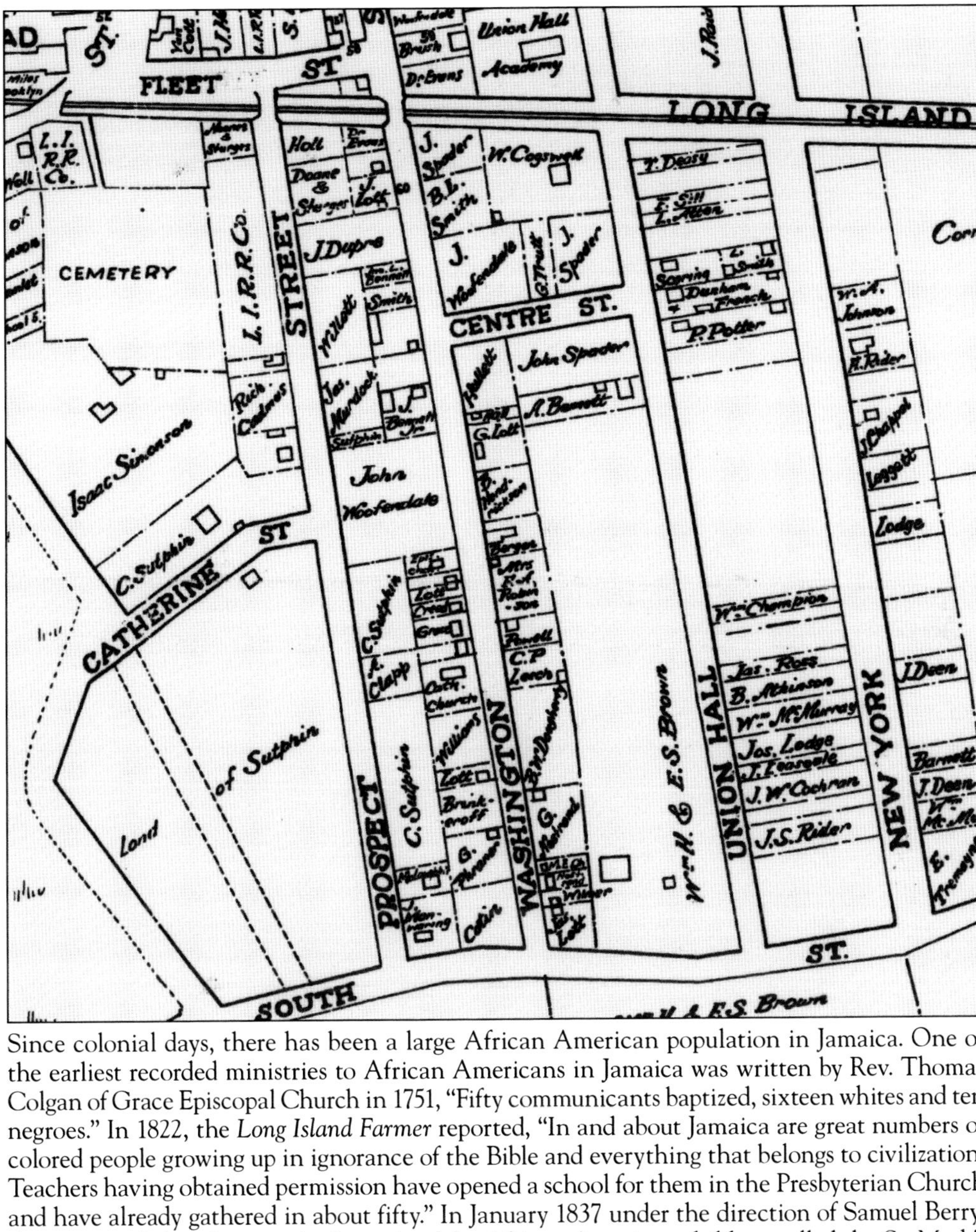

Since colonial days, there has been a large African American population in Jamaica. One of the earliest recorded ministries to African Americans in Jamaica was written by Rev. Thomas Colgan of Grace Episcopal Church in 1751, "Fifty communicants baptized, sixteen whites and ten negroes." In 1822, the *Long Island Farmer* reported, "In and about Jamaica are great numbers of colored people growing up in ignorance of the Bible and everything that belongs to civilization. Teachers having obtained permission have opened a school for them in the Presbyterian Church and have already gathered in about fifty." In January 1837 under the direction of Samuel Berry, the Episcopal church opened a free school for African American children called the St. Mark's Colored Episcopal Sunday School of Jamaica. In this 1842 map of Jamaica, the index lists an African Episcopal Church and African Methodist Church, both located on Washington Street (160th Street). "M.E Ch." is the African Methodist Episcopal, and "Epis. Church" is the African Episcopal Church. The present site of both churches is now on the York College CUNY campus.

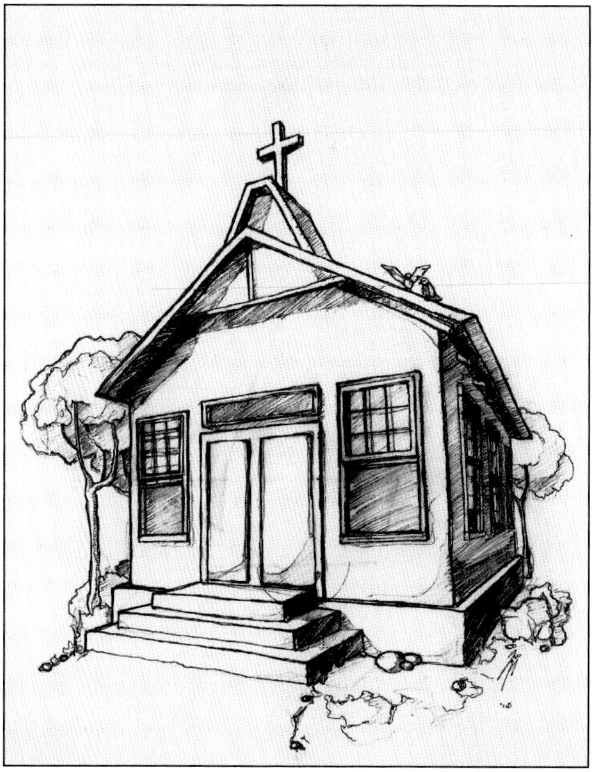

The Allen African Methodist Episcopal (AME) Church of Jamaica was incorporated on July 5, 1844, but the church was organized as far back as 1834. It was located on Washington Street (160th Street), just north of South Street (Road). At first, worship services were held in a small wooden structure (illustrated) measuring 18 by 25 feet. When a larger church was built, the old building was used as a lecture room. (Artwork by Robert Baxter.)

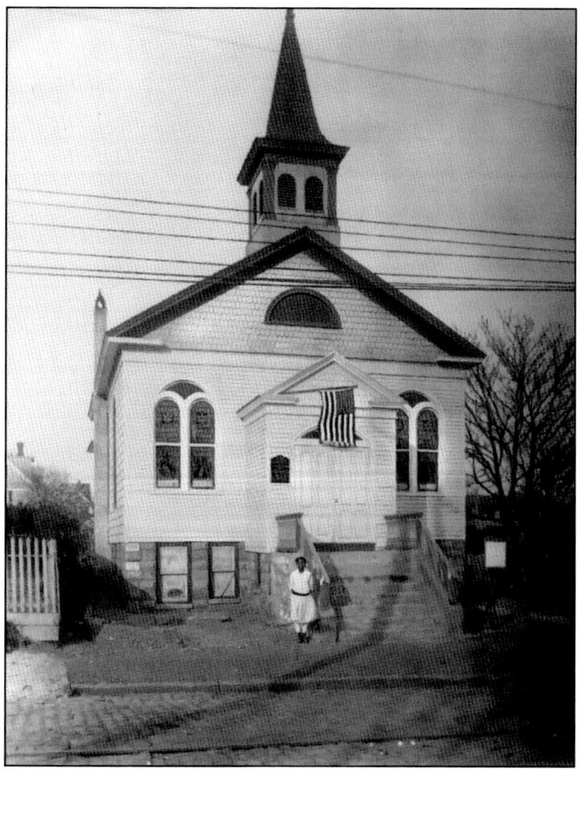

The Allen AME Church pictured here was erected in 1869. It stood on Washington Street (160th Street) north of South Street (Road). The name Allen refers to Rev. Richard Allen of Philadelphia, who founded the African Methodist Episcopal denomination in 1816 and was elected its first bishop. The Jamaica AME moved but is still a vibrant and active parish today. (Archives at Queens Library, Frederick Weber Photographs.)

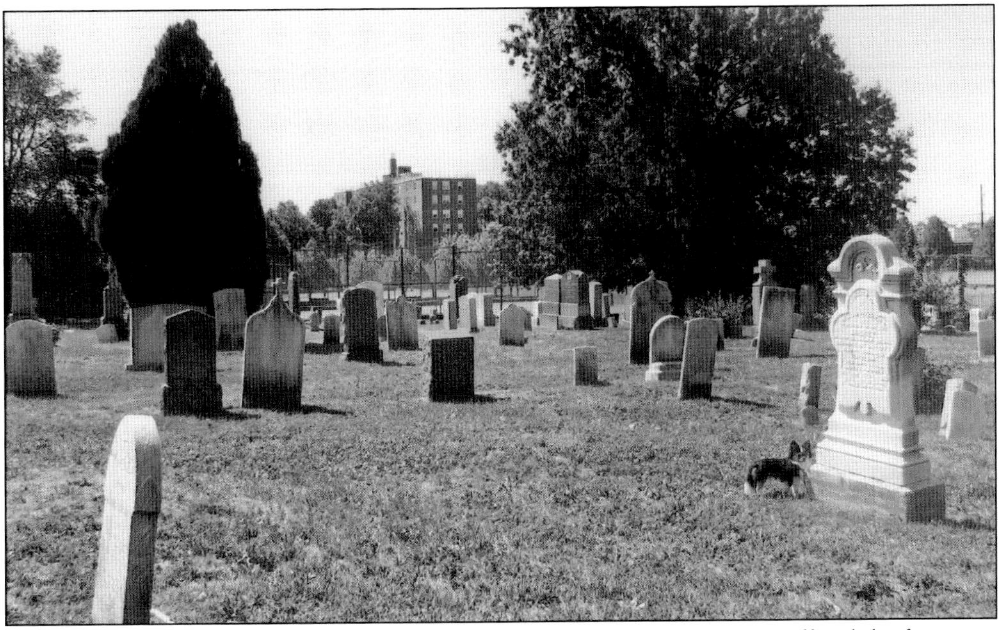

St. Monica's Catholic Church was established in 1838 when Father Curran offered the first mass in the home of blacksmith John McLaughlin for Irish laborers who came to Jamaica in 1836 to work for the railroad and local farmers. A wooden chapel was built on Washington Street (160th Street) and dedicated in 1840. When a new church was built farther north on Washington Street, the original site was made into St. Monica's cemetery.

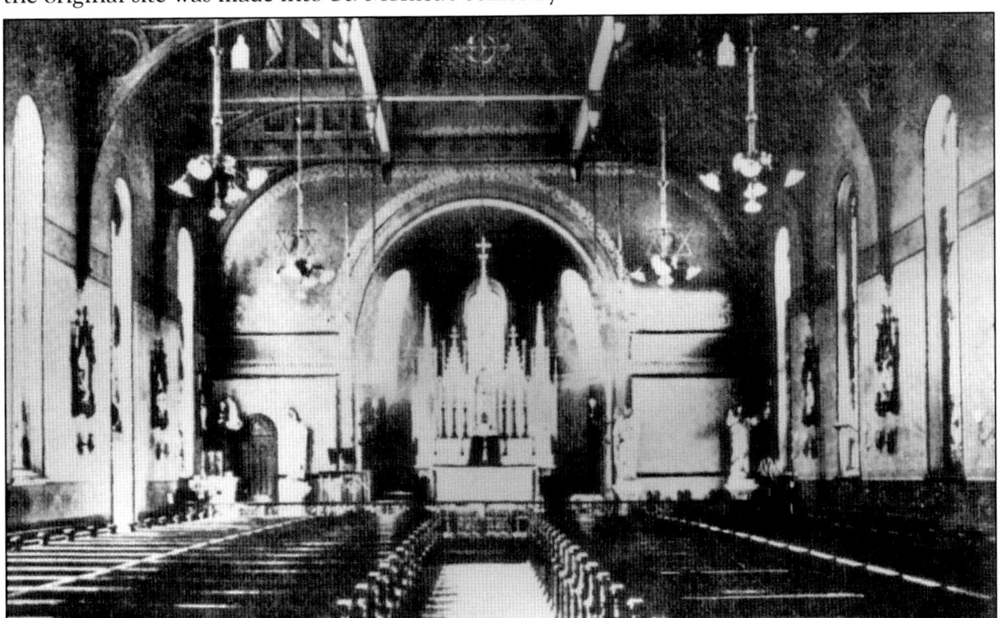

Fr. Edward Maginnis was made the first pastor in 1848. Fr. Anthony Farley became pastor in 1854 and built a brick church in 1857. It was designed by Father Farley in the Romanesque Revival style and built by contractor Anders Peterson. The new church was dedicated on August 15, 1857, by Bishop Loughlin. The apse was added by Fr. Michael Dennison in 1891. (RC Diocese of Brooklyn Archives.)

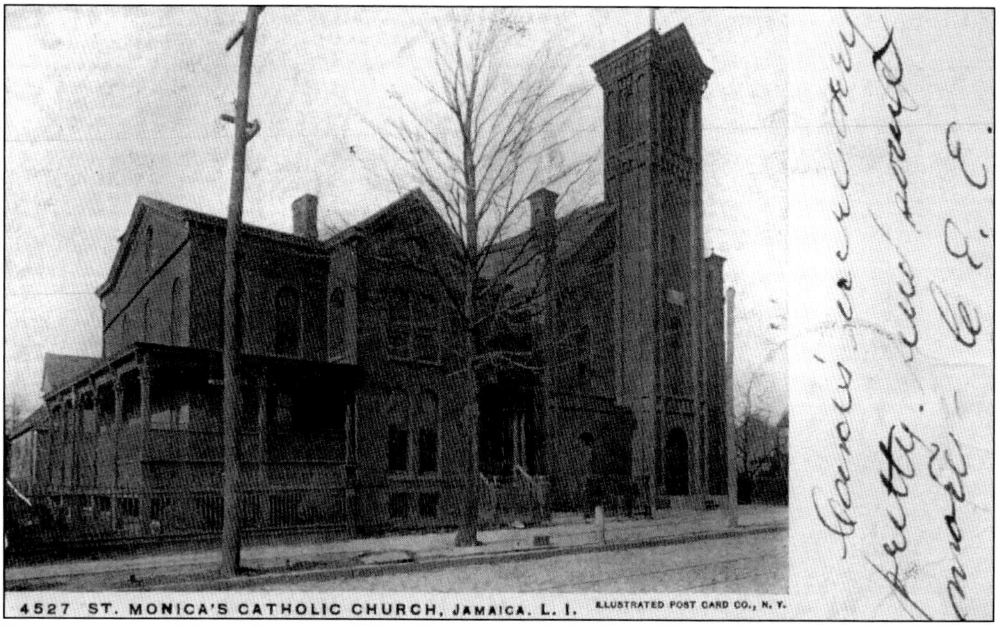

Future governor Mario Cuomo and his family attended St. Monica's Parish, where he served as an altar boy. By 1968, there were 49.8 acres of property, including St Monica's, purchased by New York City for the York College, part of the City University of New York (CUNY). The church building was designated a landmark in 1979 but fell into disrepair and collapsed. The facade, with its soaring bell tower, was saved and incorporated into a day care center building.

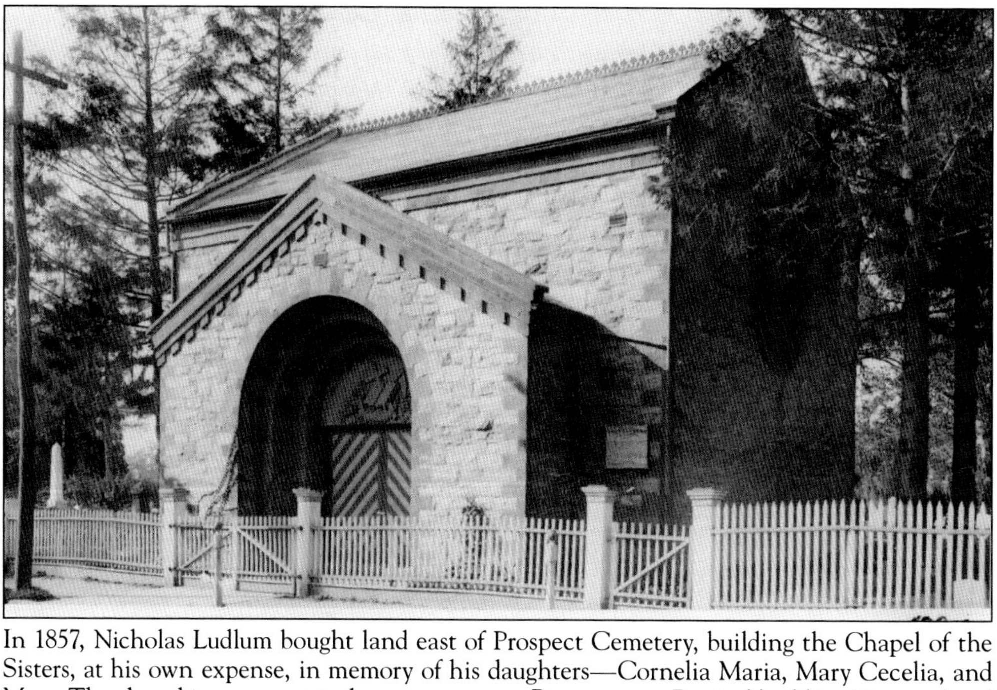

In 1857, Nicholas Ludlum bought land east of Prospect Cemetery, building the Chapel of the Sisters, at his own expense, in memory of his daughters—Cornelia Maria, Mary Cecelia, and Mary. The chapel is a symmetrical, one-story stone Romanesque Revival building. Restored and renovated as a performance and arts space, it is part of the York College campus. The cemetery remains well preserved due to the care of the Prospect Cemetery Association.

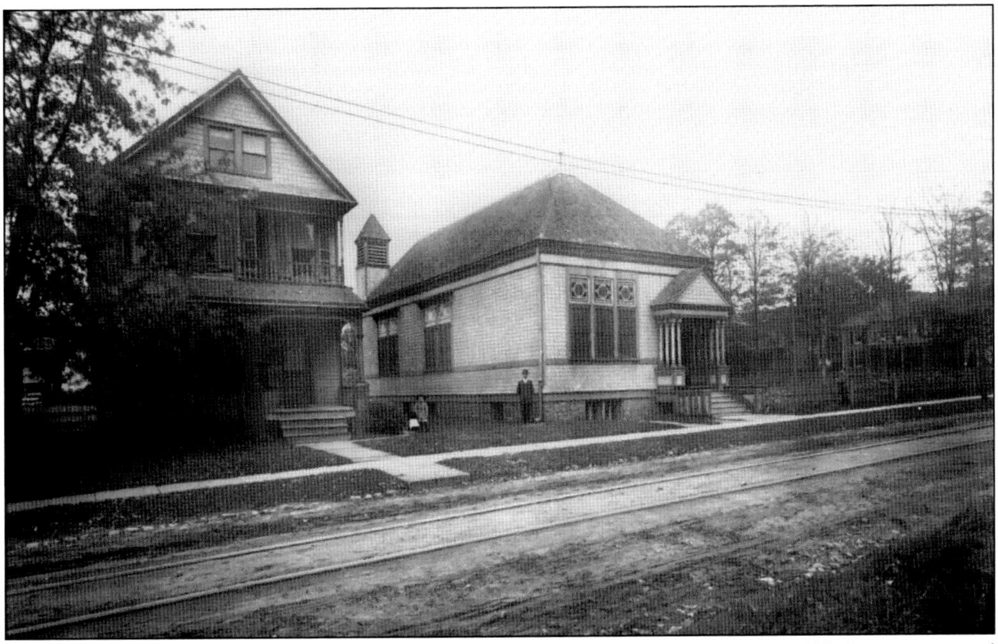

Baptist Church of Jamaica, according to the *History of Queens County, 1683–1882*, "was organized November 11, 1868. A church was built at a cost of $1,800. The pastors have been Reverends George H. Pendleton, Mr. Fuller, A. Stewart Walsh, Charles Colman, Charles Edwards and Samuel Taylor." Pictured above is the church on Ninetieth Avenue west of Parsons Boulevard. (Archives at Queens Library, Frederick Weber Photographs.)

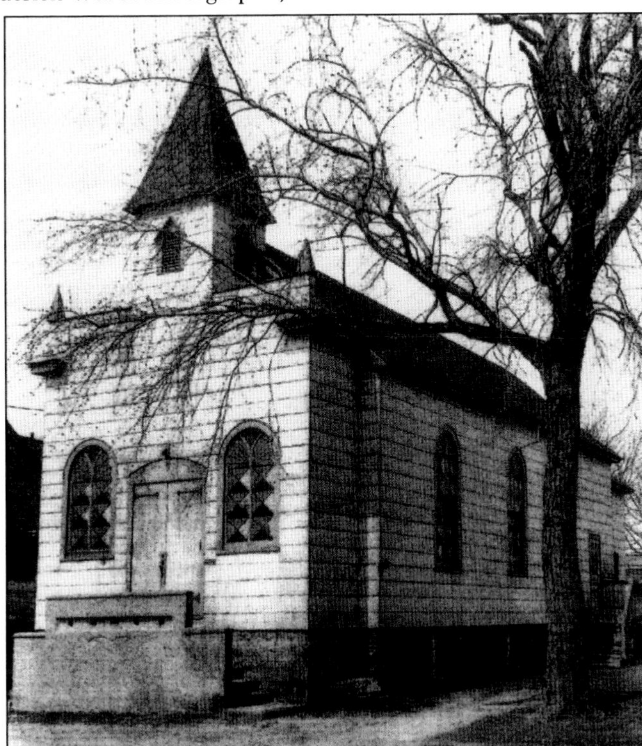

Baptist Shiloh African Church was organized December 22, 1872, and dedicated in November 1877. According to the *Brooklyn Eagle* dated May 12, 1897, "Edmund Tunnell, an old and respected Baptist negro missionary preacher, died. His funeral will be held at the Shiloh Church. He was the founder of the Shiloh church of Jamaica and preached there for many years. He visited every part of Long Island as a missionary, establishing many Baptist churches."

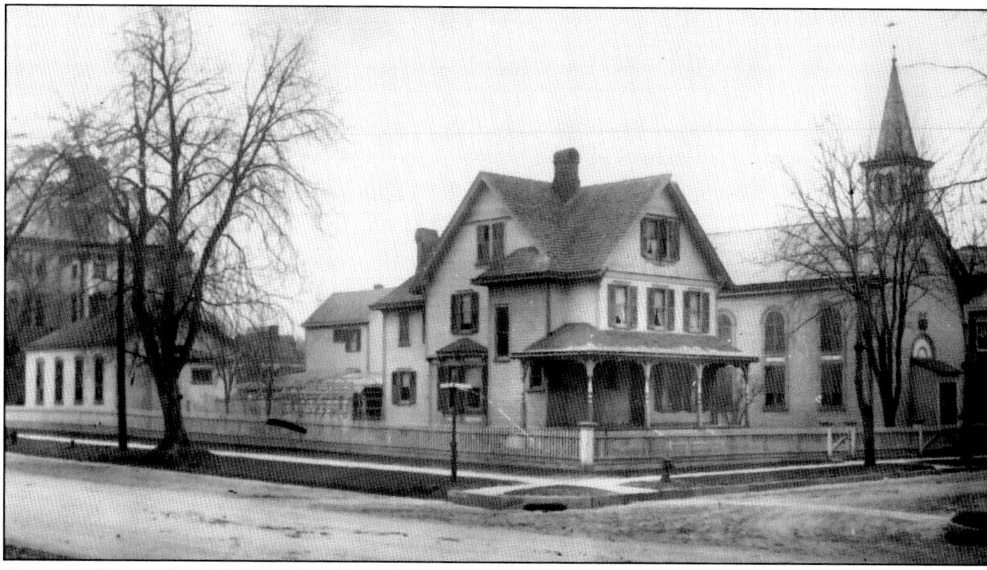

German Evangelical St. Paul's Church, according to the *History of Queens County, 1683–1882*, "was organized in 1873. The pastors have been P. Quirn, S. H. Gundt, Ernest Oxee, Julius Hones and Henry Freech." The church was located on the southeast corner of Hillside Avenue and 161st Street. The large brick building on the left is the Jamaica High School built in 1896. (Archives at Queens Library, Frederick Weber Photographs.)

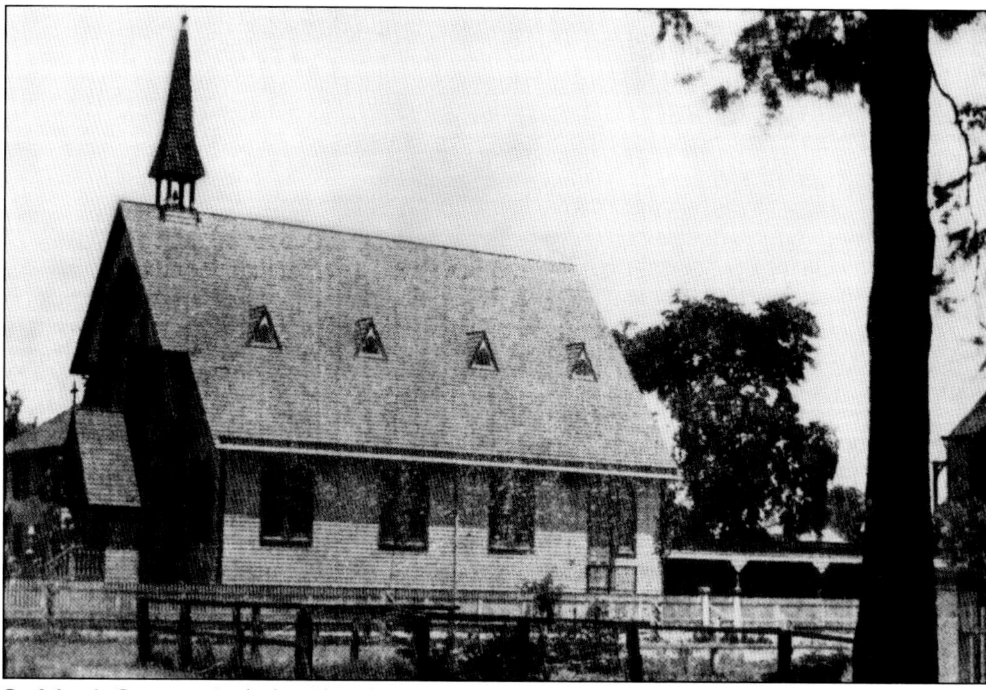

St. Mary's German Catholic Church was created when the German Catholic population grew sufficiently to warrant a parish. Land was purchased at Shelton Avenue (Eighty-ninth Avenue) and Parsons Boulevard. On May 16, 1886, the first mass was said in a 1767 farmhouse. Rev. Ignatius Zeller laid the cornerstone for a small, wooden, Gothic-style church, which is shown here on the northeast corner and facing Parsons Boulevard. (RC Diocese of Brooklyn Archives.)

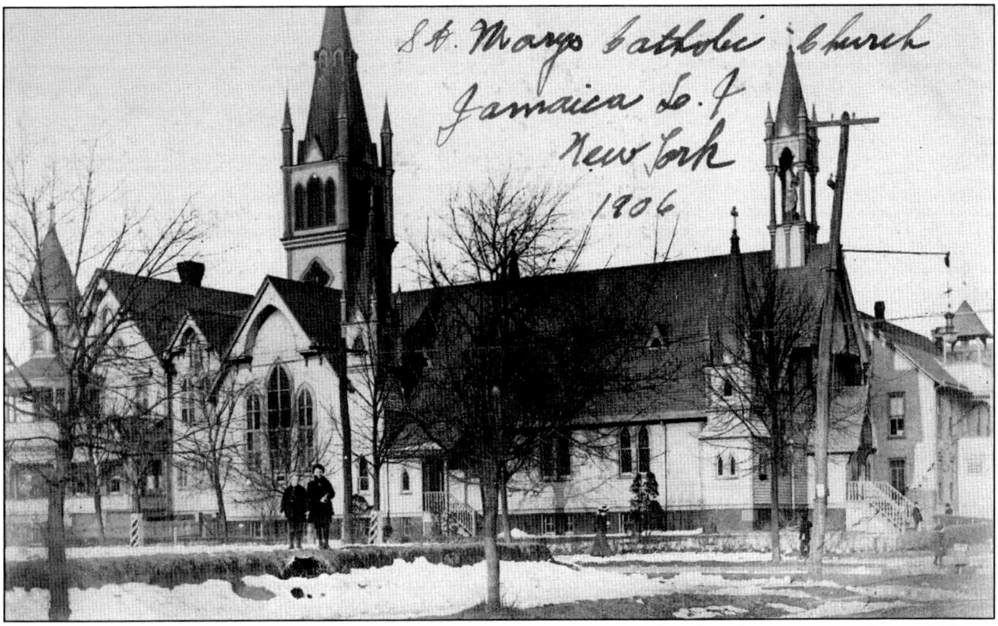

In 1887, Dominican sisters started a small orphanage. A parish school was opened in 1893. In 1894, the old church was moved to face Shelton Avenue (Eighty-ninth Avenue) and enlarged. Father Zeller planned its design and added seven steeples, each dedicated to honor a saint—St. Rose of Lima, St. Joseph, St. Elizabeth, St. Aloysius, St. Ignatius, and the huge bell tower and steeple dedicated to SS. Charles and Edward.

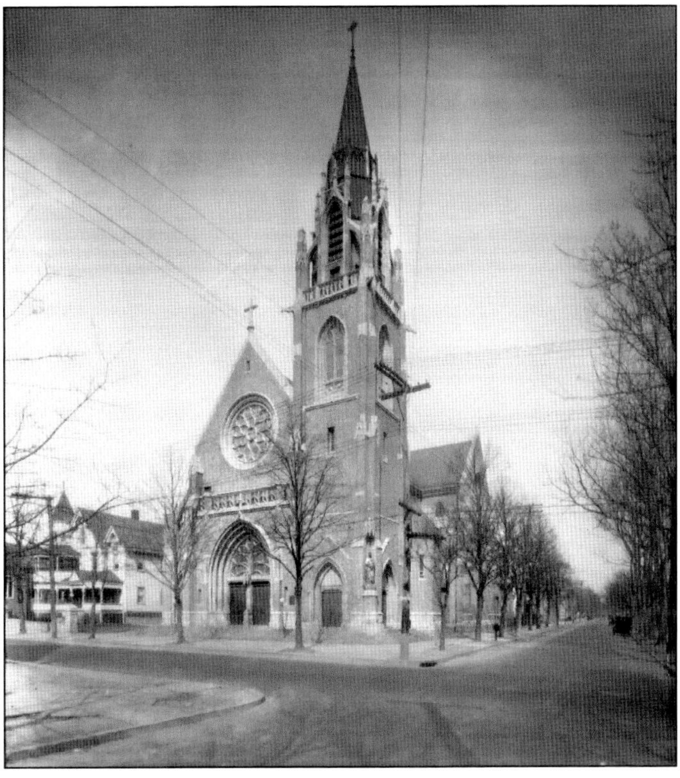

An increase in population warranted a new High Gothic–style church, which was dedicated on June 24, 1923, on the same location of the old church. The new church was turned to face Parsons Boulevard once again. Originally named St. Mary's German Catholic Church, today it is referred to as Presentation of the Blessed Virgin Mary. (Archives at Queens Library, Frederick Weber Photographs.)

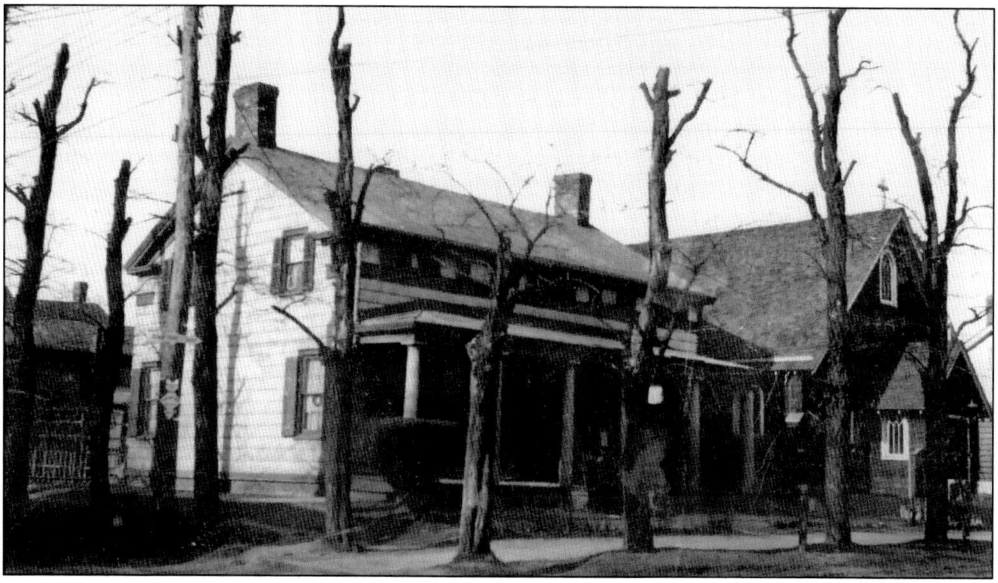

St. Stephens Episcopal Church was established in 1902, when land was purchased at Grand Street (168th Street) and Ninetieth Avenue. On the site, the house became the rectory and the barn was torn down and replaced by a small parish house. On February 15, 1903, the parish house was dedicated as a church. The mission was said to be primarily for the black population in the eastern part of Jamaica. (Archives at Queens Library, Eugene Armbruster Collection.)

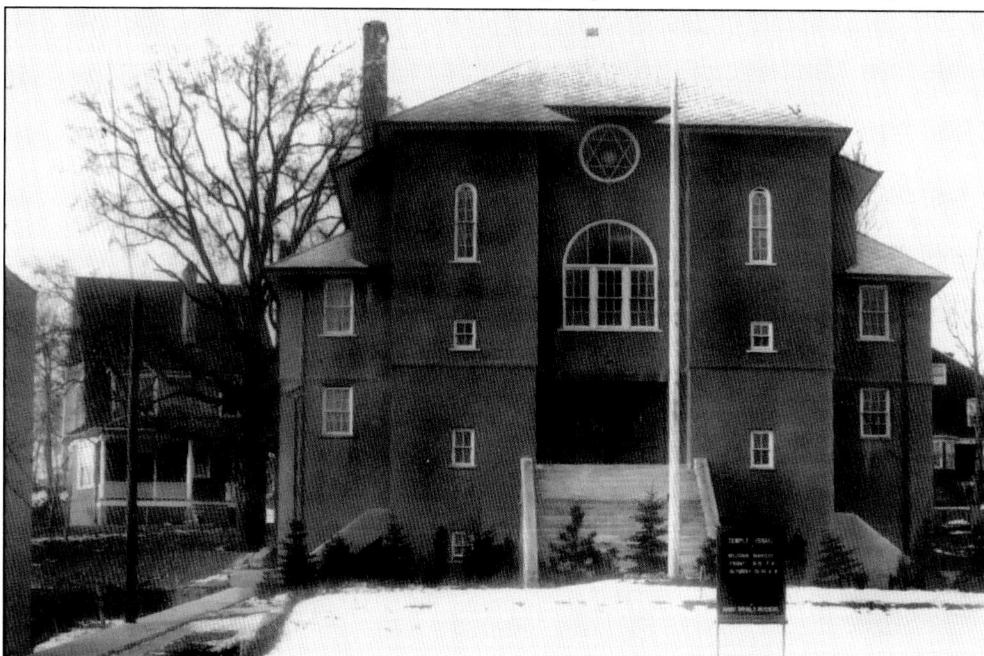

Temple Israel of Jamaica, a Reform synagogue, was established on September 13, 1918. The High Holy Days of 1918 marked the beginning of services. Rabbi Lipkin was formally installed as rabbi of Temple Israel in 1919. By 1920, land on the north side of Hillside Avenue at 160th Street was purchased, and the temple above was erected. (Archives at Queens Library, Frederick Weber Photographs.)

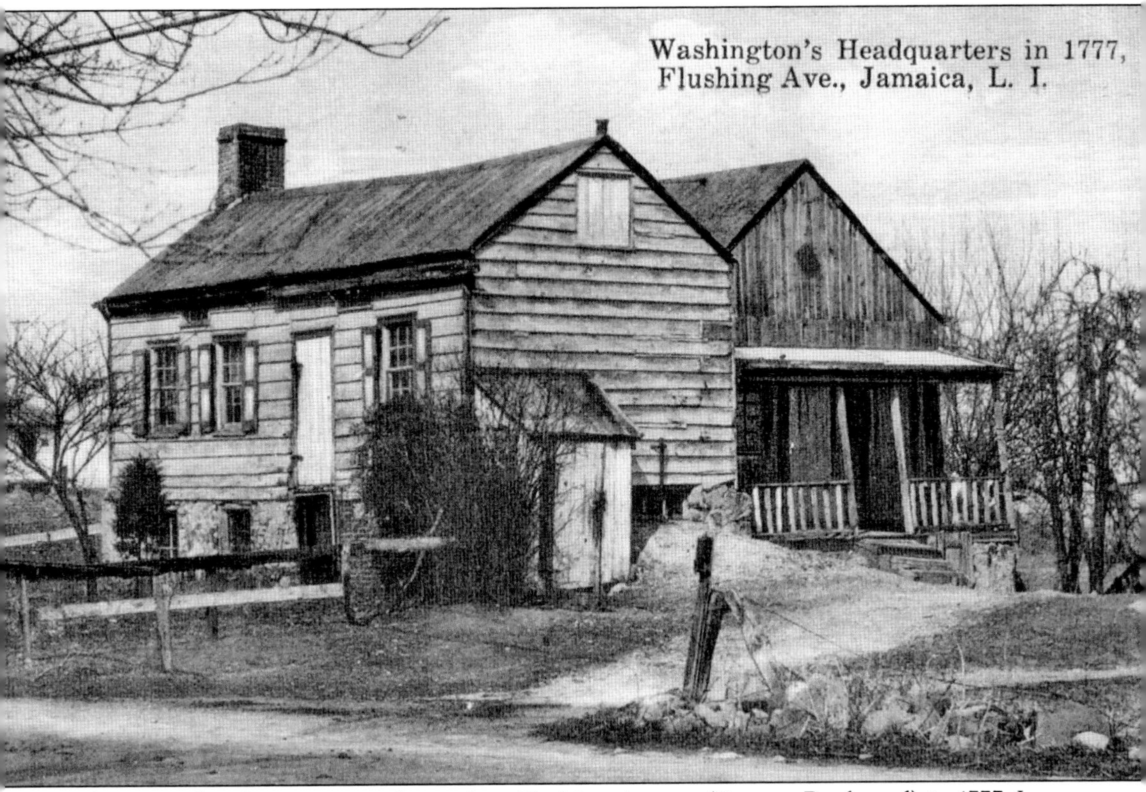

Washington's headquarters were located on Flushing Avenue (Parsons Boulevard) in 1777. In 1775, the minutemen of Jamaica formed to defend American liberty. Among them were sons of prominent Jamaica families, including Samuel Higbie, Isaac Baylis, Hope Rhoades, William Ludlum, Cornelius Amberman, Derick Amberman, Hendrick Hendrickson, Benjamin Everitt, Stephen Rider, Richard Betts, Daniel Skidmore, Andrew Oakley, and John Innis. Their uniform dress was a linen frock reaching below the knee, a fringe around the neck and arms, and a white feather in the hat. Following is the "Song of the Jamaica Minute Men": "Arouse, my brother Minute Men! And let us bear our chorus; the braver and the bolder, the more they will adore us. / Now to our station let us march and rendezvous with pleasure, behaving like brave Minute Men to save so great a treasure. / We'll let 'em see immediately that we are men of mettle, American boys who fear no noise, and ne'er will flinch from battle. / That Troy brood that has withstood this great and glorious jovial, if they advance, we'll make 'em dance the tune of 'Yankee Doodle.' "

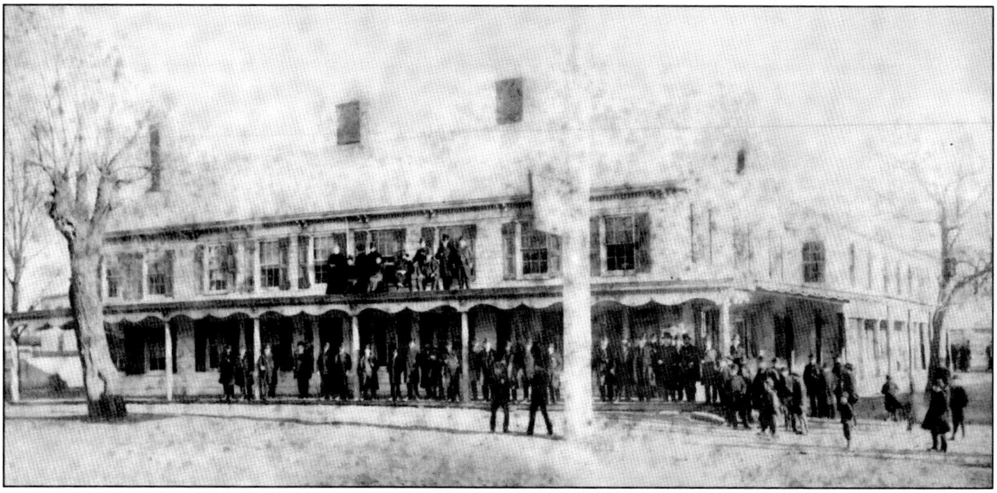

According to the *New York Times* on July 21, 1900, "Pettit's Tavern, on Jamaica Avenue is one of Long Island's oldest road houses. George Washington slept here in 1790, calling it a 'pretty good and decent house.' Known first as Queens Head, Thomas Rochford kept the tavern with an elegant tea garden." The structure was torn down in 1906, and the Joseph P. Addabbo Federal Building now occupies the site. This photograph was taken in 1880. (Archives at Queens Library, George Winans Collection.)

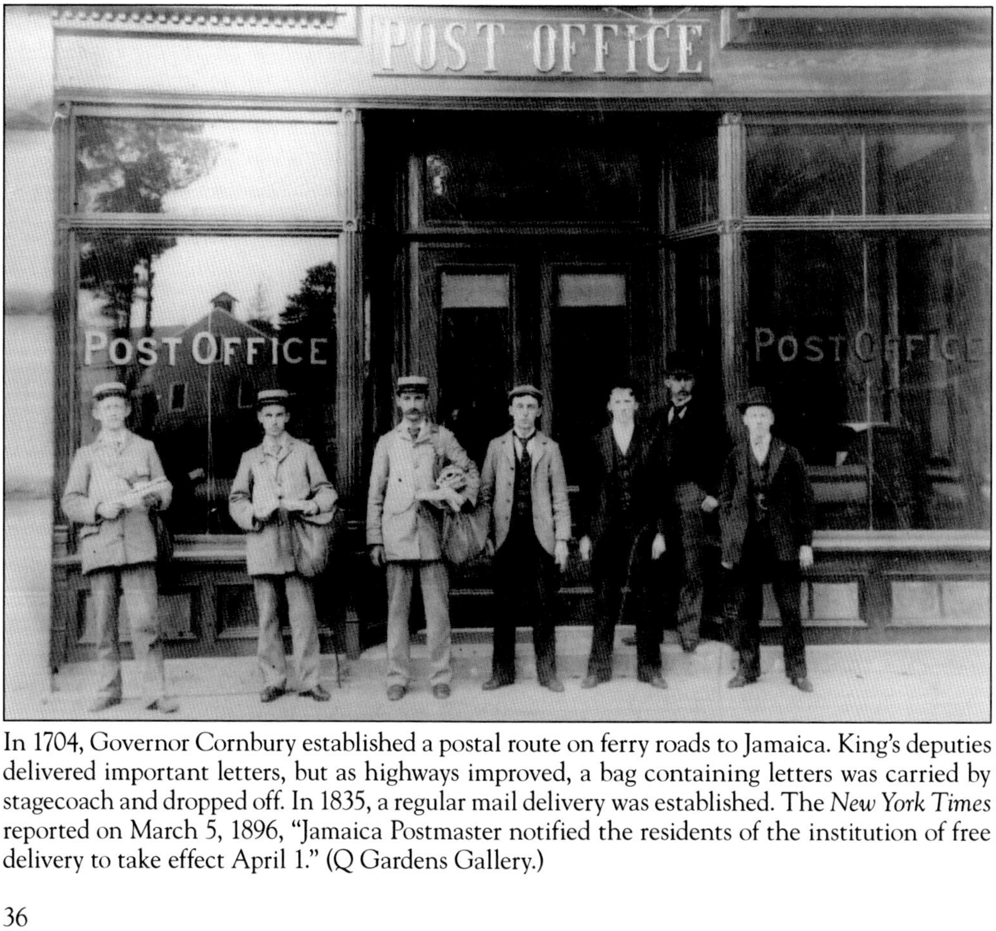

In 1704, Governor Cornbury established a postal route on ferry roads to Jamaica. King's deputies delivered important letters, but as highways improved, a bag containing letters was carried by stagecoach and dropped off. In 1835, a regular mail delivery was established. The *New York Times* reported on March 5, 1896, "Jamaica Postmaster notified the residents of the institution of free delivery to take effect April 1." (Q Gardens Gallery.)

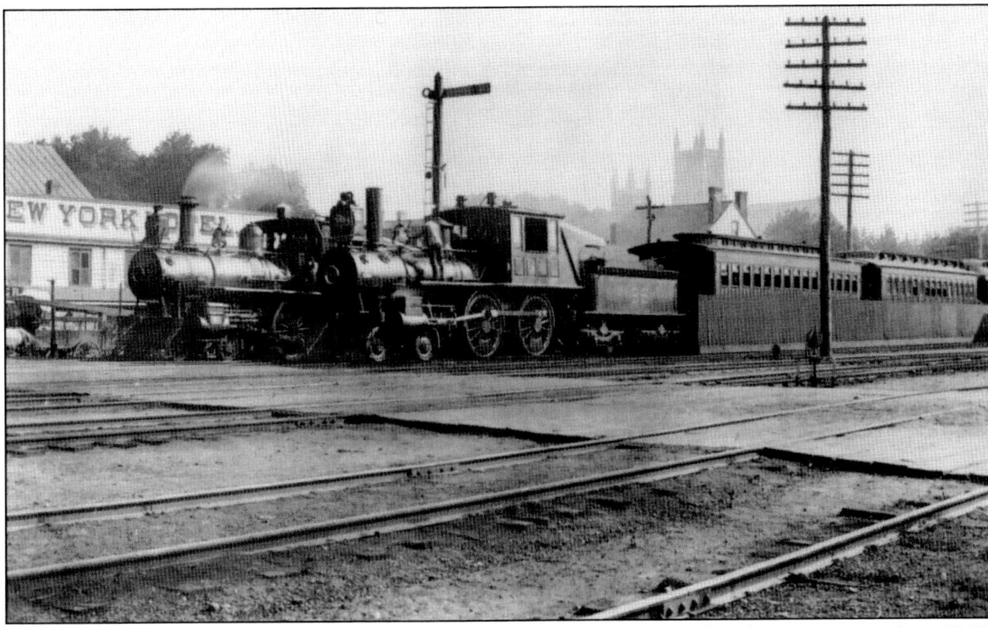

The Brooklyn and Jamaica Railroad, the first railroad on Long Island, incorporated in 1832. Completed on April 18, 1836, it ran from the East River to Jamaica and was operated by the Long Island Rail Road (LIRR) under lease. According to the *New York Times* on July 30, 1896, "John Areson of Jamaica, 86 years old, died yesterday. In 1832 he worked laying the tracks of the Brooklyn and Jamaica Railroad system." (Archives at Queens Library, Ron Ziel Collection.)

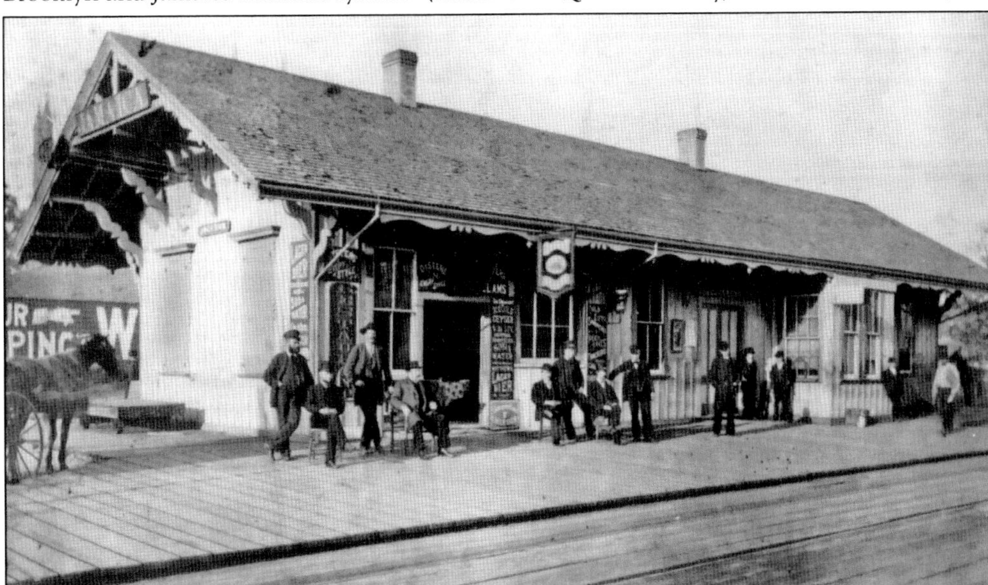

The Long Island Rail Road's original Jamaica Station (Old Jamaica) was erected in 1836, the terminus of the LIRR. It was remodeled in 1869 and rebuilt in 1871 (pictured). In 1867, a second depot was built nearby at the South Side Railroad and was called Jamaica Beaver Street Station for the Atlantic Branch. Both stations were discontinued as stops and razed between 1912 and 1913, and a new station was erected at Sutphin Boulevard. (Archives at Queens Library, Frederick Weber Photographs.)

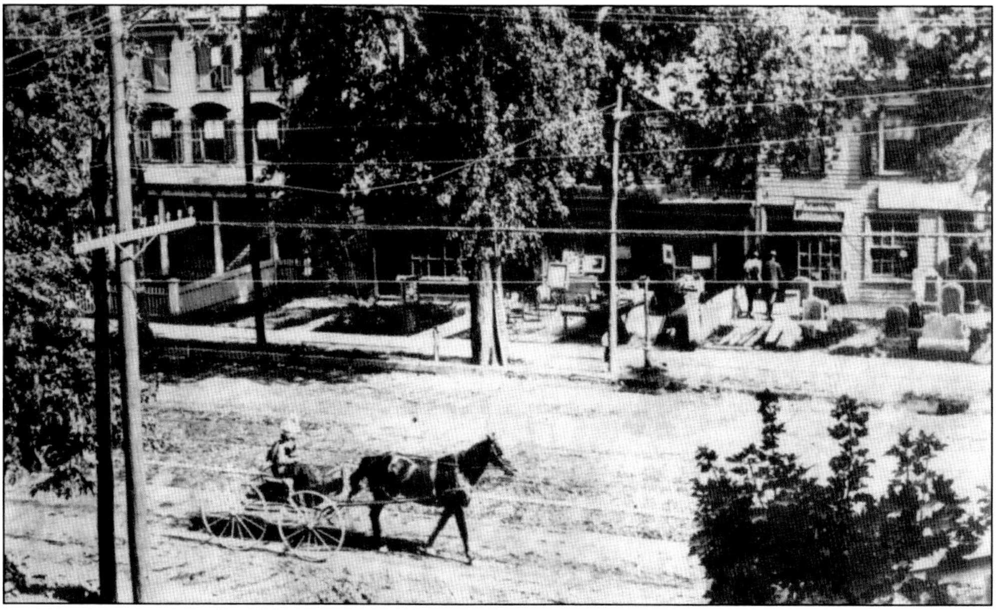

In 1809, deteriorated conditions of highways on Long Island led a group of private citizens to organize the Brooklyn, Jamaica, and Flatbush Turnpike Company. Given a long-term lease on the highways by the New York State Legislature, the company agreed to widen Jamaica Avenue, lay pavement, and keep it in good repair. The turnpike company was allowed to collect tolls, and tollhouses were established. Jamaica Avenue is pictured here in 1890. (Archives at Queens Library, Borough President Collection.)

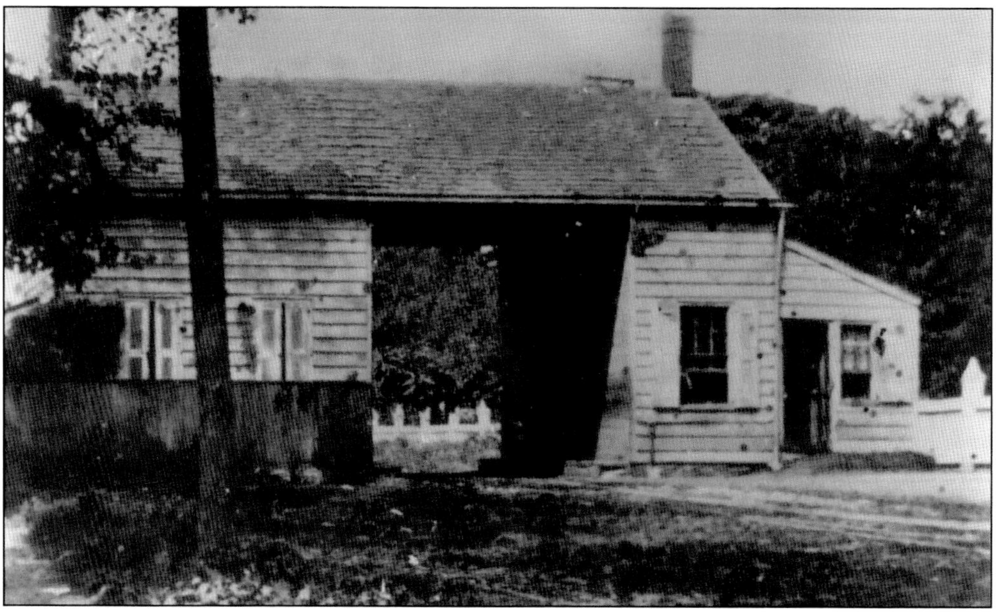

Fulton Street (Jamaica Avenue) to the Brooklyn Ferry had toll gates. One near Van Wyck Avenue (between 137th and 138th Streets) is pictured here. Tolls were not to exceed 1.5¢ a mile for a vehicle drawn by two animals, plus half a cent for every additional animal; three-quarters a cent per mile for every vehicle drawn by one animal; and half a cent a mile for each horse and rider or lead horse. (Archives at Queens Library, Borough President Collection.)

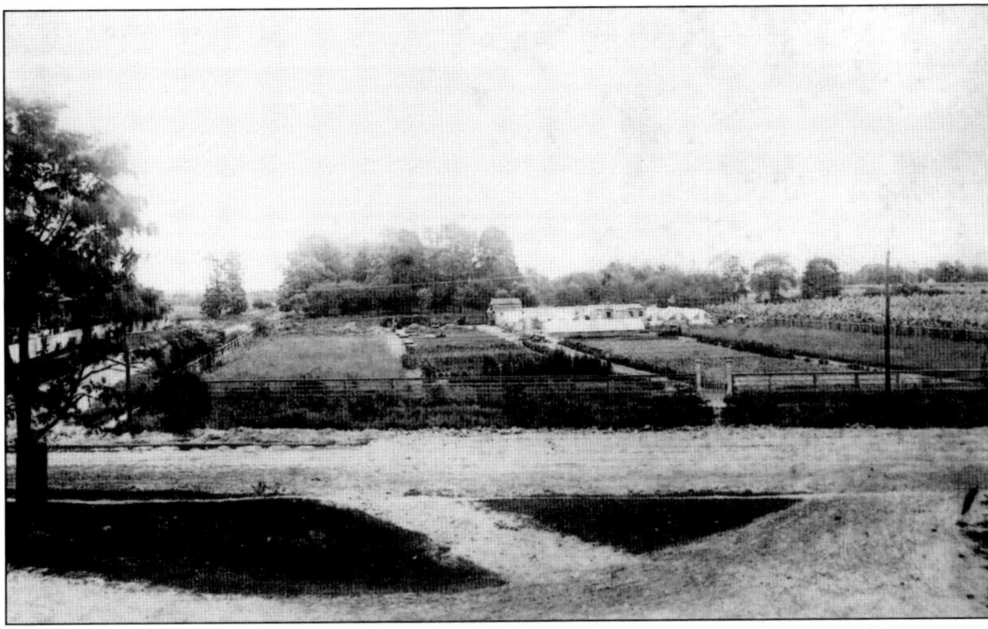

Pictured here are Jamaica Avenue and, at the left, the single-lane Van Wyck Avenue (Expressway) heading south that was opened by Abraham Van Wyck in 1834. Florist Henry Grebe turned this corner into a so-called Garden of Eden. The cluster of trees in the back is now the location of Jamaica Hospital. Today, the Van Wyck is a major six-lane highway. Turnpikes were fairly good for travel, except during spring, when rain turned them into mud and made them almost impassable.

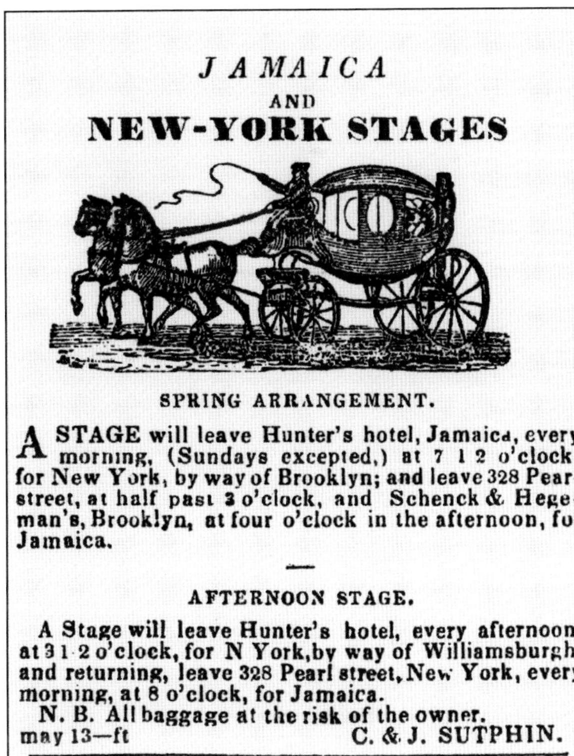

JAMAICA

AND

NEW-YORK STAGES

SPRING ARRANGEMENT.

A STAGE will leave Hunter's hotel, Jamaica, every morning, (Sundays excepted,) at 7 1 2 o'clock, for New York, by way of Brooklyn; and leave 328 Pear-street, at half past 3 o'clock, and Schenck & Hegeman's, Brooklyn, at four o'clock in the afternoon, fo Jamaica.

AFTERNOON STAGE.

A Stage will leave Hunter's hotel, every afternoon at 3 1 2 o'clock, for N York, by way of Williamsburgh; and returning, leave 328 Pearl street, New York, every morning, at 8 o'clock, for Jamaica.

N. B. All baggage at the risk of the owner.

may 13—ft C. & J. SUTPHIN.

The era of popular plank roads began as a result of poor traveling conditions. Hemlock, pine, or oak planks, eight feet long and three to four inches thick, were laid across the road. The Jamaica and Brooklyn Plank Road Company was incorporated and, by 1851, had laid a plank road through the village. Jamaica Avenue was called the Jamaica Plank Road. An 1835 *Long Island Democrat* advertisement shows the means of transportation in the 1700s and early 1800s.

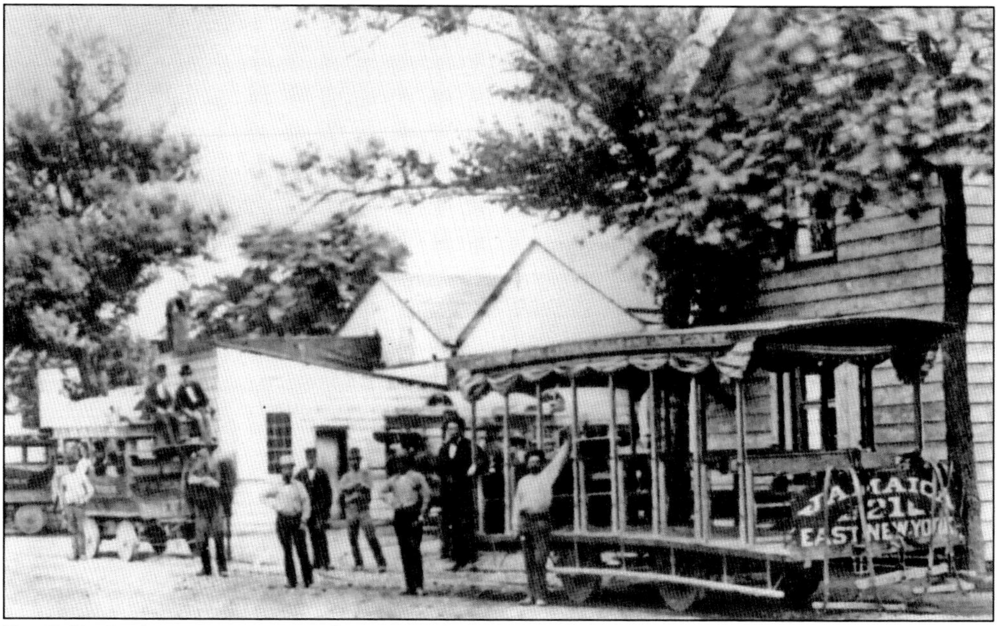

By 1863, the horsecar was popular. A single track was laid, and cars like the ones in this 1880 photograph glided along pulled by a single horse or, later, two horses. Owned by the East New York and Jamaica Railroad Company, this horsecar's fare from Brooklyn to Jamaica was 10¢. In the older models, the driver sat on top. When passengers wished to get off, they pulled a strap attached to the driver's boot.

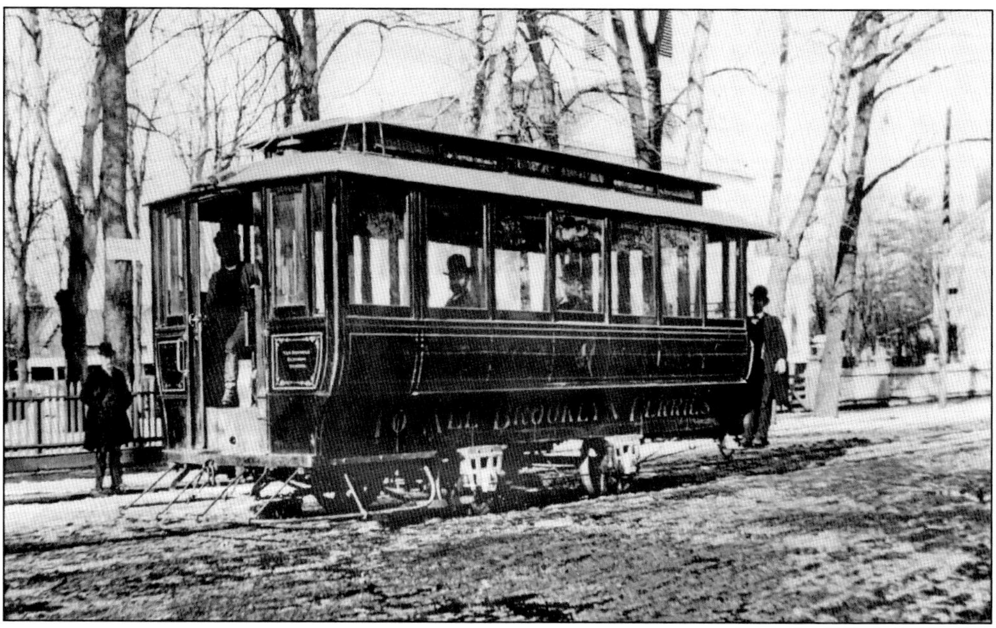

In 1886, Charles Van Depoele designed the first motor and power plant that generated electricity to propel streetcars in New York City, and he selected Jamaica to test his invention. The Jamaica and Brooklyn Road Co. leased its horse-pulled streetcar line to Van Depoele. The electricity-run cars debuted on December 7, 1887. People were in awe, some claiming horses were hidden inside. This photograph shows the trolley on Jamaica Avenue between 163rd and 164th Streets.

This 1916 photograph shows the elevated subway line construction on Jamaica Avenue, looking west with Queens Boulevard at the right. The *New York Times* on September 9, 1917, read: "The residents of Queens Borough along the elevated extensions on Jamaica Avenue can now ride for a five cent fare not only to Park Row but through the new subway in Manhattan." (Q Gardens Gallery.)

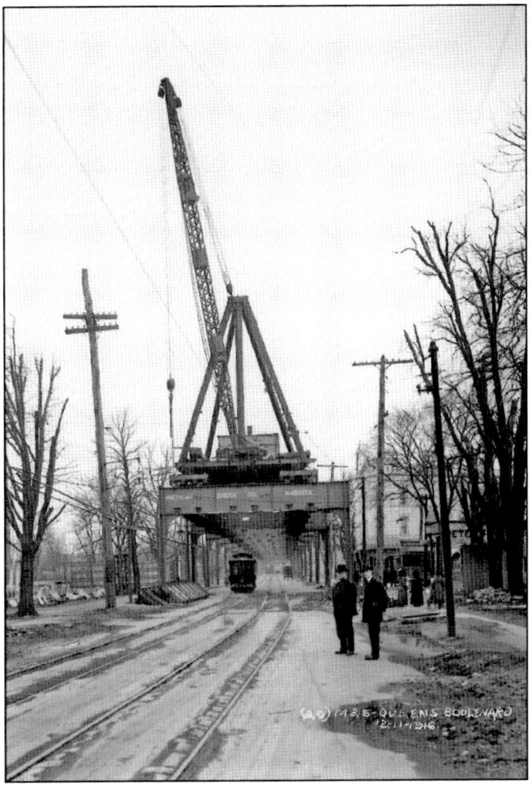

According to the *New York Times* on September 9, 1917, "Many new factories are being built and others under construction. Demand for apartments to house the influx of mechanics. The Jamaica Avenue extension from Cypress Hills, opened on May 25 of 1917 as far as Richmond Hill, and expected to reach Jamaica within the next few months." This view looks west on Jamaica Avenue, with 163rd Street at the right. (Q Gardens Gallery.)

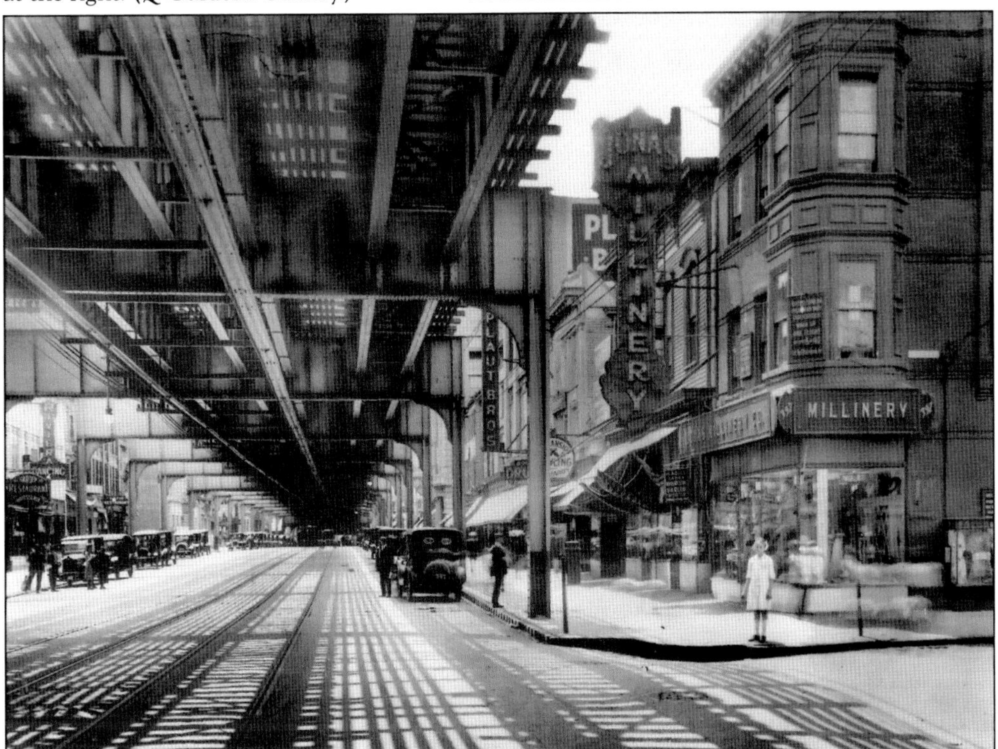

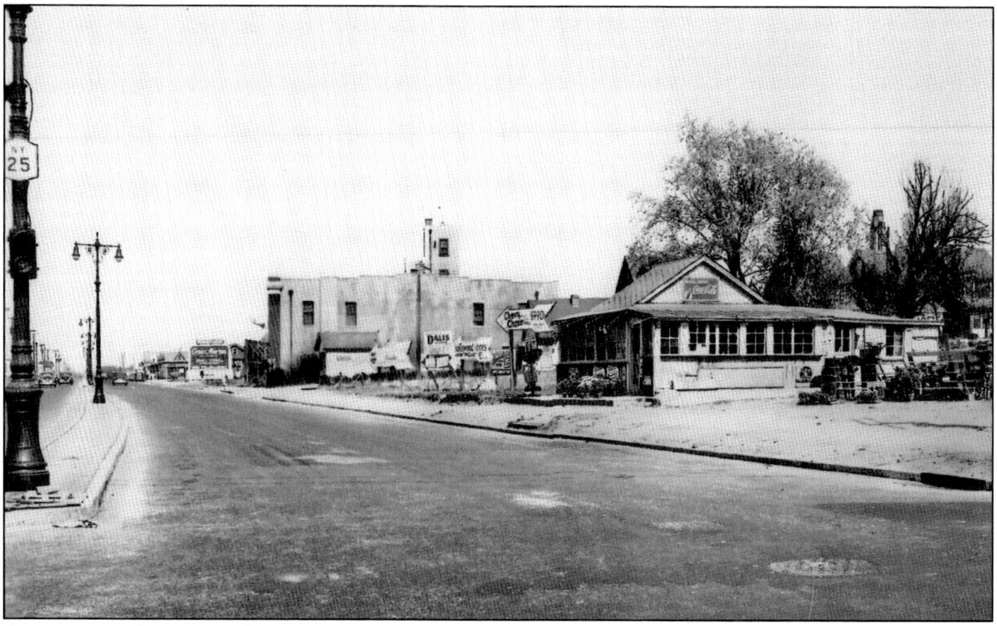

A report in the *Long Island Farmer* on March 6, 1855, remarks on "Union Turnpike—Some of the enterprising inhabitants of our town of Jamaica, have organized a turnpike company and will proceed to open a turnpike from Black Stump (73rd Avenue/Utopia Parkway) a little south of Quarrelsome Lane (75th Avenue), to Myrtle Avenue." This photograph shows Union Turnpike looking east from Parsons Boulevard. (Q Gardens Gallery.)

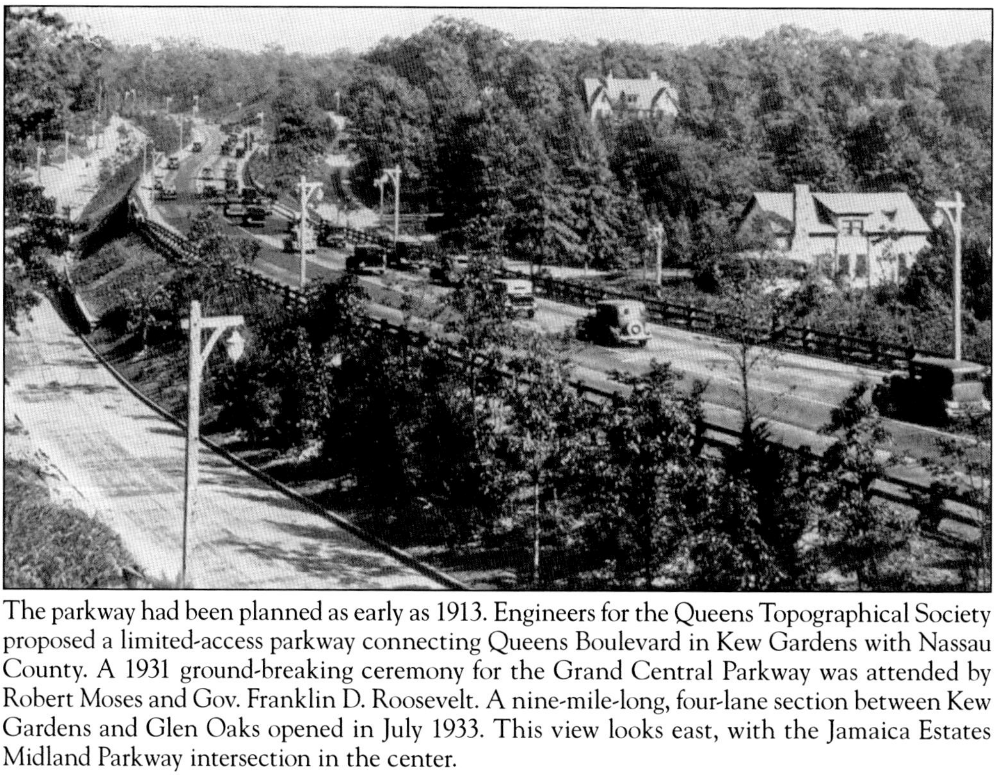

The parkway had been planned as early as 1913. Engineers for the Queens Topographical Society proposed a limited-access parkway connecting Queens Boulevard in Kew Gardens with Nassau County. A 1931 ground-breaking ceremony for the Grand Central Parkway was attended by Robert Moses and Gov. Franklin D. Roosevelt. A nine-mile-long, four-lane section between Kew Gardens and Glen Oaks opened in July 1933. This view looks east, with the Jamaica Estates Midland Parkway intersection in the center.

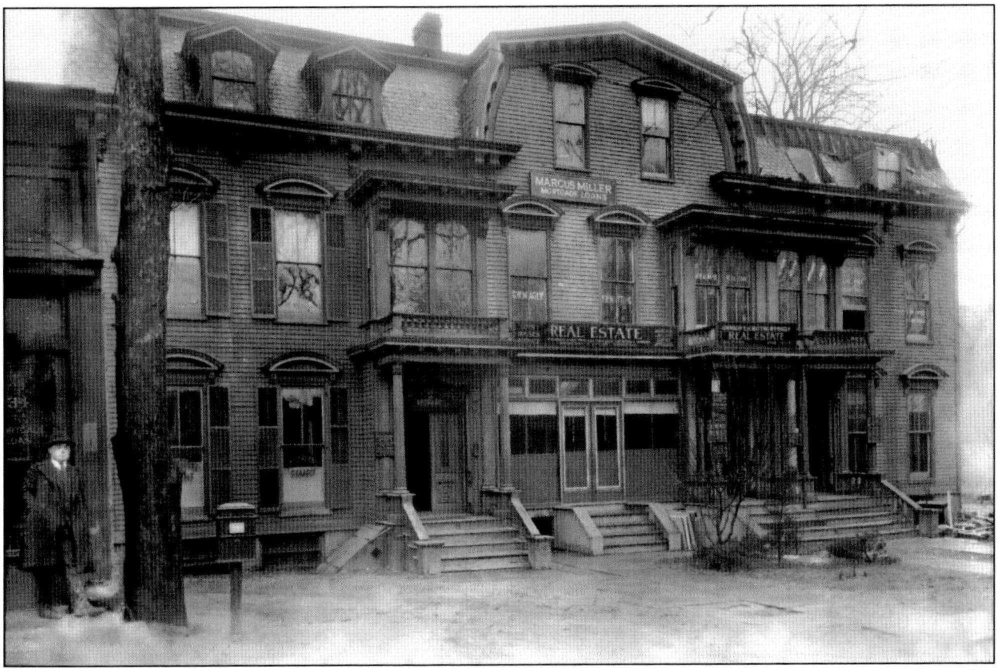

The first record concerning a school is from 1676, when Richard Jones started a school in the town meetinghouse. On May 1, 1792, Union Hall Academy opened, so named because it was a union of Jamaica, Flushing, and Newtown. The academy became famous as an educational center, with students coming from South America and even Europe. This photograph is of the second 1842 school building on Union Hall Street. (Archives at Queens Library, Frederick Weber Photographs.)

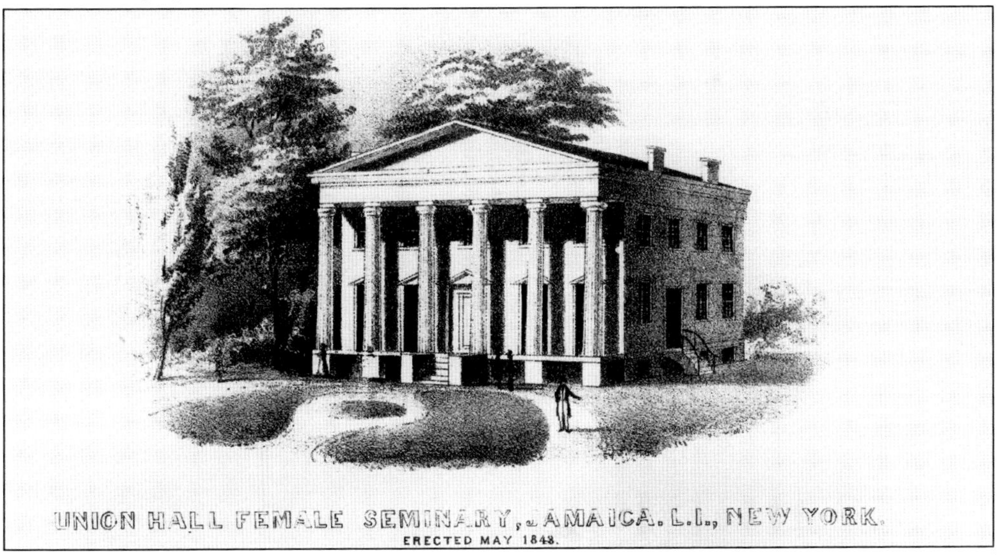

As noted in the *50th Anniversary Address of Union Hall* in 1842, "It was resolved, at a meeting of the inhabitants in 1825, to establish a Female Academy, and in 1832 it was united to Union Hall until it destruction in a fire two years ago." The new 1843 building, illustrated here, was located on Jamaica Avenue between Guy Brewer Avenue and 165th Street. Union Hall Academy closed its doors in 1873 after 81 years.

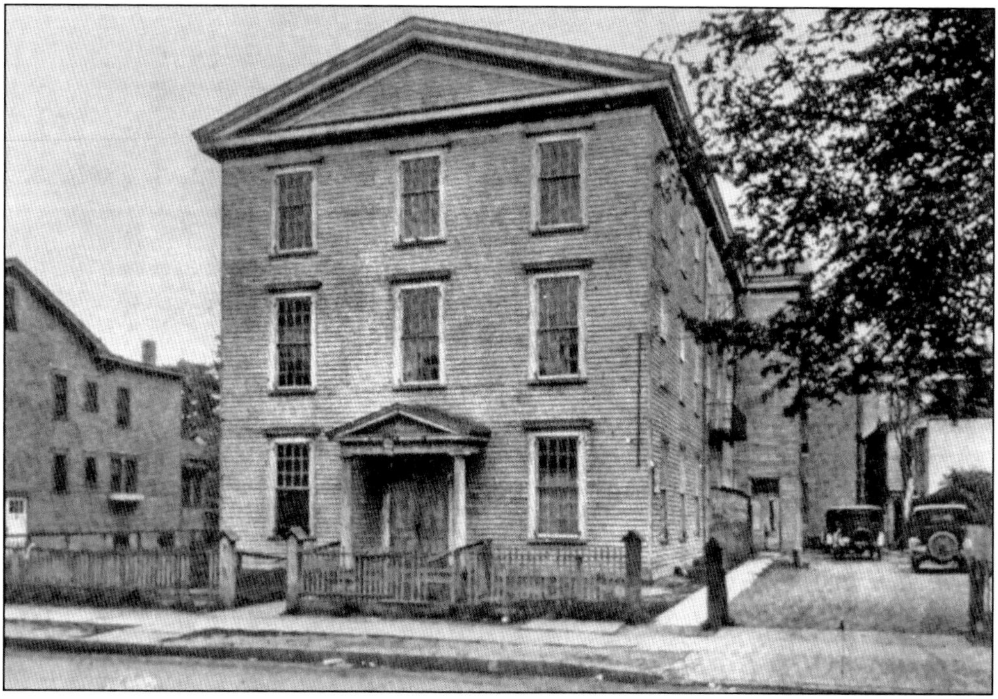

According to the *Brooklyn Eagle* on July 20, 1853, "An act establishing a Board of Education, and providing for a Free School for Jamaica passed the Assembly and Senate." A three-story wooden school building was erected on Herriman Street (161st Street) in 1854. The *Brooklyn Eagle* stated on July 12, 1854, "Jamaica public school opened on the July 6, with 200 pupils." At first, it was named Public School No. 1.

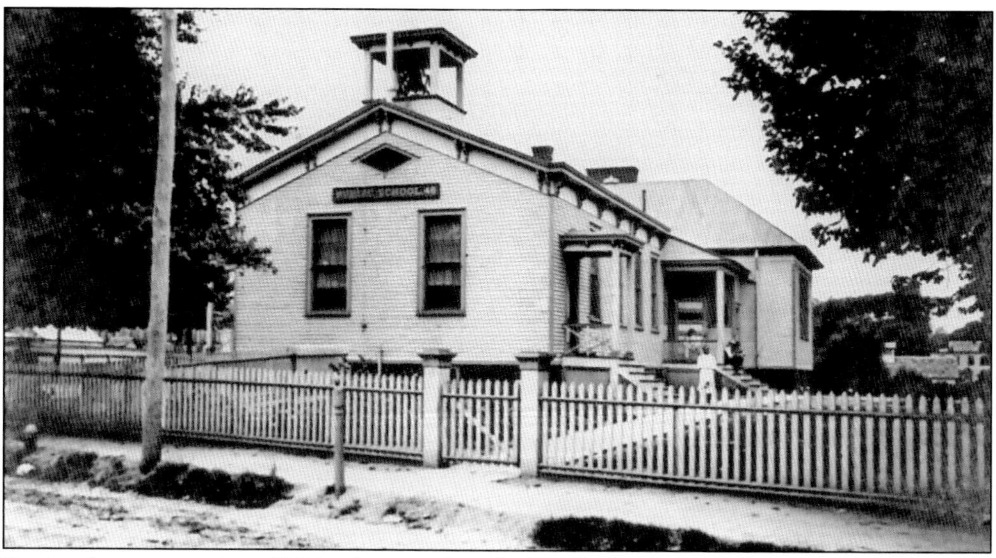

During the construction of PS 1, a location for a "colored" school was underway. Jamaica followed an education policy of separate but equal. On January 17, 1854, a school for African Americans opened in rented rooms at the Allen AME Church on Washington Street (160th Street), with 36 pupils and a Miss Hicks as teacher. It remained in rented rooms until 1886, when a school building was constructed on South Street (Road). First called PS 2, the school was later renamed PS 48.

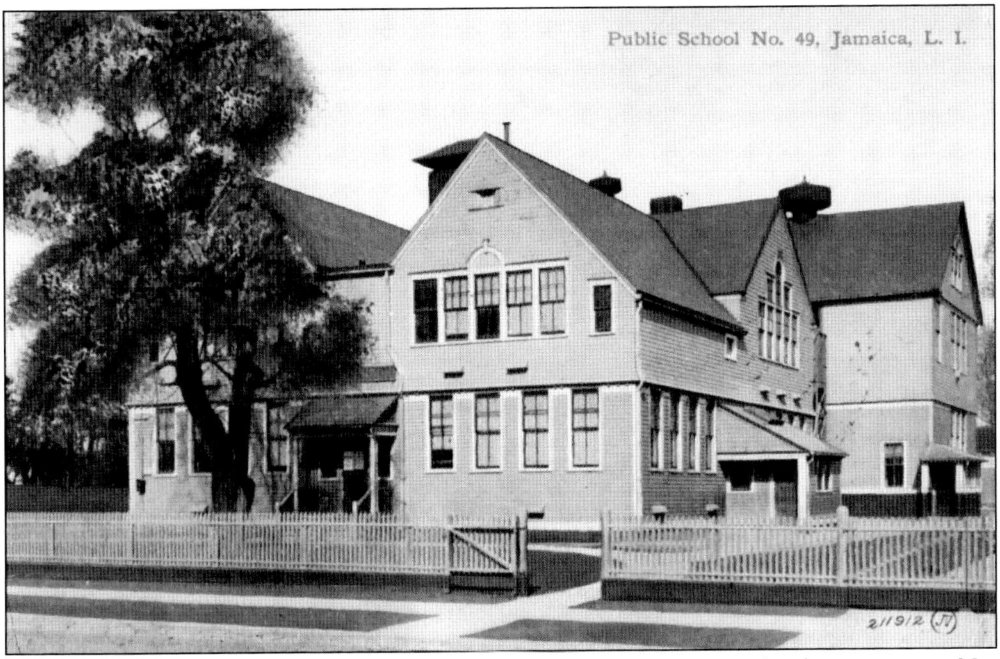

The *Long Island Farmer* on September 6, 1895, reported: "New primary school is now in use. No. 3 school is on Brenton Avenue (170th Street). It has four classrooms, with an assembly-room on the second floor and two teachers." It would later be known as PS 49. Samuel Cisco lived near this new school and, in September 1896, brought his son Jacob to be enrolled.

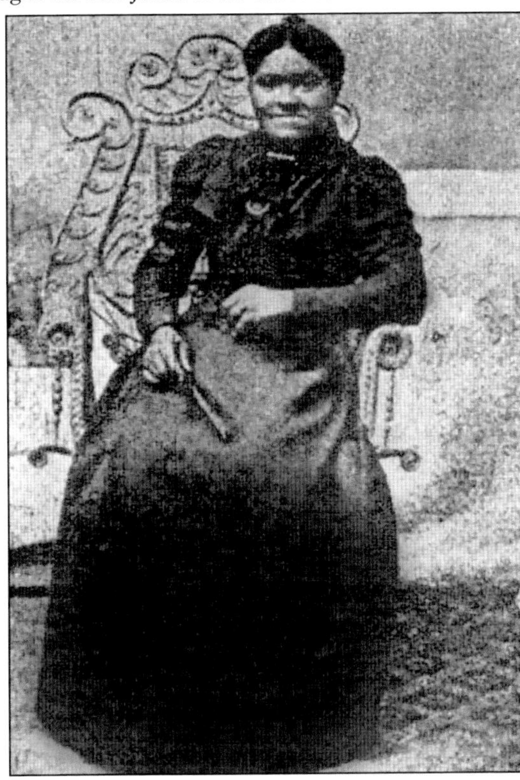

Reported in the *Long Island Farmer* in 1896, "Samuel Cisco was arrested for refusing to send his children to the colored school. 'They were refused admission because they were colored and sent to the colored school.'" Cisco's wife, Elizabeth, continued to fight after Samuel died in 1897. In 1900, her lawyer drafted a bill to end school segregation in New York State. It passed the assembly and was signed by Gov. Theodore Roosevelt. At right is a photograph of Elizabeth Cisco.

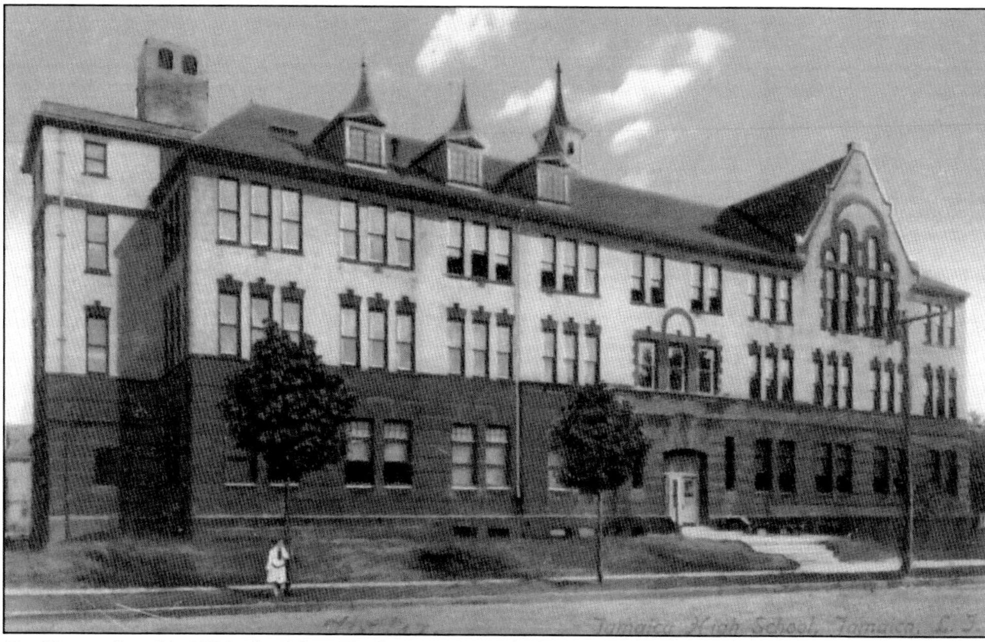

On December 14, 1892, the New York State Board of Regents granted a charter for Jamaica High School, which began in the old schoolhouse on Herriman Street (161st Street). A building was later constructed on Hillside Avenue and 162nd Street. As reported in the *Brooklyn Eagle* on December 4, 1896, "The new high school building was dedicated to the cause of free education, and hundreds of people who inspected the structure were well pleased."

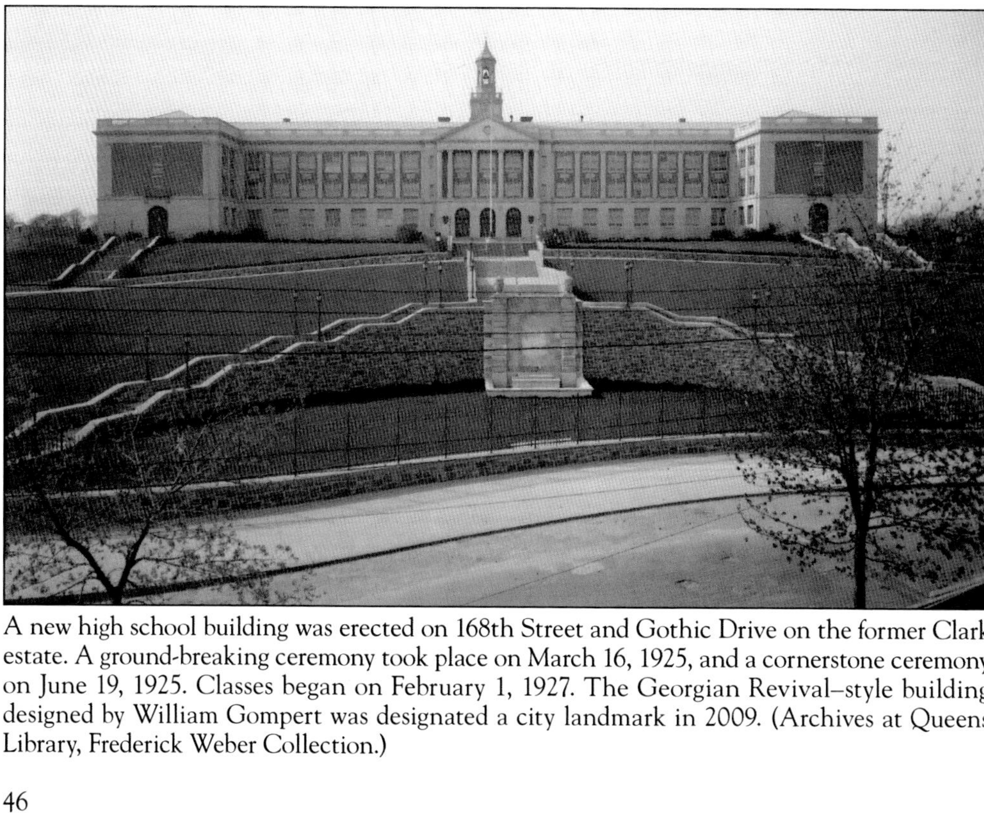

A new high school building was erected on 168th Street and Gothic Drive on the former Clark estate. A ground-breaking ceremony took place on March 16, 1925, and a cornerstone ceremony on June 19, 1925. Classes began on February 1, 1927. The Georgian Revival–style building designed by William Gompert was designated a city landmark in 2009. (Archives at Queens Library, Frederick Weber Collection.)

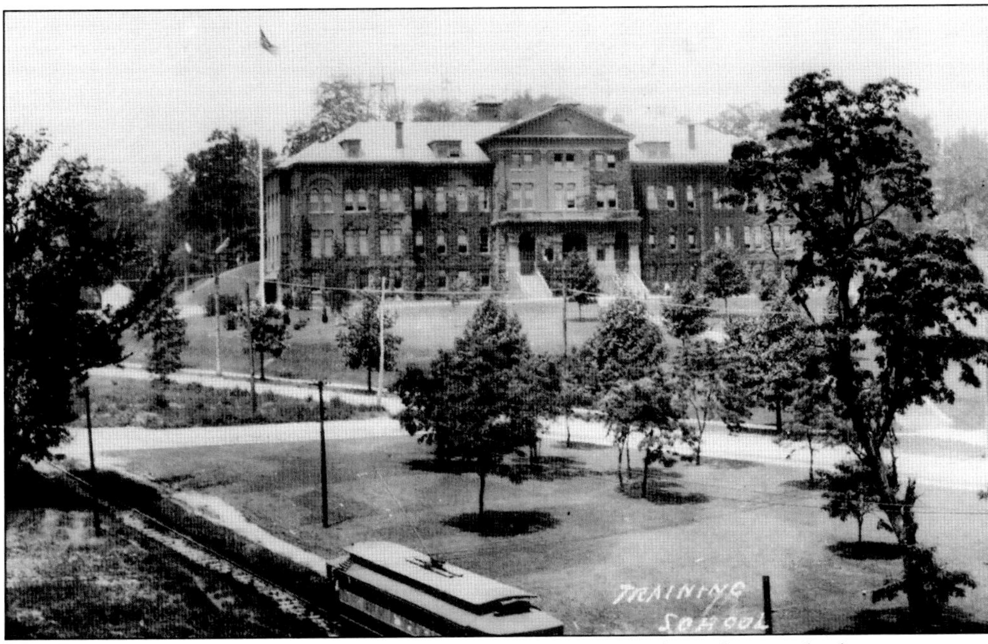

The Jamaica Normal School opened in 1897 for training teachers the standards, or norms, of teaching. "The buildings, which are surrounded by lawns, are situated in a grove of trees on the crest of hills overlooking Jamaica and facing the ocean," stated the *Long Island Farmer*. It stood on Parsons Boulevard and Hillside Avenue and was torn down in the early 1970s. In 1974, Hillcrest High School was built on the site. (Bob Stonehill Collection.)

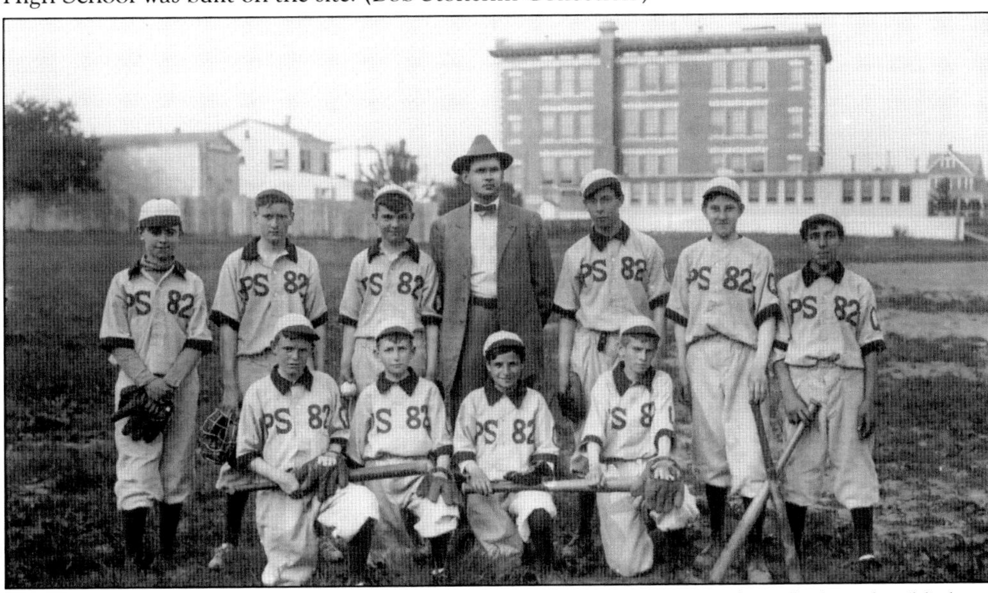

The PS 82 team poses at the Woodhull Baseball Ground (139th Street), with the school behind them. According to the *Long Island Democrat* in 1892, "The game of baseball between the Cincinnati Reds (female) and the 'Young Giants' (colored) took place in Jamaica and witnessed by 350 people. The game was called by the manager of the Reds at 4 o'clock. Their pitcher, first and second base players were excellent, but that was all." (Archives at Queens Library, Frederick Weber Collection.)

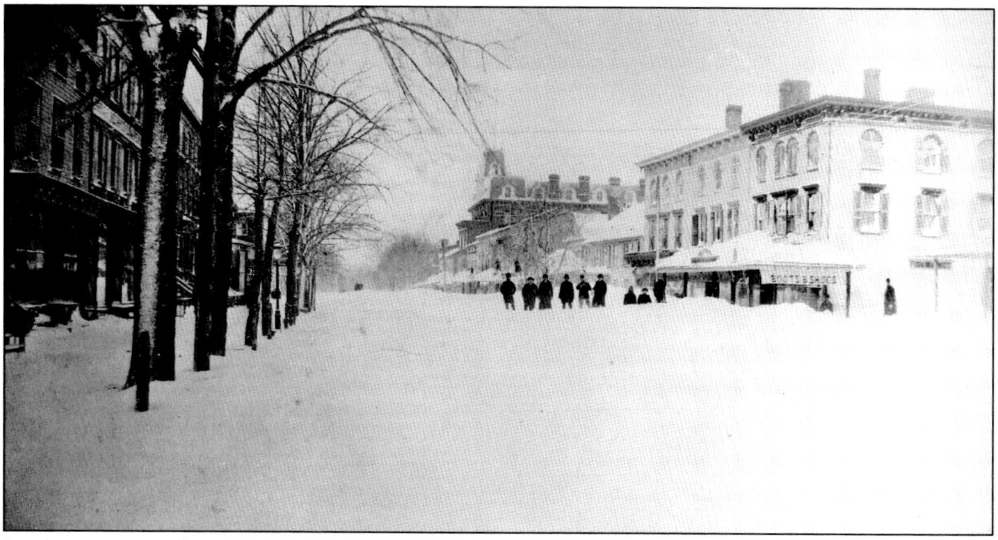

Looking west on Jamaica Avenue, town hall is in the distance in this view of the Great Blizzard of 1888. According to the *Long Island Democrat*, "The snow was found in many places waist deep. In front of Edward's Bakery a drift had formed 12 feet in height and so on down the north side of Jamaica Avenue, 10 feet was about the general rule to Town Hall and beyond."

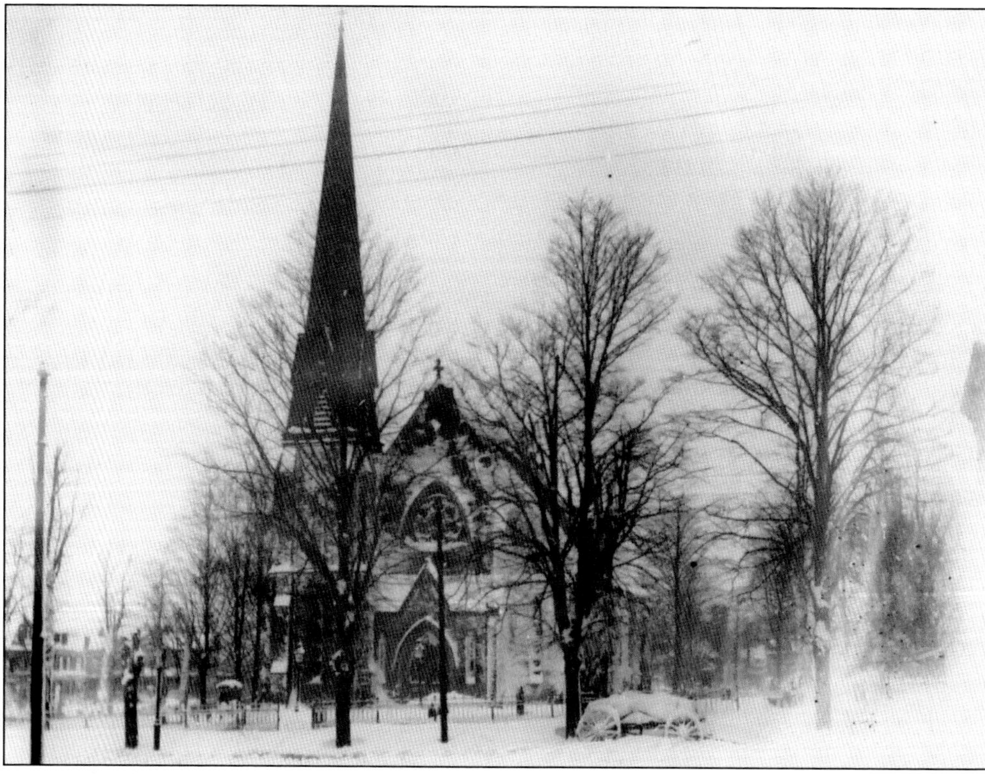

Grace Church is shown in a blizzard in 1898. According to the *Long Island Democrat*, in the Great Blizzard of 1888, "'Blizzard stories' are all the rage. A man seeing a hitching post in the snow drift, tied his horse. The next morning after the snow had settled he saw his poor horse hanging to the spire of a church steeple." (Archives at Queens Library, William Murray Photographs.)

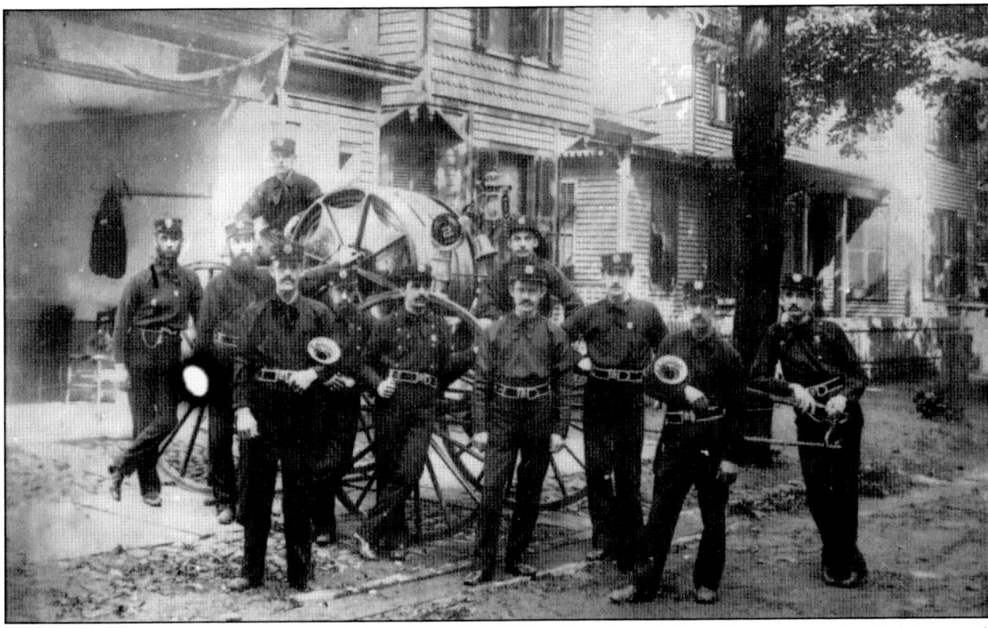

The *New York Times* reported on May 13, 1895, "The Excelsior Hose Company No. 2 (pictured) prides itself on member's promptness to fires. When several failed to respond, a resolution was adopted. Resolved, That, no fines be imposed the newly-married members for the non-attendance during what is commonly known as the 'honeymoon,' which for the purposes of this company, shall be deemed to last for months." (Archives at Queens Library, Frederick Weber Photographs.)

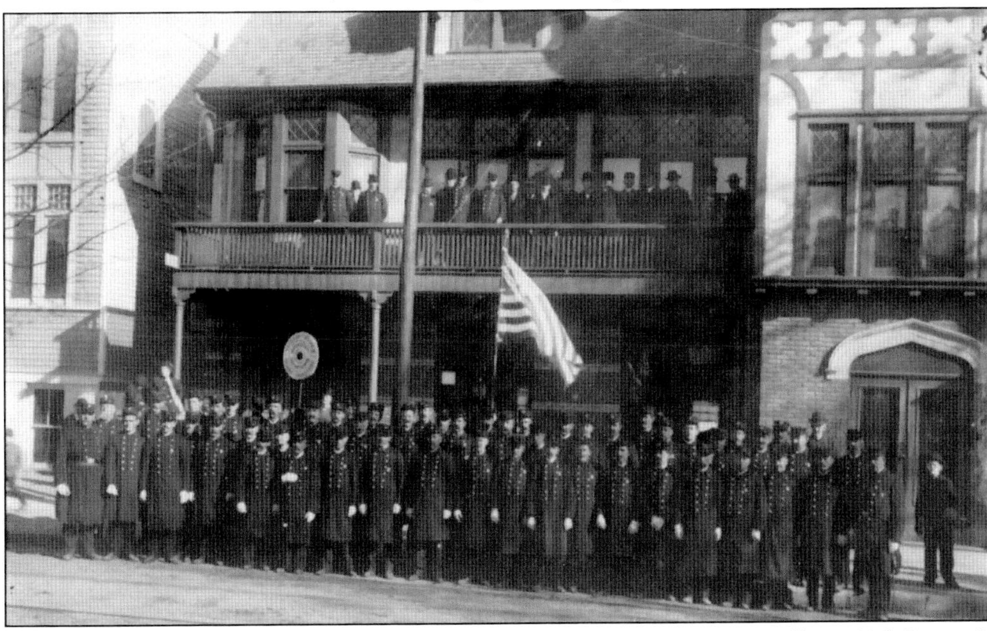

A 1906 photograph shows the Veteran Firemen Sharp Shooters at Firemen's Hall on 160th Street. In 1797, James Waters, owner of an engine, petitioned for the better extinguishing of fires. Proprietors of a fire engine in Jamaica were authorized to form an organization of three to five trustees who would choose 13 volunteer firemen. This number was later increased to 24. (Archives at Queens Library, Frederick Weber Photographs.)

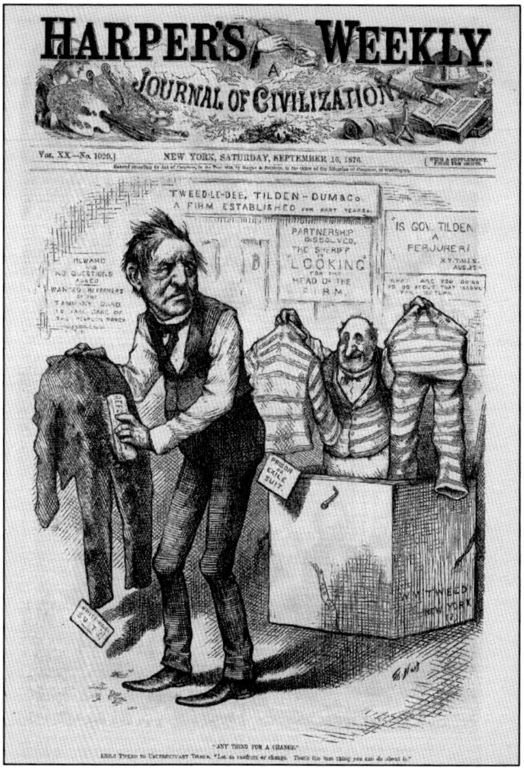

Harper's Weekly's September 16, 1876, edition includes a political cartoon by Thomas Nast of William M. Tweed, sometimes called Boss Tweed, a New York City politician who was convicted for stealing over $100 million from city taxpayers. "Sale of Tweed Place at Jamaica. Historic homestead sells for $73,000. The property belonged to William Tweed, and its parlors are credited with having been the scene of many secret affairs concocted and discussed," reported the *New York Times* on April 13, 1893.

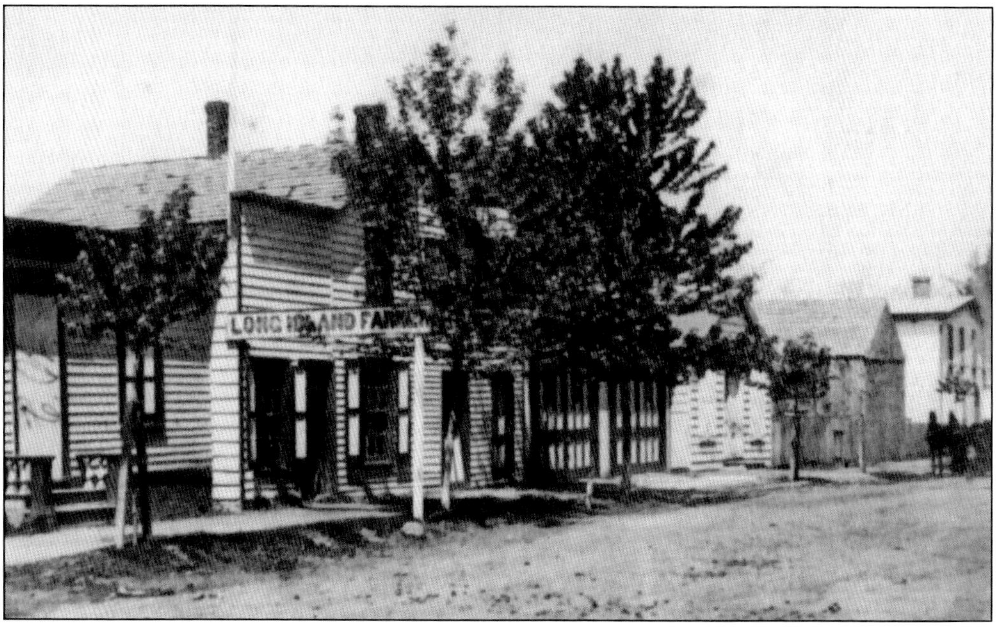

An 1885 photograph shows the Long Island Farmer office located on the west side of Herriman Avenue (161st Street) near Jamaica Avenue. The *Long Island Farmer* was published in 1819. The weekly newspaper eventually became a daily and in 1920 became the *Long Island Daily Press* (shortened to the *Long Island Press* in the 1960s). The paper ended a 150-year-plus run when it closed in 1977. (Archives at Queens Library, George Winans Collection.)

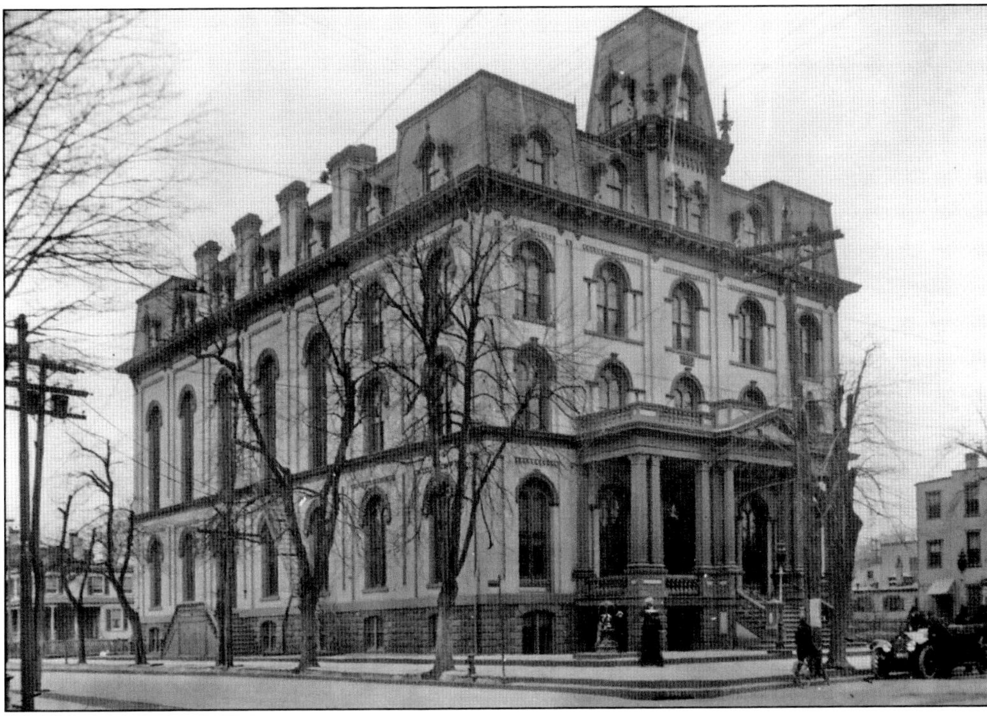

According to the *Long Island Farmer* on December 22, 1868, "Our New Town Hall—The dimensions of the building is 71 feet front and 116 feet deep. Three stories high, faced with O. K. Crotos brick, with iron and brown stone trimming. Surmounted by a mansard French roof, covered with the best Susquehanna slate and a cupola with flag staff of suitable dimensions." (Archives at Queens Library, Frederick Weber Photographs.)

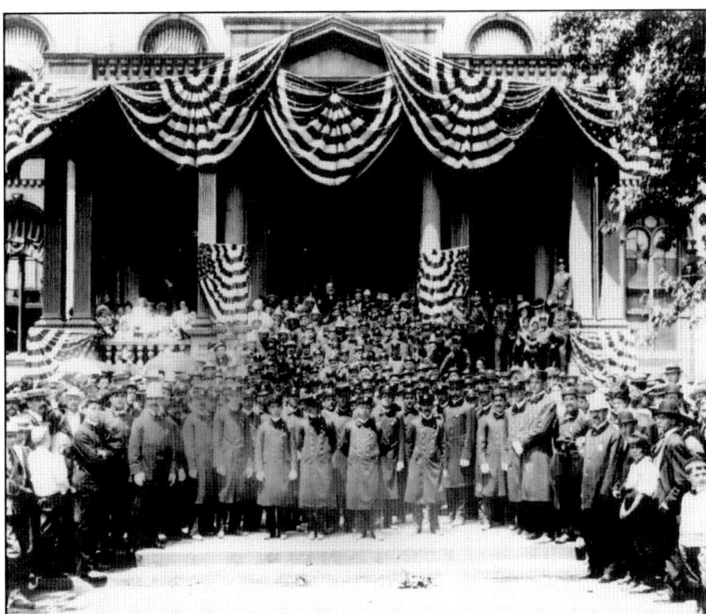

The town hall served as a courthouse, opera house, and jail and included meeting rooms for various clubs. After the 1898 consolidation of the five boroughs, it became the municipal courthouse, sheriff's office, and traffic court. This graceful Victorian structure was razed in 1941. This view shows the Jamaica Volunteer Firemen on the steps of the town hall on July 4, 1907. (Archives at Queens Library, Frederick Weber Photographs.)

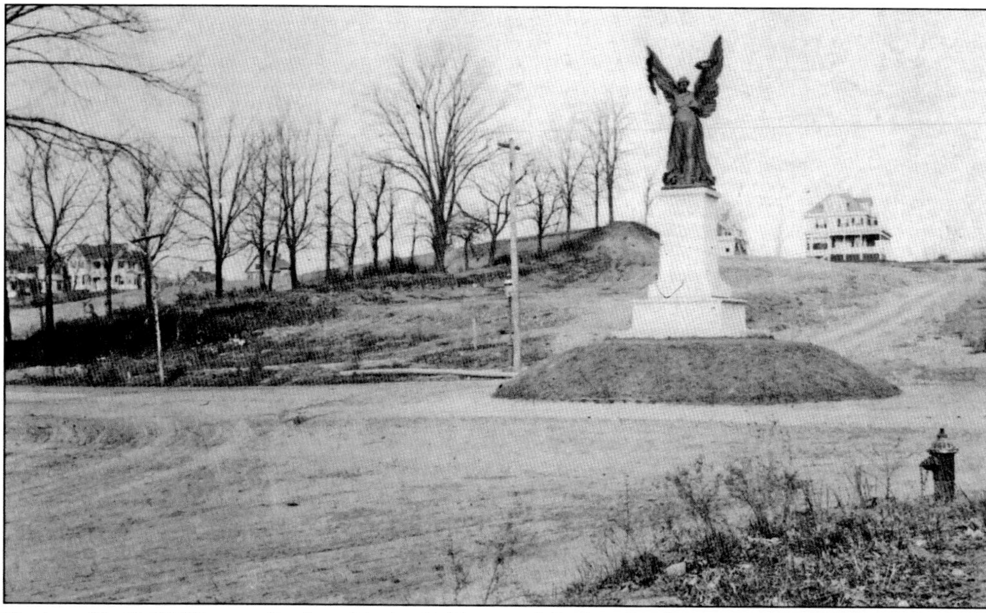

Designed by F. Wellington Ruckstuhl, the Soldiers and Sailors Civil War Monument depicts Victory alighting from the clouds. Her drapery is filled with the rushing wind, giving the figure motion. She holds a palm branch symbolizing fame and a crown of laurel standing for immortality. For the soldiers of Jamaica who died for their country, it indicates that they will now live victorious in history. (Archives at Queens Library, George Winans Collection.)

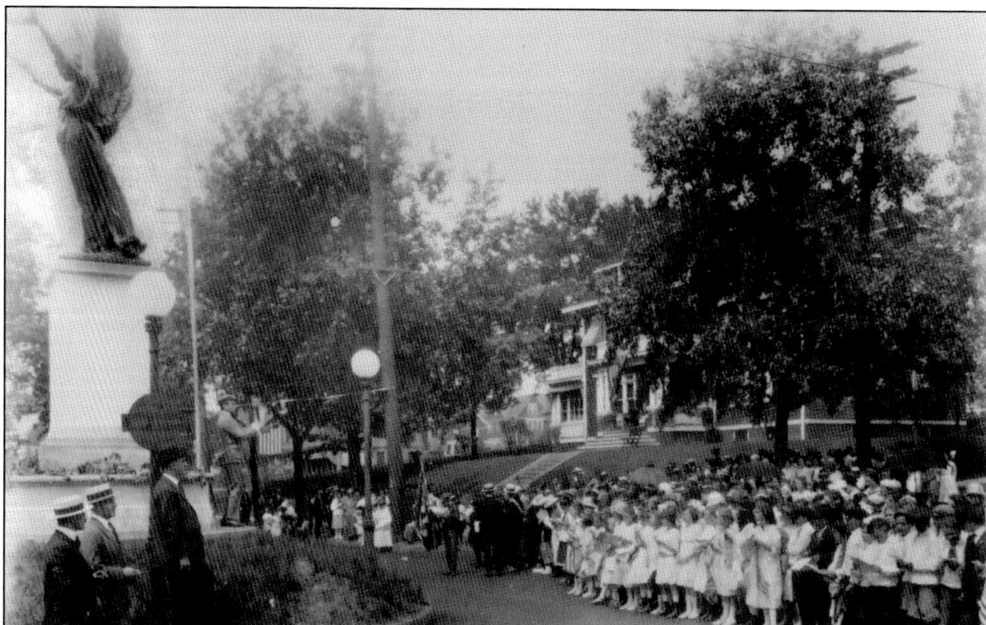

The monument was erected at Hillside Avenue and Bergen Avenue (Merrick Boulevard) and unveiled on May 30, 1896. On the granite pedestal, designed by Julius Harder, are the dates 1861–1865. According to the *New York Times*, on May 31, 1896, "In the pedestal there is a box containing the names of all men, white and black, who went to the front." (Archives at Queens Library, Joseph Burt Photographs.)

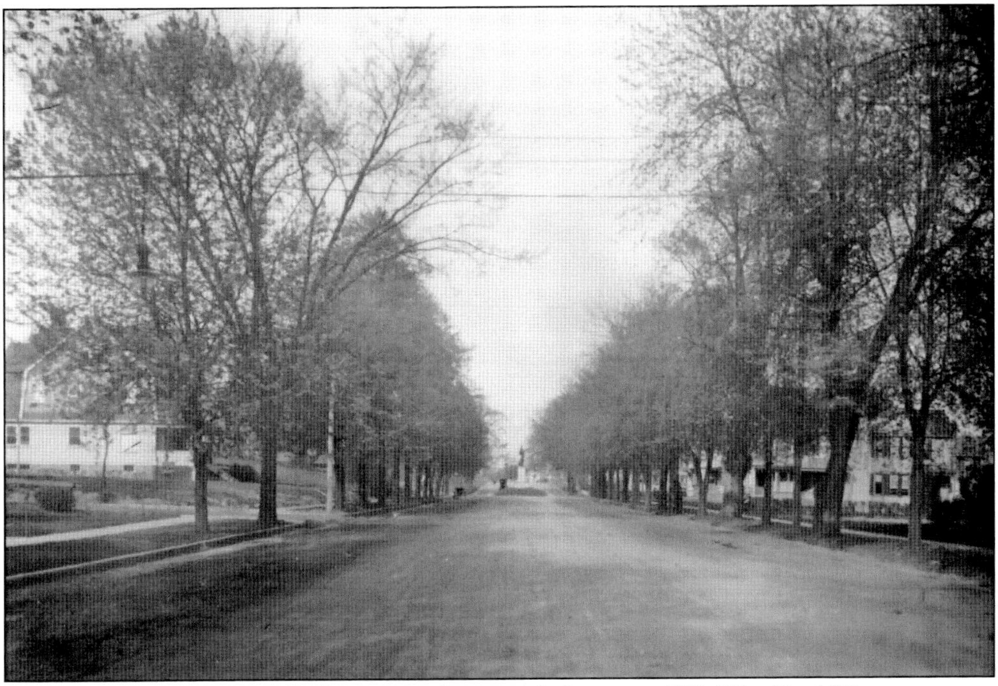

This view looks east on Hillside Avenue from 164th Street in 1910. The Civil War monument stands in the center of the avenue. On March 1, 1870, the *Long Island Democrat* wrote, "There is a bill before the legislature to open an avenue (Hillside) on the north side of Jamaica under the hills, 100 feet in width, and lay sidewalks and plant trees." (Archives at Queens Library, Frederick Weber Photographs.)

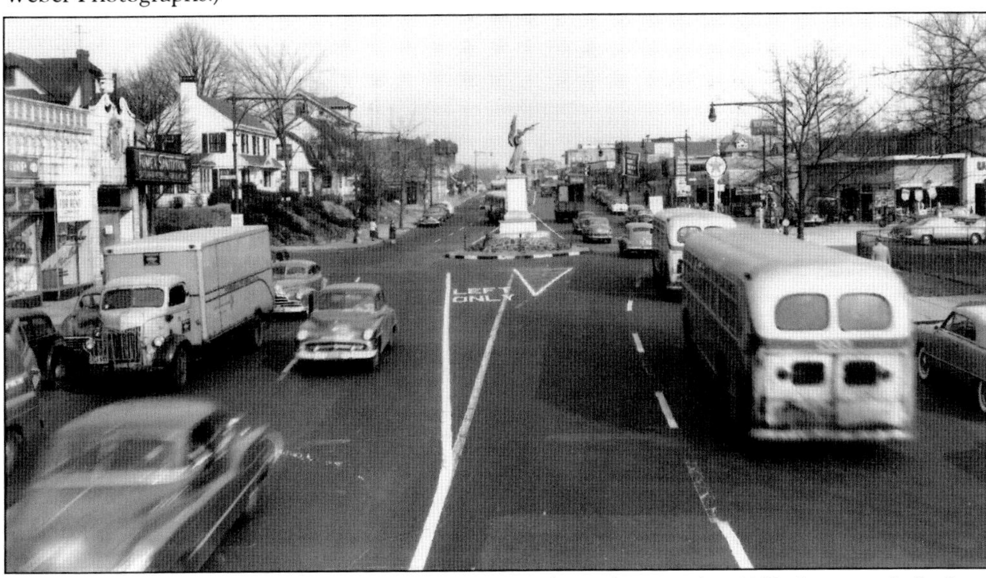

The view changes dramatically four decades later, as shown here in this 1952 photograph, looking east on Hillside Avenue at the Merrick Boulevard intersection. The Soldiers and Sailors Civil War Monument faces Merrick Boulevard, looking south. It became a major obstacle with the increased flow of traffic and in 1960 was moved to a park on the south side of Hillside Avenue and 175th Street.

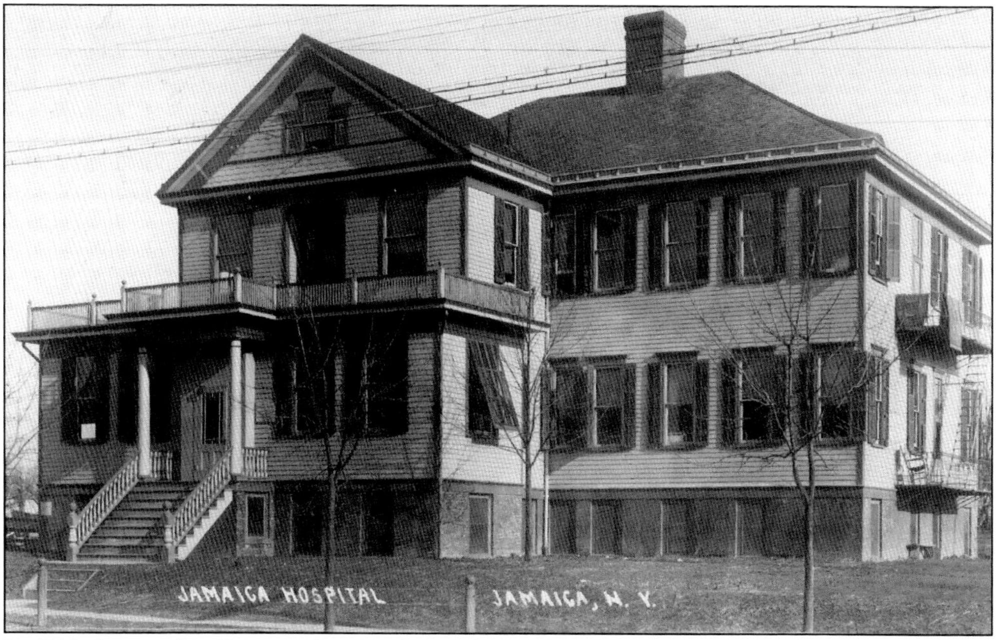

In 1883, the people of Jamaica foresaw the need for an institution where the ill could be made well. A hospital fair raised $179.40, but the possible location was an issue. "If the hospital is located in our Town Hall, there will be trouble, clubs have decided to vacate. Small-pox, typhoid fever, or the piercing screams of persons undergoing amputation will be everything but pleasant," reported the *Long Island Democrat* in 1888. A temporary hospital opened in 1891 in rented space at Jamaica Avenue and Canal Street (168th Street). The first permanent hospital (above) was erected and opened in 1898 at New York Avenue (Guy Brewer Boulevard). Razed years ago, the site is on the York College campus. In 1924, a new larger hospital was opened on Van Wyck Boulevard (Expressway). (Below, Archives at Queens Library, Frederick Weber Photographs.)

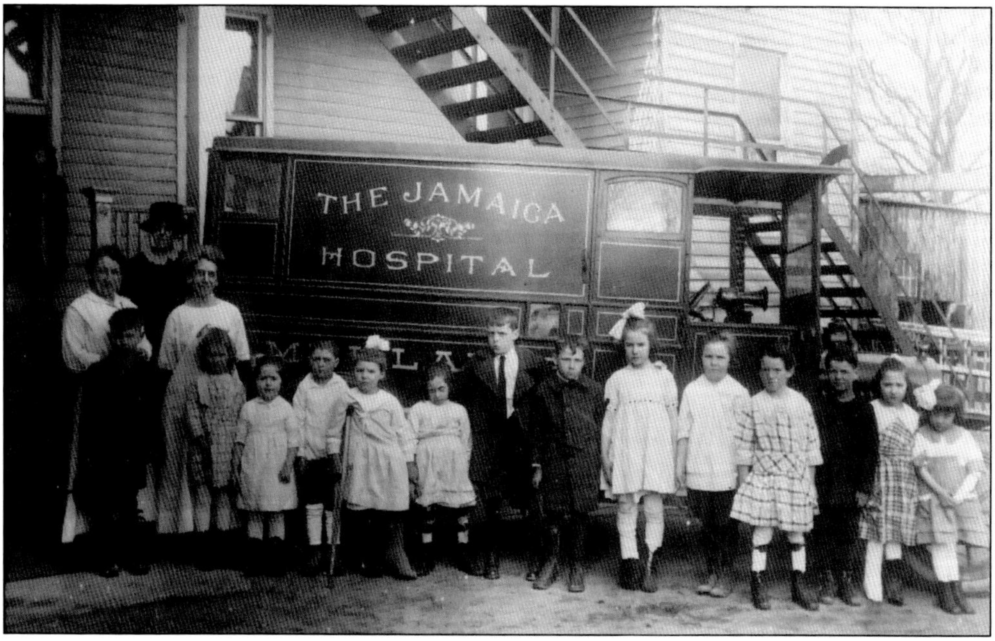

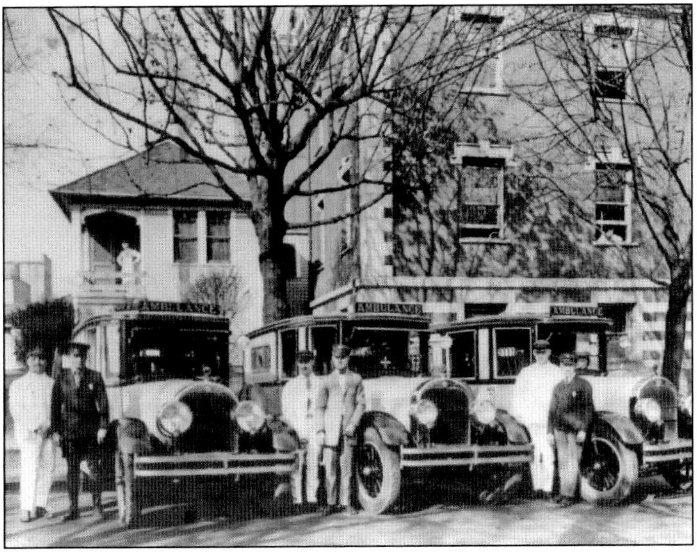

Father Zeller of St. Mary's Catholic German Church persuaded doctors to form a Catholic hospital. Opened on Jamaica Avenue in 1902, it was named St. Mary's Hospital. Land and two cottages on Shelton Avenue (Eighty-ninth Avenue) and Ray Street (153rd Street) were donated, and in 1904, this 300-patient brick hospital opened. (Archives at Queens Library, Frederick Weber Photographs.)

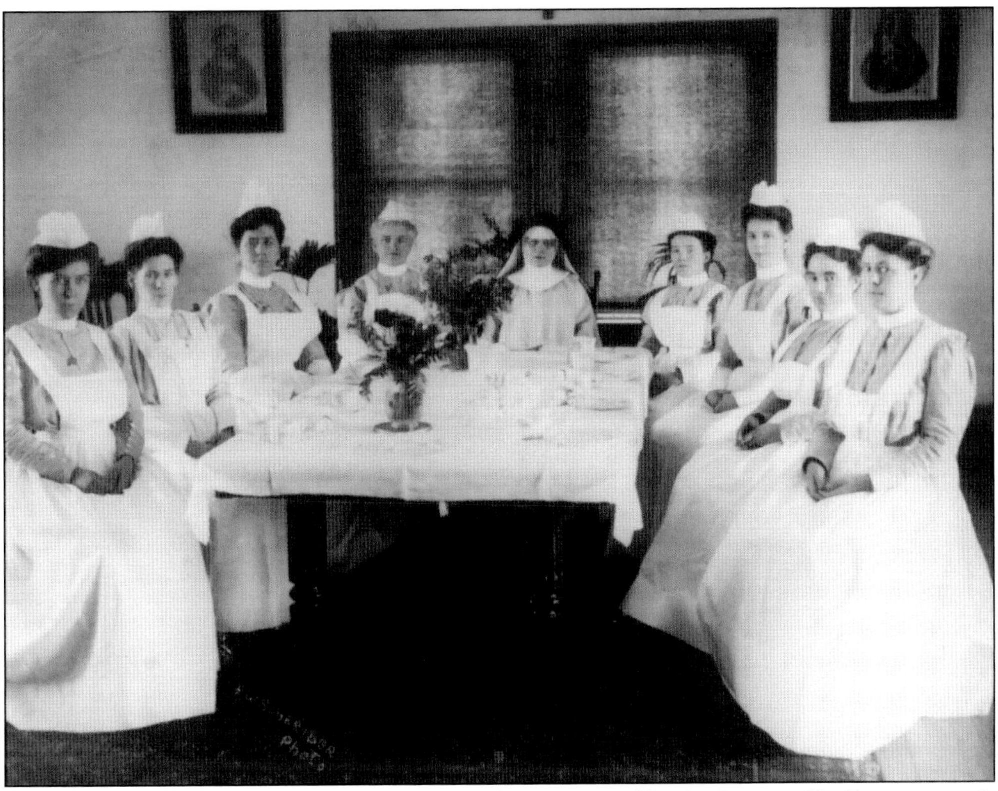

Renamed Mary Immaculate in 1920, the hospital was operated by the Sisters of St. Dominic, with Mother Prioress Sister Mary Catherine. In 1925, a 10-story facility accommodating 7,500 patients was erected, adjoining the older building. The *New York Times* reported in 1905, "Shep, a collie haunts St. Mary's since his master was admitted for appendicitis. He has not been admitted but food has been sent out to him." (Archives at Queens Library, Frederick Weber Photographs.)

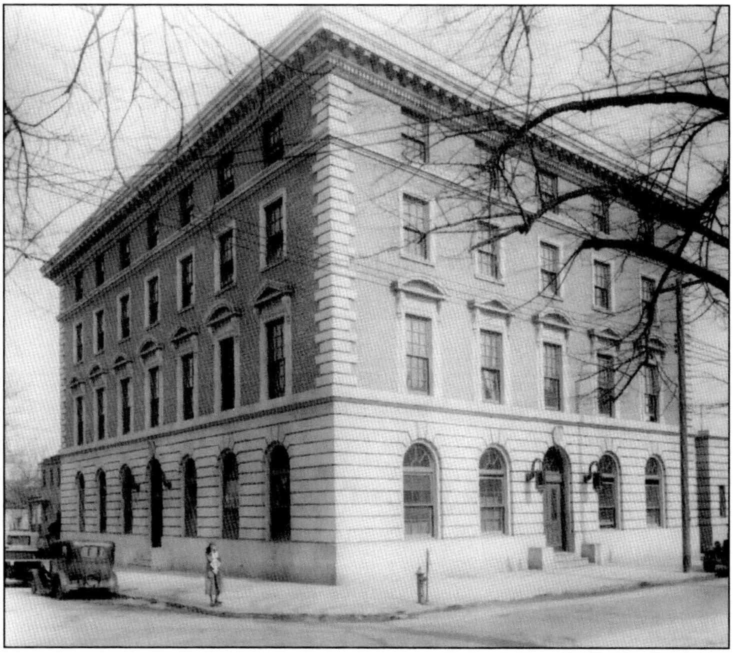

The 103rd Precinct at 168th Street and P.O. Edward Byrne Avenue is shown here. An article in the *New York Times* on May 15, 1889, noted that "Jamaica is suffering from the depredations of sneak thieves and burglars. During the last two weeks a dozen chicken roosts have been robbed and two houses entered. The citizens will hold a meeting to devise some way to secure police protection." (Archives at Queens Library, Frederick Weber Photographs.)

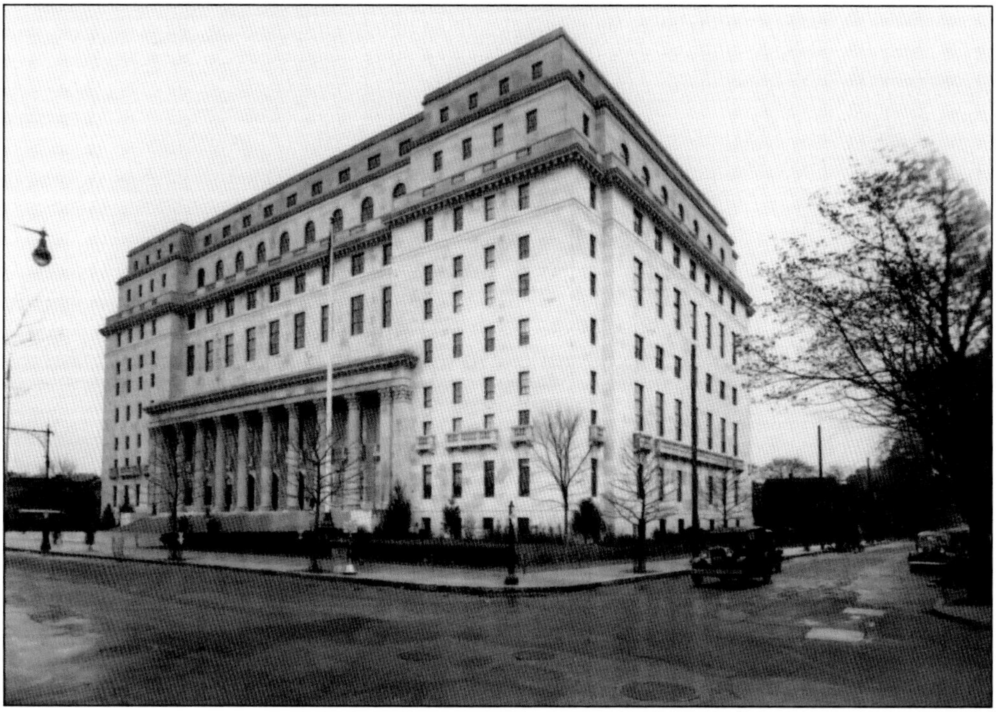

The General Court House of Jamaica was dedicated in 1939. A *New York Times* July 15, 1883, article relates, "Justice Betts asks. 'Fritzpatrick, same old trouble?—Mother-in-lawism?' In reply, 'No, your worship! Now peace and happiness reign supreme, sunshine in our home does beam, one more angel has gone above, that kind, affectionate, beautiful dove, my wife's mother.' Betts answered, 'Those lines are every affecting. You are discharged,' with court poet ambling out." (Archives at Queens Library, Frederick Weber Photographs.)

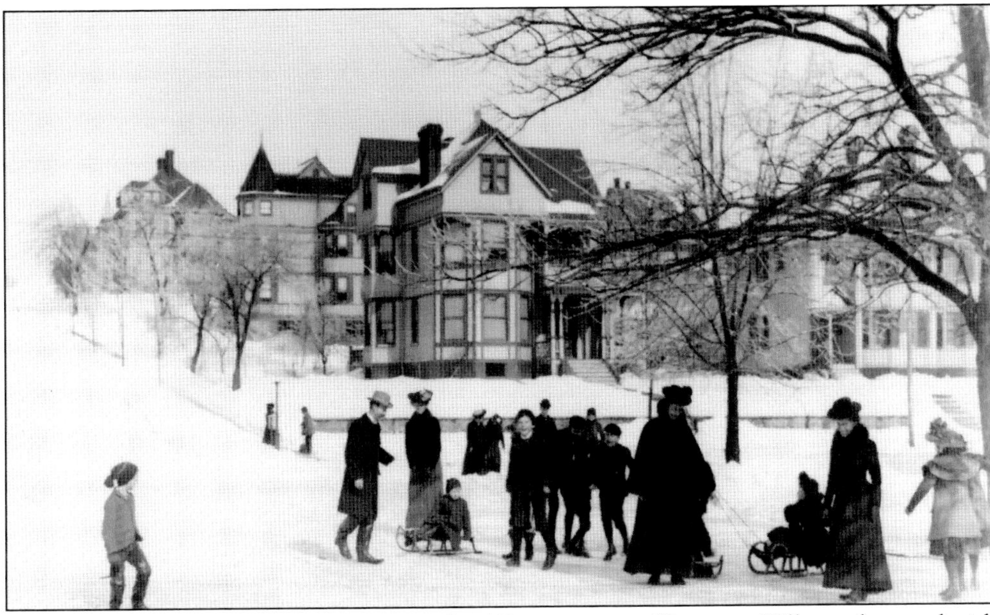

A write-up in the January 19, 1886, *Long Island Democrat* says, "Prospect Hill was thronged with coasting parties of boys and girls. The hills in a good condition, and a long run could be made. As a 'bob' was coming down, the front runners broke and threw all the occupants off." Here the view looks north on Union Avenue (162nd Street) and Hillside Avenue. (Archives at Queens Library, George Winans Collection.)

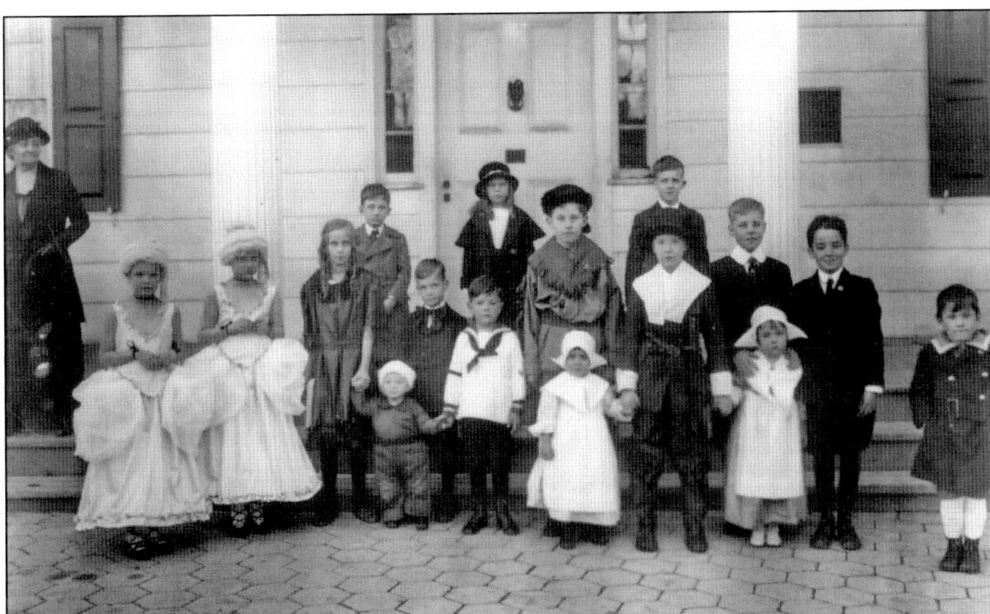

At a patriotic celebration at the Rufus King house in 1921, children are dressed in period colonial costumes. According to the *New York Times* on March 8, 1903, "The care of the house has been given to an organization of women known as the King Manor Association. The Daughters of the Revolution and other patriotic societies have also assisted in restoring the house." (Archives at Queens Library, Frederick Weber Photographs.)

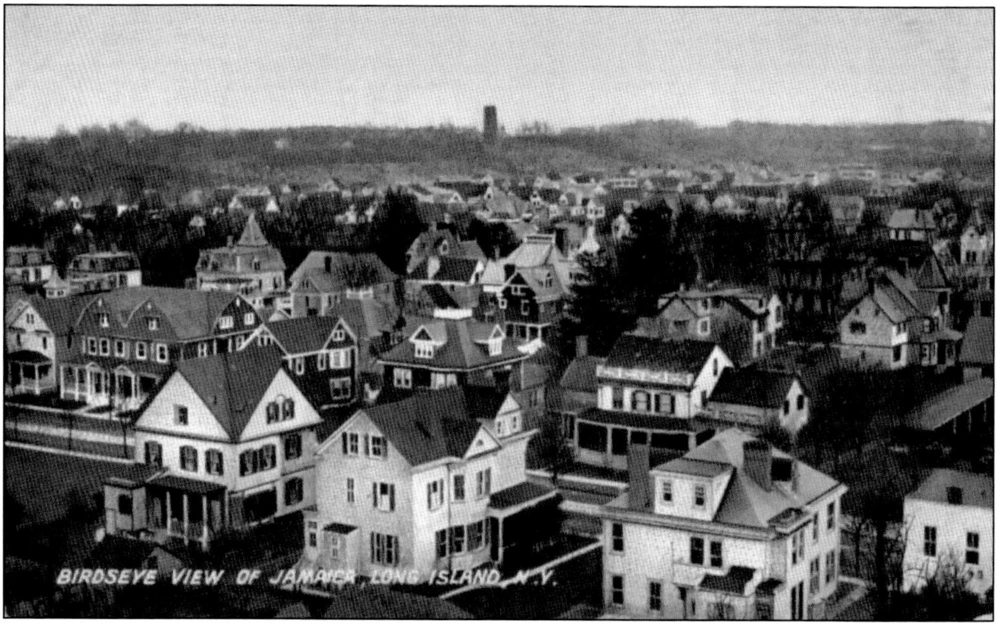

This view looks north of Jamaica to the hills created by glacial movements some 18,000 years ago. The *Brooklyn Eagle* on April 10, 1858, reported "the recent discovery of some bones of the Mastodon in the excavation made at Baisley Pond, the Village of Jamaica, we availed ourselves to visit to witness the disinterment of the remains of so interesting a monster." The workmen had shoveled up several molar teeth.

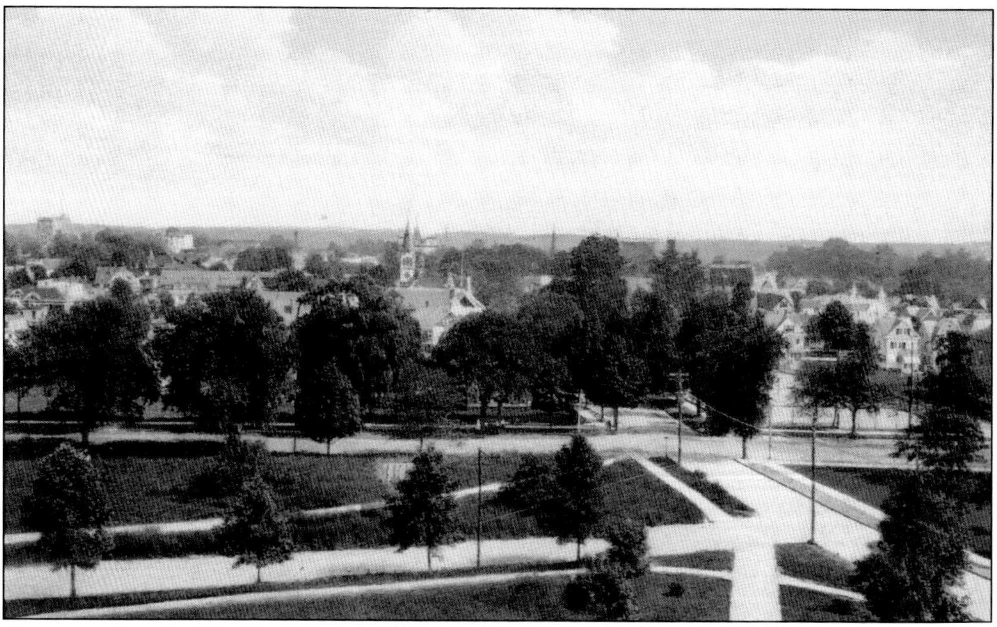

As reported in the *New York Times* on March 7, 1897, "The light harness horsemen have secured the right to use as a speedway Hillside Avenue, Jamaica, a stretch of country that will make an ideal course for the speeding horses by the Board Public Improvements. The horsemen are jubilant at their success which was opposed by property owners." Hillside Avenue is seen in the center, with the Parsons Boulevard intersection at right, looking south. (Bob Stonehill Collection.)

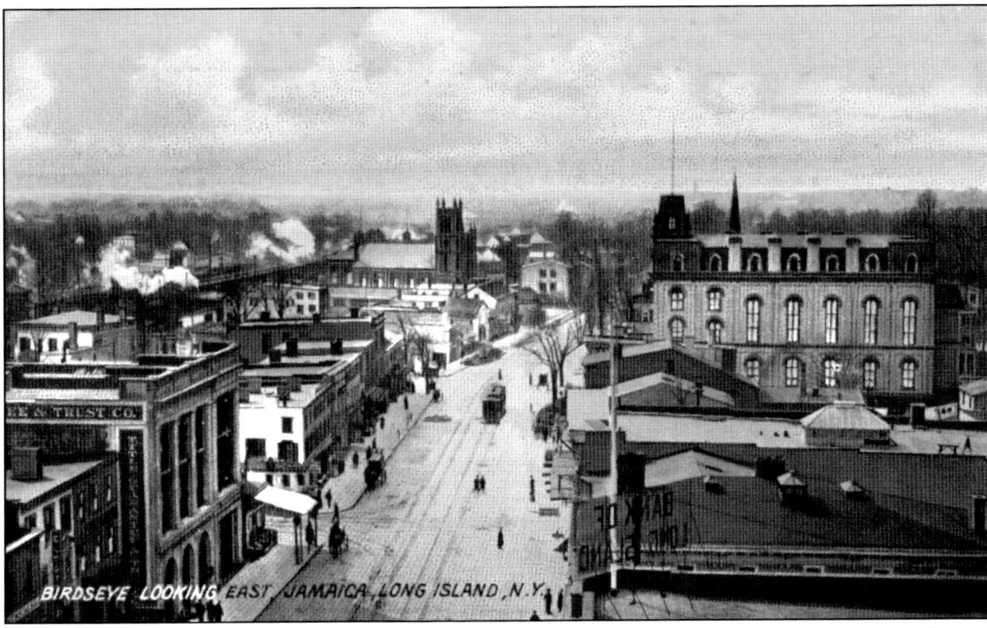

This mislabeled postcard looks west, not east, on Jamaica Avenue, with the town hall at right. "At 3:10 an earthquake lasting five seconds was felt. The town hall was seriously shaken. At several hotels glasses danced, billiard balls moved and people were terrorized. P. Riley, a liveryman at Pettit's Hotel, buried himself in the hay loft. It was late last evening before he could be induced to venture out," reported the *Brooklyn Eagle* on March 15, 1893.

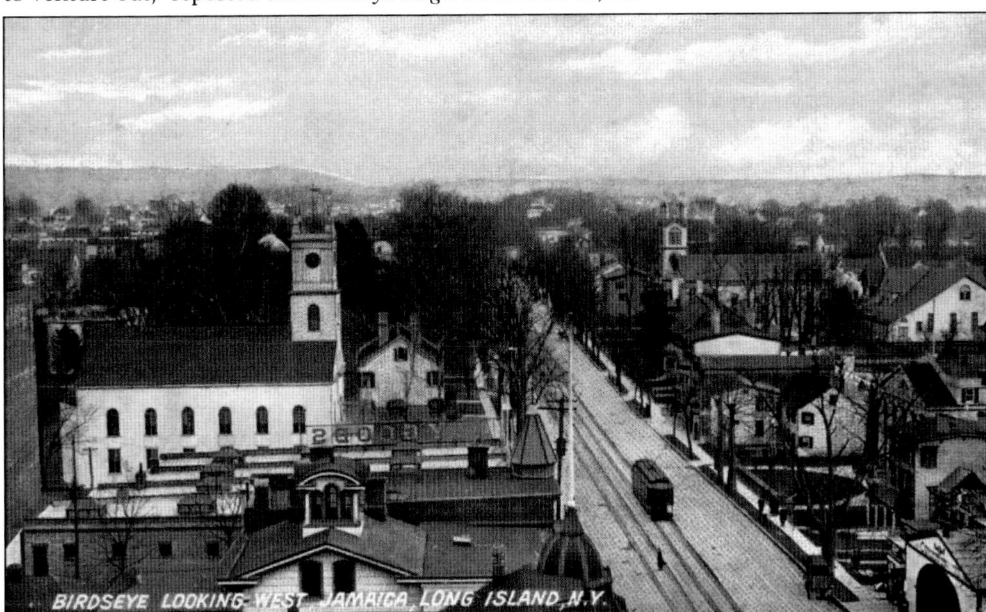

A mislabeled postcard looks east, not west, on Jamaica Avenue, with the Presbyterian church on the left at 164th Street. An article in the March 5, 1891, *New York Times* says, "The Trustees of the Presbyterian Church decided to continue without a choir. For several Sundays the choir loft is said to be very cold. Choir members suffered so much they became hoarse. Thereupon certain congregation members made fun of them. The choir refused to sing until apologies were made."

There is only one

PROSPECT HILL

and few places like it anywhere.

In New York City, in sight of the Ocean, but 145 feet above it, with real country at its back door and real city at its front gate.

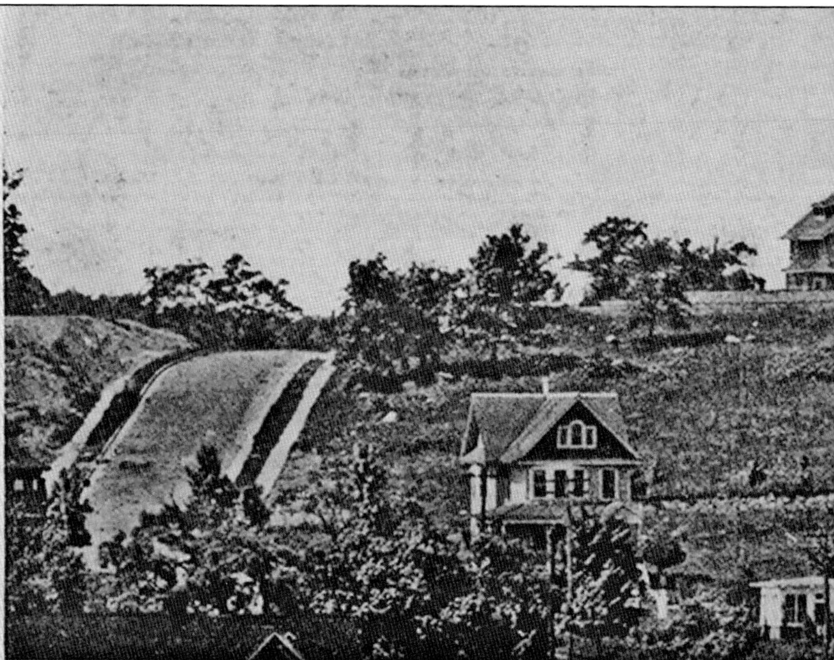

Reproduced from a recent photo of Prospect Hill, Jamaica

This is a rare four-folded postcard advertisement about the Prospect Hill development located north of Hillside Avenue on the terminal moraine, the backbone of Long Island. The complex offered commanding views of the Atlantic Ocean before the area was overdeveloped with multistory apartments. The *Long Island Democrat* reported on May 29, 1883: "On Thursday night a great many persons went up to Prospect Hill to view the illumination of the newly opened Brooklyn

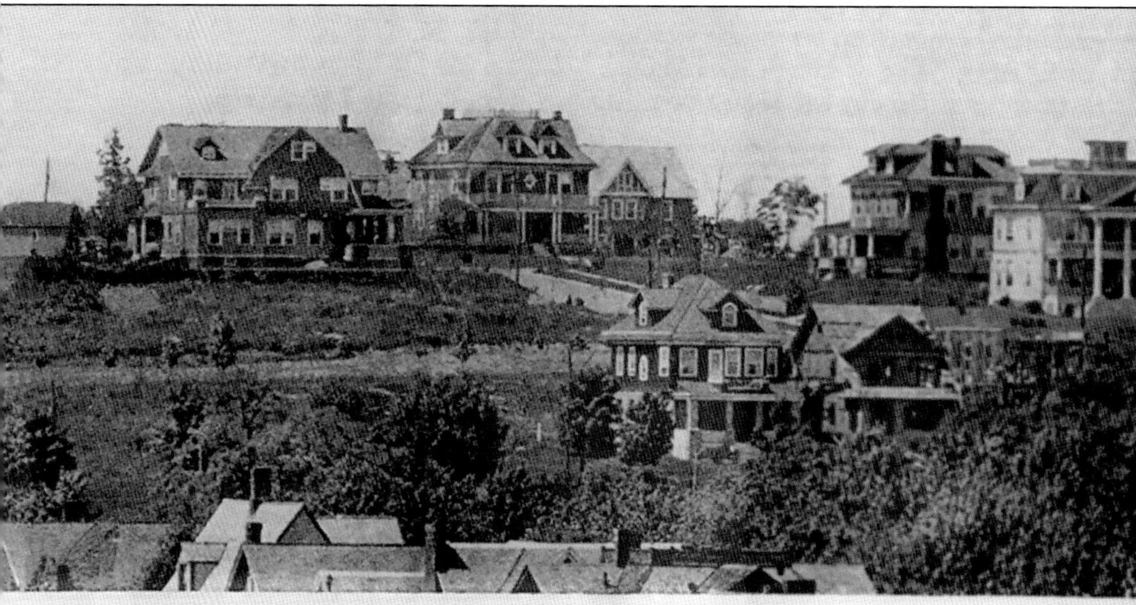

25 minutes from Wall Street

Particulars by mail, or 'ph

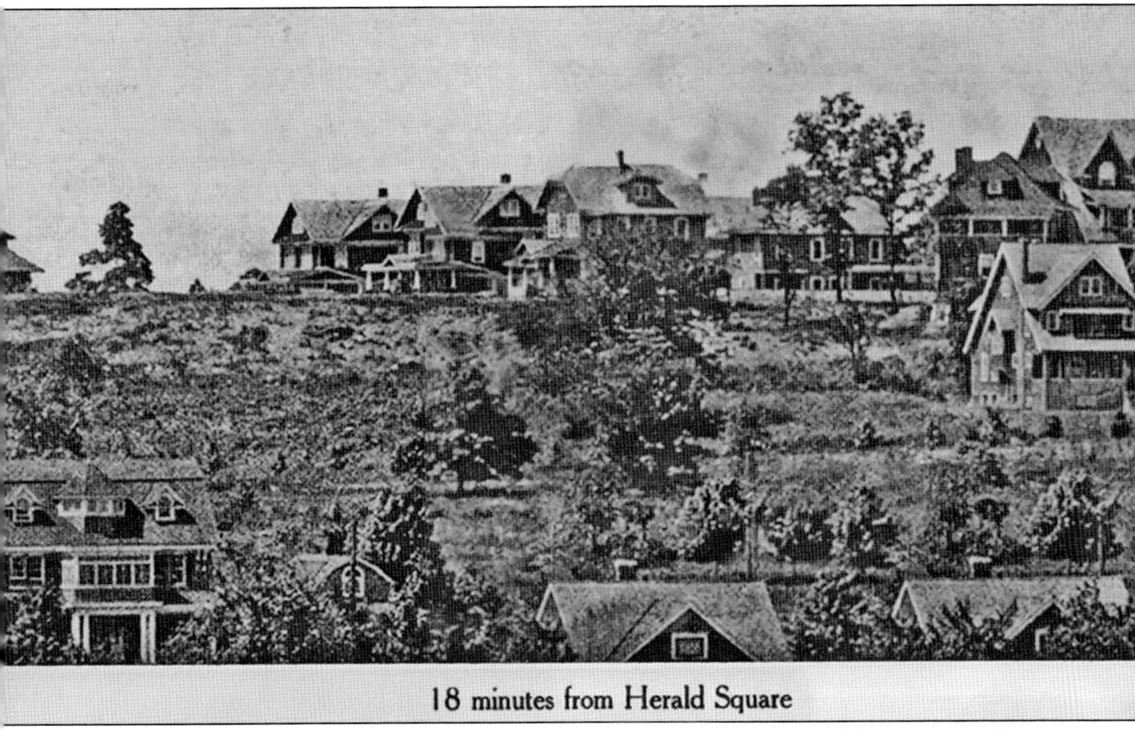

Bridge and the fireworks. Even at that great distance the night was a beautiful one, the rockets and colored lights being distinctly visible. Some of the younger spectators, being either of sharper sight, or of more imagination than the rest, professed to see figure pieces and all sorts of fiery devices." (Bob Stonehill Collection.)

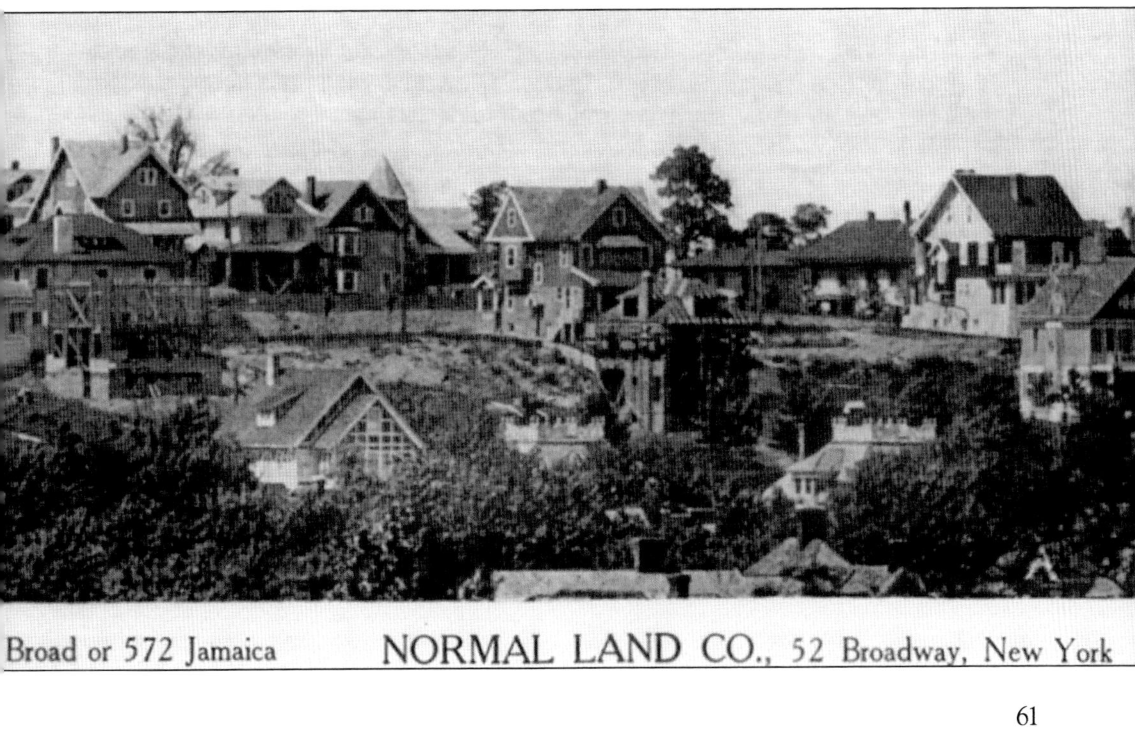

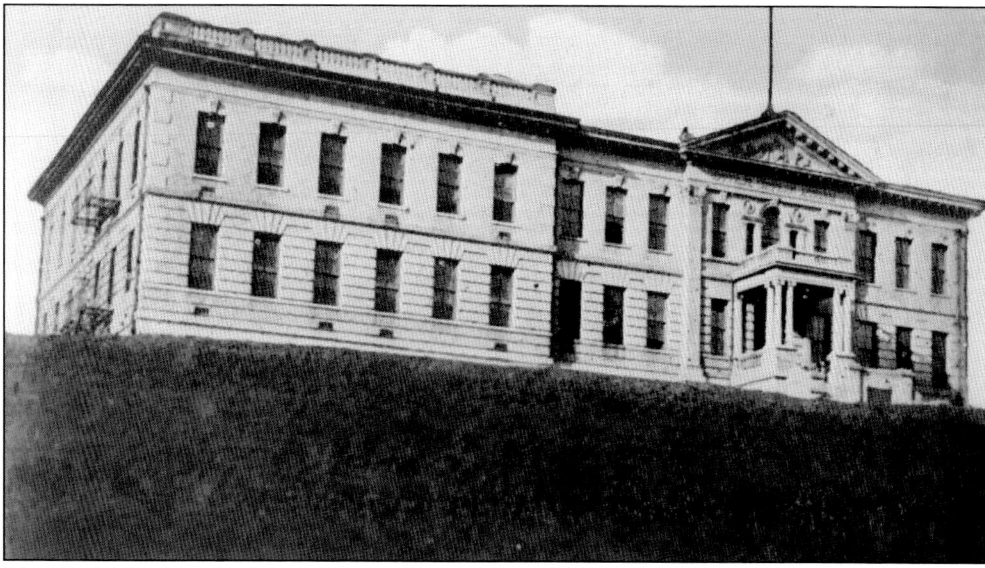

The Ottilie Orphan Asylum was started by a society of German ministers and laymen of Brooklyn in 1892 and named in memory of the daughter of a Mr. Miller, the group's president. The asylum moved to Jamaica and dedicated the building shown here on April 12, 1907. A separate hospital was erected in 1911, as was a school for the first six grades. It is located north of Eighty-seventh Avenue between 144th and 148th Streets.

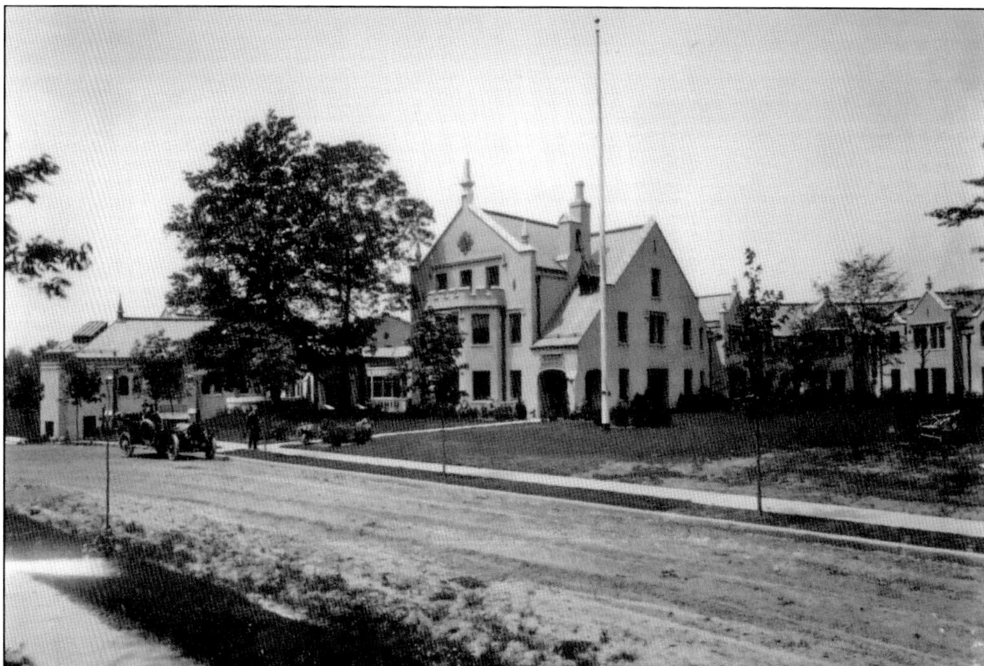

The *New York Times* reported on August 28, 1910, "The Chapin Home for the Aged and Infirm is to be located in Jamaica at Chapin Avenue (Parkway) and 164th Street. The Chapin Home organization was incorporated in 1869 and founded by the wife of Rev. E.H. Chapin D.D., a contemporary of Henry Beecher." The home was dedicated on October 24, 1911. (Courtesy of the Archives at Queens Library, Frederick Weber Photographs.)

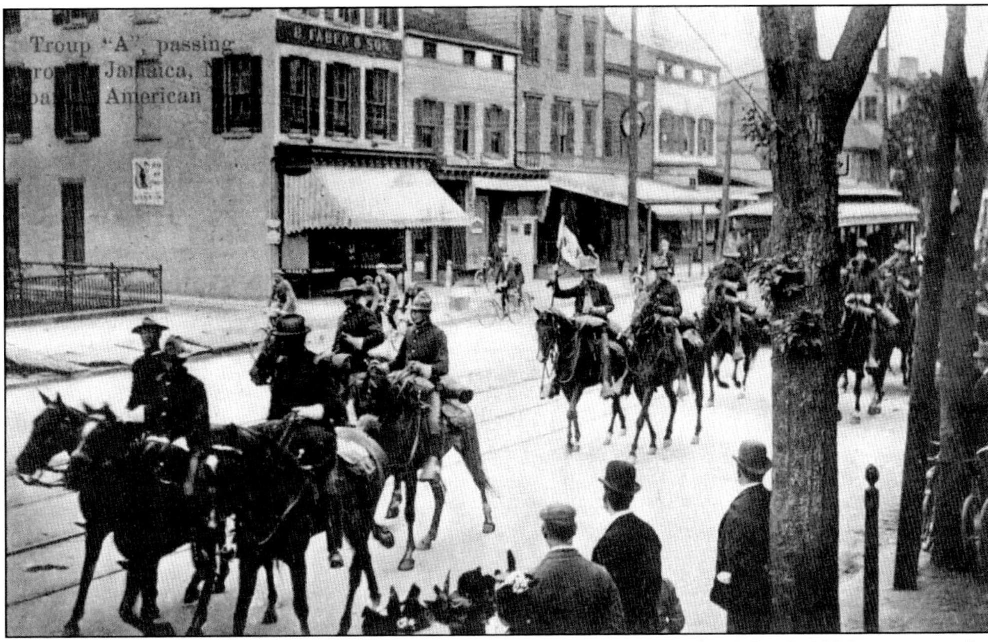

According to *History of Troop "A" New York Cavalry 1899*, "On Monday, May 2, 1898, we arrived at Jamaica at noon, where a halt was made at Pettit's Hotel for lunch. With ham sandwiches of Jamaica in our throats we came upon the board plain of Hempstead at Camp Black for training." Rough Riders are about to pass in front of the town hall, whose garden fence is seen across the street.

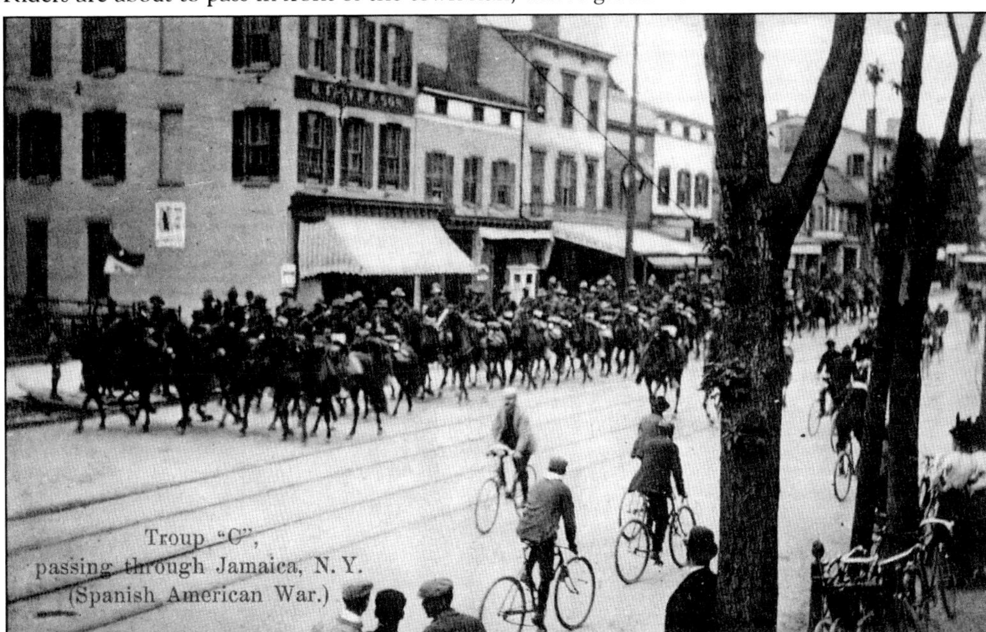

As reported in the *New York Times* on May 23, 1898, "Troops A and C Depart! New York's enthusiastic farewell to her cavalrymen bound south to war. Big Street demonstrations! Great throngs of people cheer the troopers on their ride through Queens, Brooklyn, and Manhattan Boroughs! The popular greetings to the troops practically began at Jamaica, where they stopped for luncheon early in the afternoon, after a ride from Camp Black."

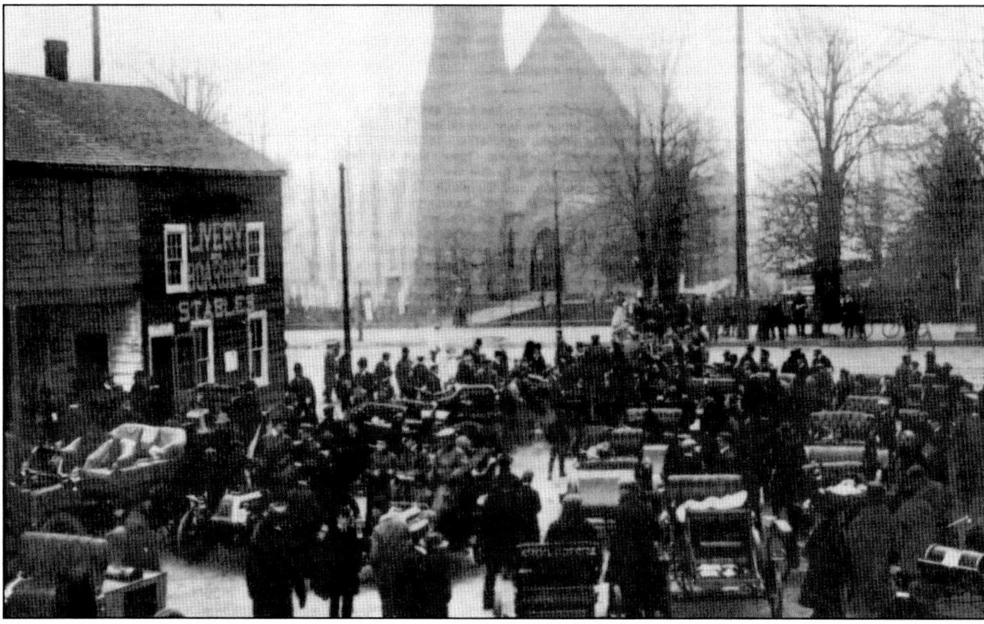

An article in the *New York Times* on April 27, 1902, states, "Automobiles virtually owned the Long Island Roads within the territory bounded by Jamaica, Oyster Bay, and Massepequa. Never before have so many machines propelled by gasoline, steam, and electricity been seen together. The occasion was the 100-mile endurance test run held under the auspices of the Long Island Automobile Club." Jamaica Avenue is seen in the background, with Grace Church shrouded in fog.

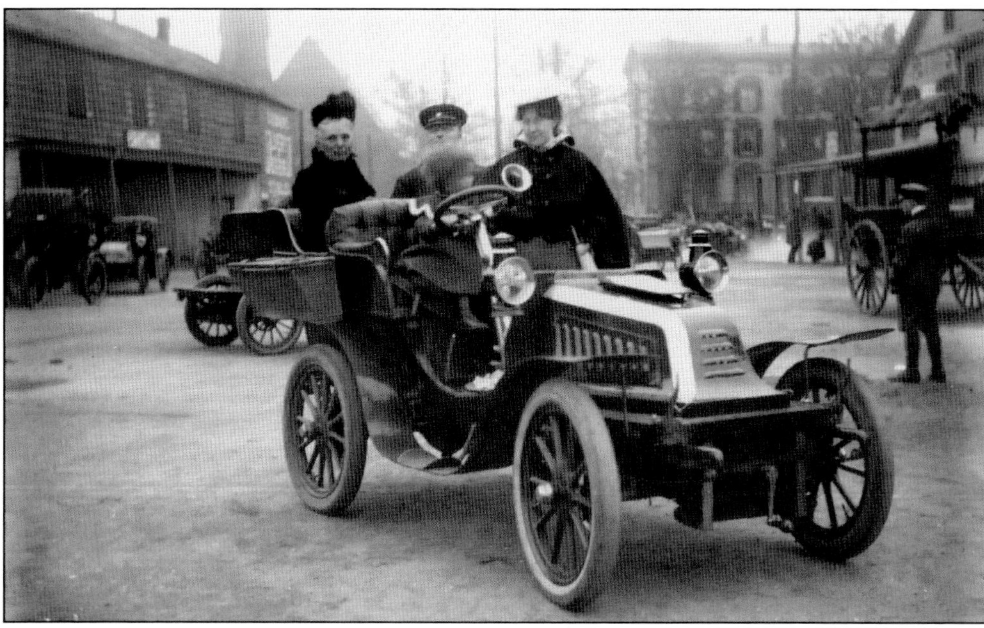

Fannie Fullerton (left), her daughter-in-law Edith Fullerton (right), and her granddaughter Hope Fullerton have arrived in a Haynes-Apperson automobile to see the endurance race. An April 27, 1902, *New York Times* write-up says, "With the exception of a strong wind, the conditions were excellent, and a vast throng of motor vehicles crowded with passengers assembled early in the morning at Jamaica to watch the start." (Archives at Queens Library, Hal Fullerton Photographs.)

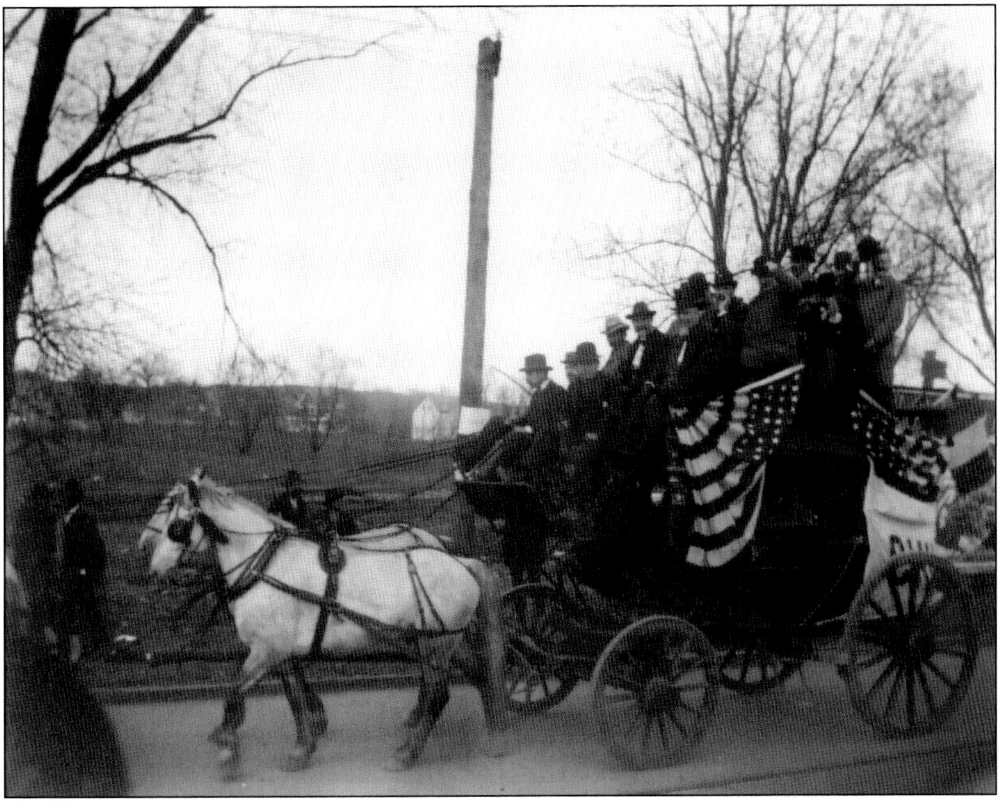

In 1908, Jamaica celebrated the connection of the subway with Manhattan. The motto was "Twenty-five minutes from Broadway." The *New York Times* on June 5, 1908, quoted Governor Hughes: "The center of political power is destined to move from Manhattan to Queens and Brooklyn and in the future we shall have a very different political history." (Archives at Queens Library, Winans Collection.)

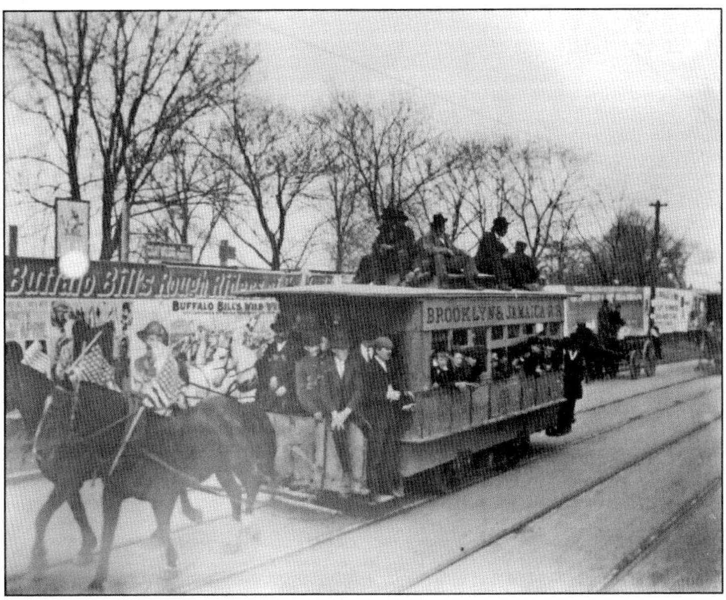

As reported in the *New York Times* on June 4, 1908, "At 10:30 this morning the people will form. Counting in all the volunteer firemen, the girl cadets, the soldiery, and all the rest, it is estimated that the parade should have 20,000 persons in it." Pictured here is a display showing the horsecar means of transportation. (Archives at Queens Library, George Winans Collection.)

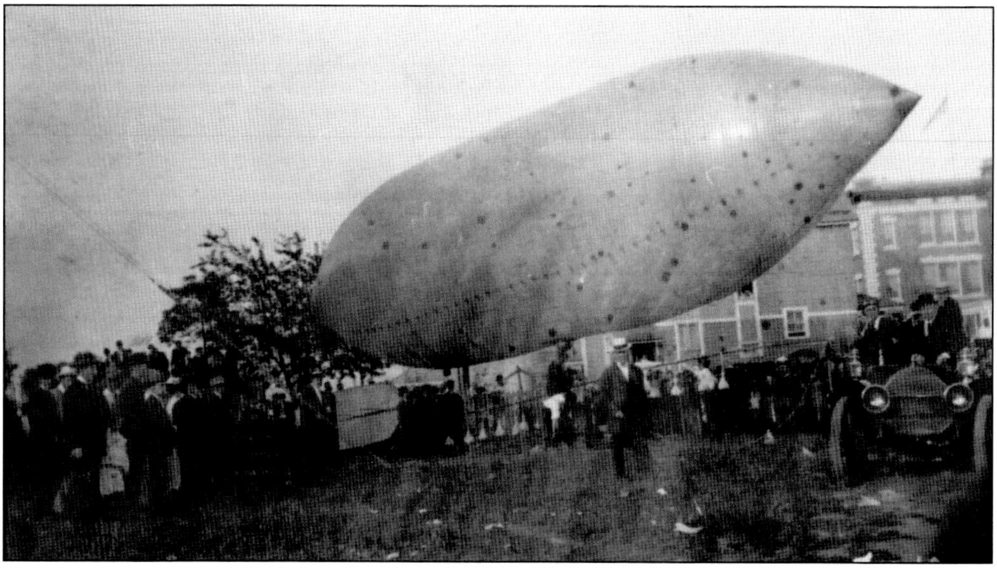

An attraction of the gala, located at Woodhull baseball grounds at Maple Street (139th Street) with PS 82 in the background, was aeronaut Lincoln Beachey, who flew a dirigible-type balloon that was cigar-shaped and made of oiled silk. Beneath it was a 100-foot bamboo pole with a seven-horsepower gasoline engine to drive the propeller. (Archives at Queens Library, Frederick Weber Photographs.)

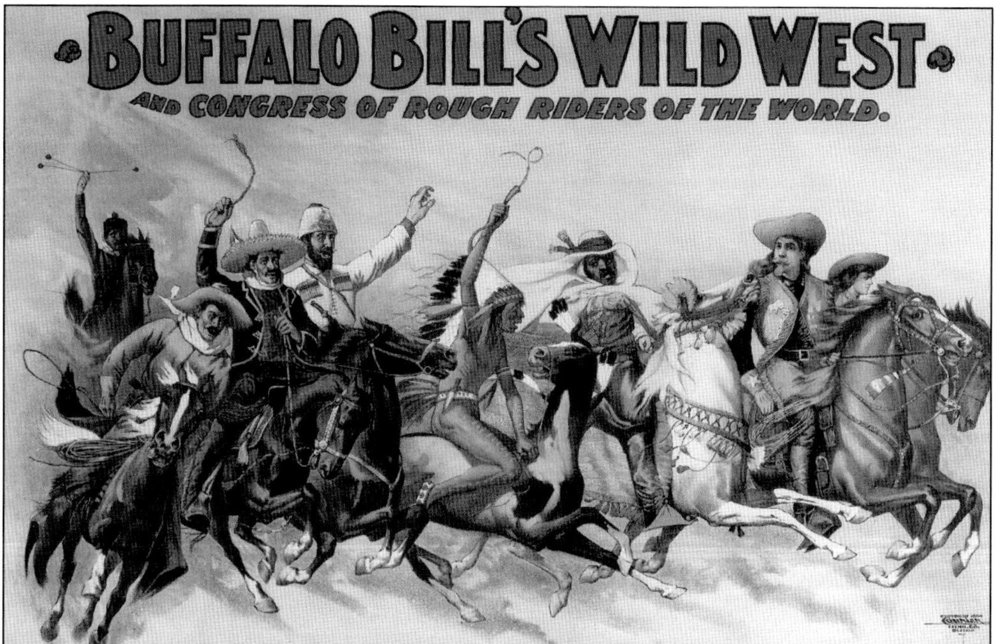

Another attraction of the gala was Buffalo Bill's Wild West Show. On June 5, 1908, the *New York Times* said, "All in all, the 'Wild West Show' is good for the blues. Doctors should recommend it to dyspeptics. At first all the Kissena Park Indians, Arabian acrobats, (always part of a real Western show), and other dare-devil people paraded around the ring. This is, of course, the grand review."

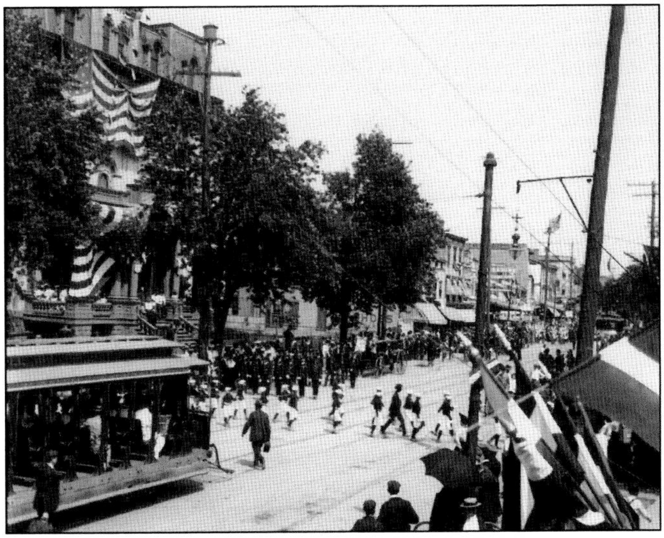

"Jamaica Firemen Parade. The Centennial and Final Public appearance of a time honored department before being absorbed in Greater New York. The Jamaica Engine, Hook and Ladder Company organized January 30, 1797 has expanded, until now at the end of only one century has five hose companies and two hook and ladder companies numbering 200 men," reported the *New York Times* on September 17, 1897. (Archives at Queens Library, William Murray Photographs.)

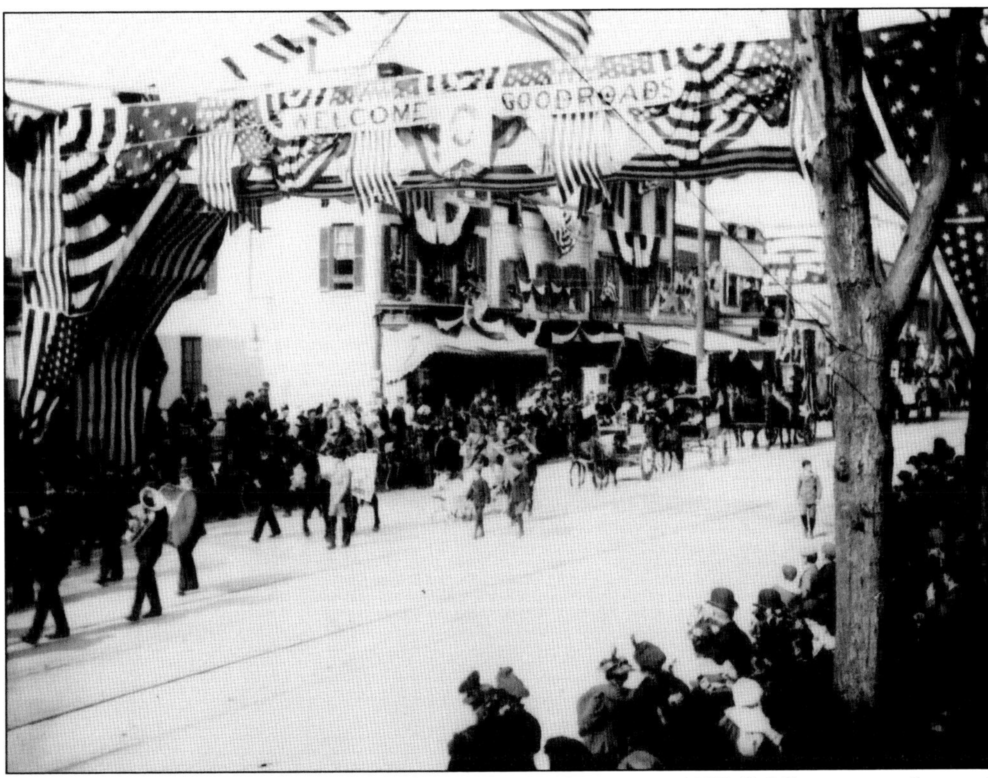

A Jamaica parade welcomes good roads on Jamaica Avenue in 1897. "Millions spent for good roads!—Great movement in public improvements before being absorbed in Greater New York. The old Jamaica Plank Road for years paved with an irregular assortment of cobblestones in being paved from curb to curb with asphalt laid on a heavy concrete foundation," reported the *New York Times* on November 14, 1897. (Archives at Queens Library, George Winans Collection.)

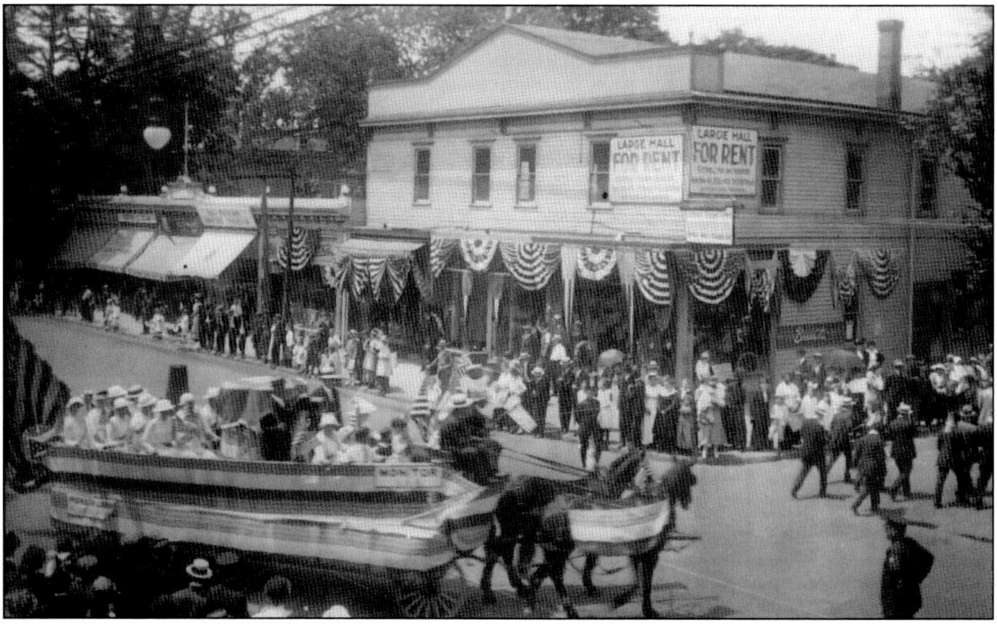

The 1915 Decoration Day Parade is pictured. The marchers' route on Jamaica Avenue turns north onto Merrick Boulevard and heads to Hillside Avenue, where wreaths are laid at the Soldiers and Sailors Civil War Monument. This holiday is now known as Memorial Day. The building with the "For Rent" sign is the old Theodore Archer building, named for a local auctioneer and real estate developer. (Archives at Queens Library, Frederick Weber Photographs.)

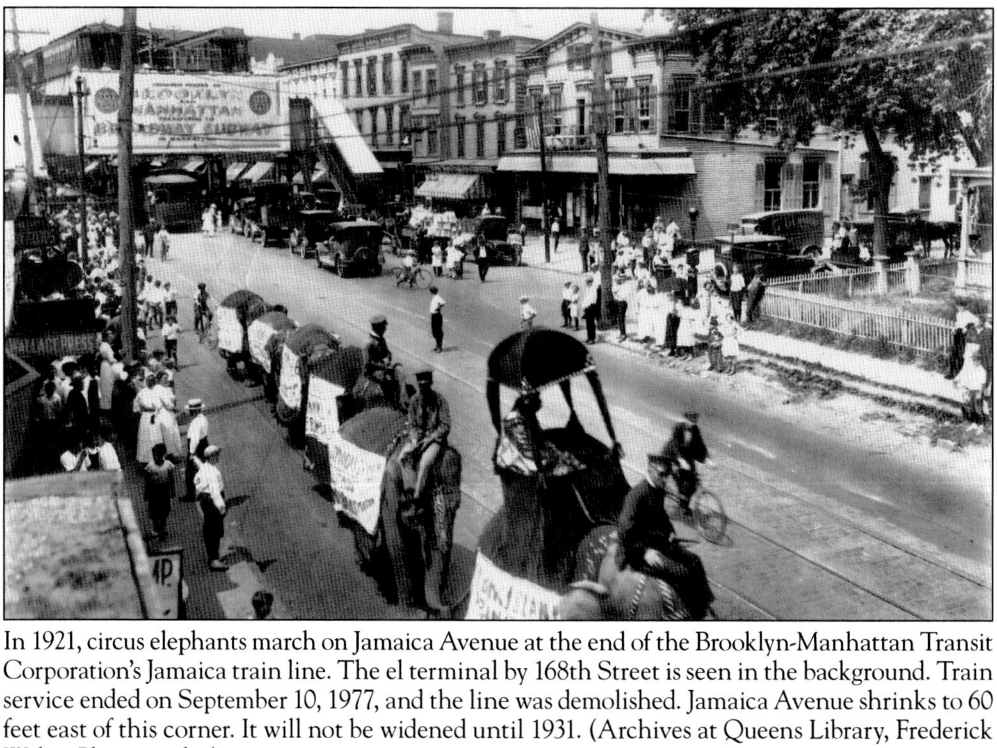

In 1921, circus elephants march on Jamaica Avenue at the end of the Brooklyn-Manhattan Transit Corporation's Jamaica train line. The el terminal by 168th Street is seen in the background. Train service ended on September 10, 1977, and the line was demolished. Jamaica Avenue shrinks to 60 feet east of this corner. It will not be widened until 1931. (Archives at Queens Library, Frederick Weber Photographs.)

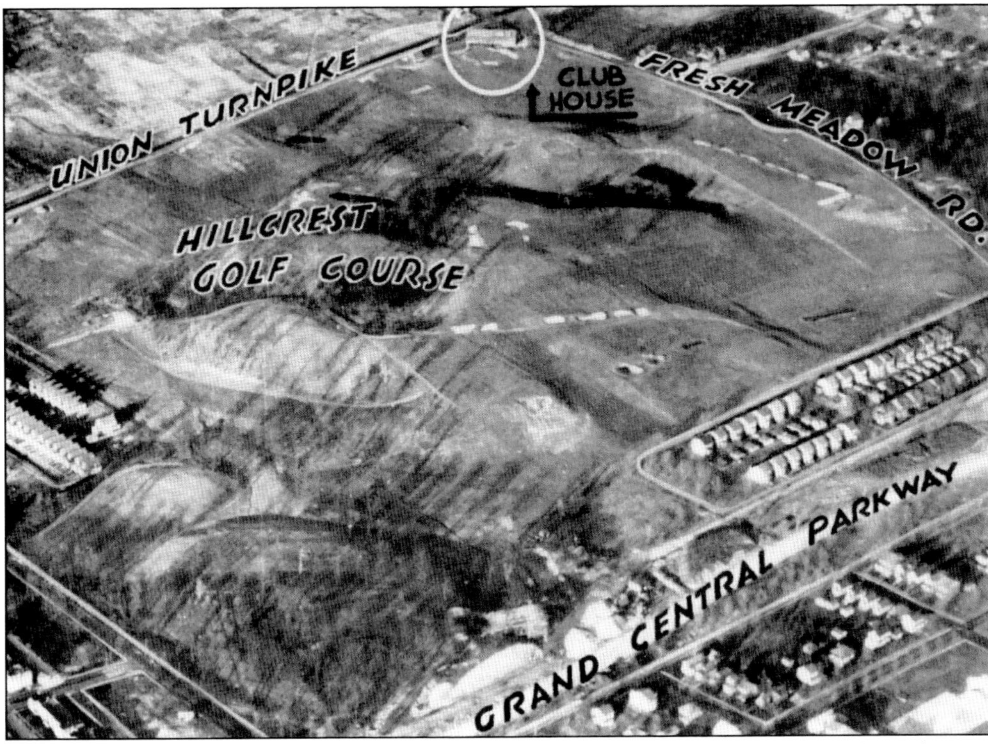

On January 19, 1908, the *New York Times* reported, "Engineers are now are work on the new golf course which is to be laid out on the Jamaica Estates property. The course has been laid out under the supervision of Willie Tucker, who planned the links at Ardaley, St. Andrew's and other important clubs." Fresh Meadows Road had various names, including Black Stump Road and Utopia Parkway.

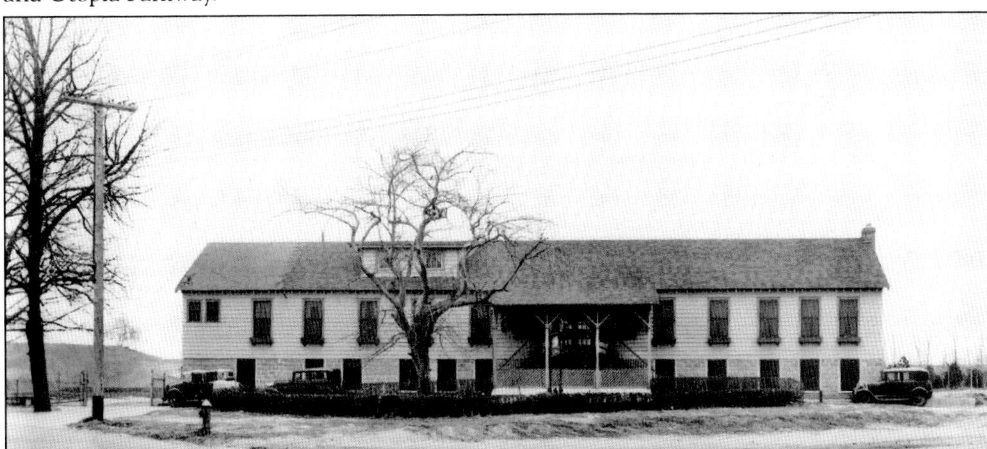

It was called the Hillcrest Golf Course. A 1924 Hillcrest brochure boasts, "It is an eighteen-hole course fully completed and second to none. The links were designed and built under the supervision of Devereux Emmett, the eminent golf architect." On February 11, 1936, the Vincentian University of St. John University purchased the 100-acre Hillcrest Golf Course for its Jamaica campus. The clubhouse on Union Turnpike is pictured here. (Q Gardens Gallery.)

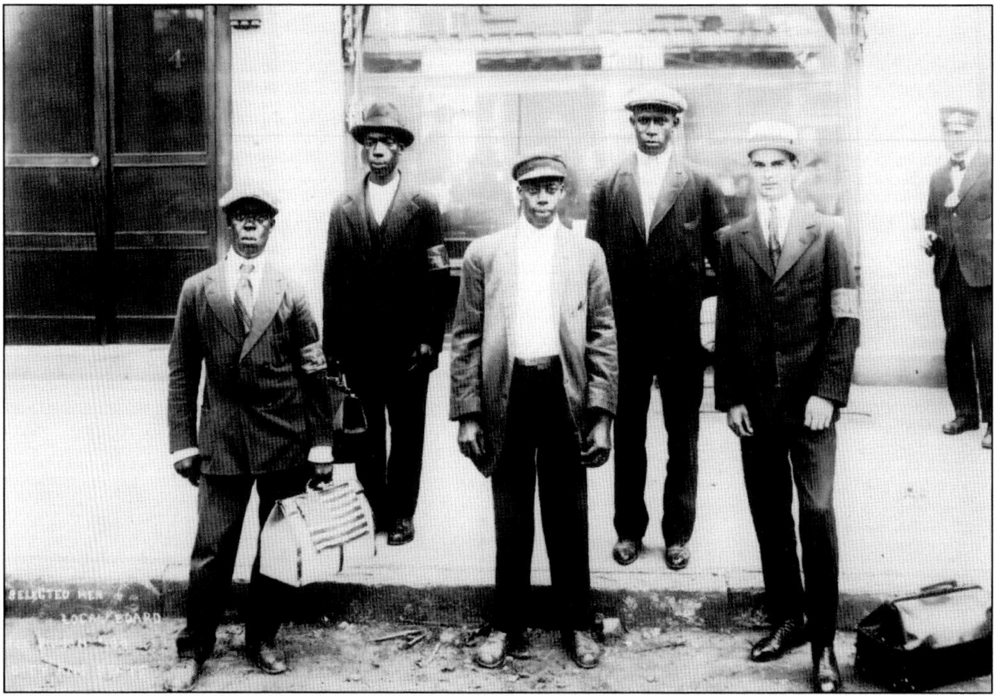

Five young draftees pose for a photograph before boarding the Long Island Rail Road for training at Camp Upton in Suffolk County. LIRR employees stand in the back. They wear arm bands marked Jamaica LI Local Board No. 184 NA (National Army). From left to right are Robert D. Watkins, Charles Robinson, Edward N. Holling, Charles Walker, and Harry Cole. (Archives at Queens Library, Frederick Weber Photographs.)

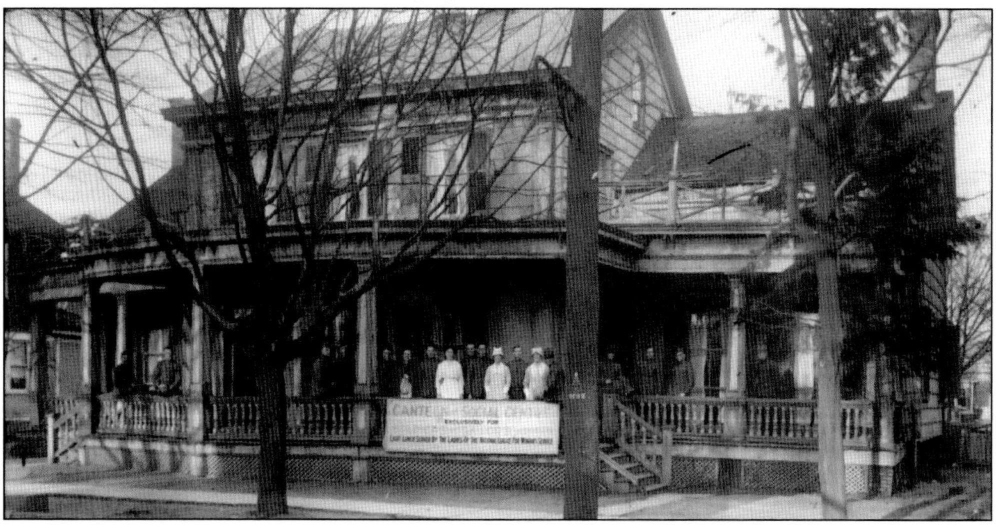

The Jamaica Canteen Social Center was organized during World War I and located in the Hardenbrook Mansion. Soldiers and sailors stand with volunteers for this photograph in 1918. The community had established the center for members of the armed forces that passed through Jamaica to and from Camp Upton. It was run by volunteers and equipped with a dining room, circulating library, and a hall for entertainment. (Archives at Queens Library, Frederick Weber Photographs.)

The Jacobs family includes Frank and Cleo with their three-year-old daughter, Marguerite. Frank Jacobs, a descendant of Blackfoot Indians, came from Virginia to find work, becoming a waiter for the Pennsylvania Railroad and eventually a Pullman porter. He married Cleo, who was from the West Indies, and settled in Harlem. On July 1, 1930, they moved to Jamaica and eventually purchased a house on 174th Street, which was described by Marguerite as "surrounded by farmland."

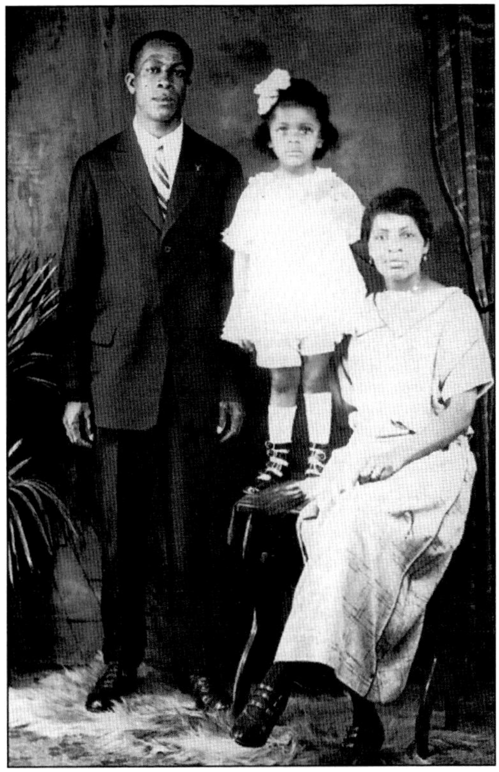

The Queens Library Jamaica branch opened in 1911 at Colonial Hall, formerly Union Hall Ladies Seminary. The Central Library built on Parsons Boulevard (pictured) opened on April 1, 1930. Designed by R.F. Schirmer and J.W. Schmidt, it featured marble staircases, bronze railings, high vaulted ceilings, and ornate chandeliers. The Queens Central Library moved to a new building on Merrick Boulevard in 1966. (Archives at Queens Library, Queens Borough Public Library Collection.)

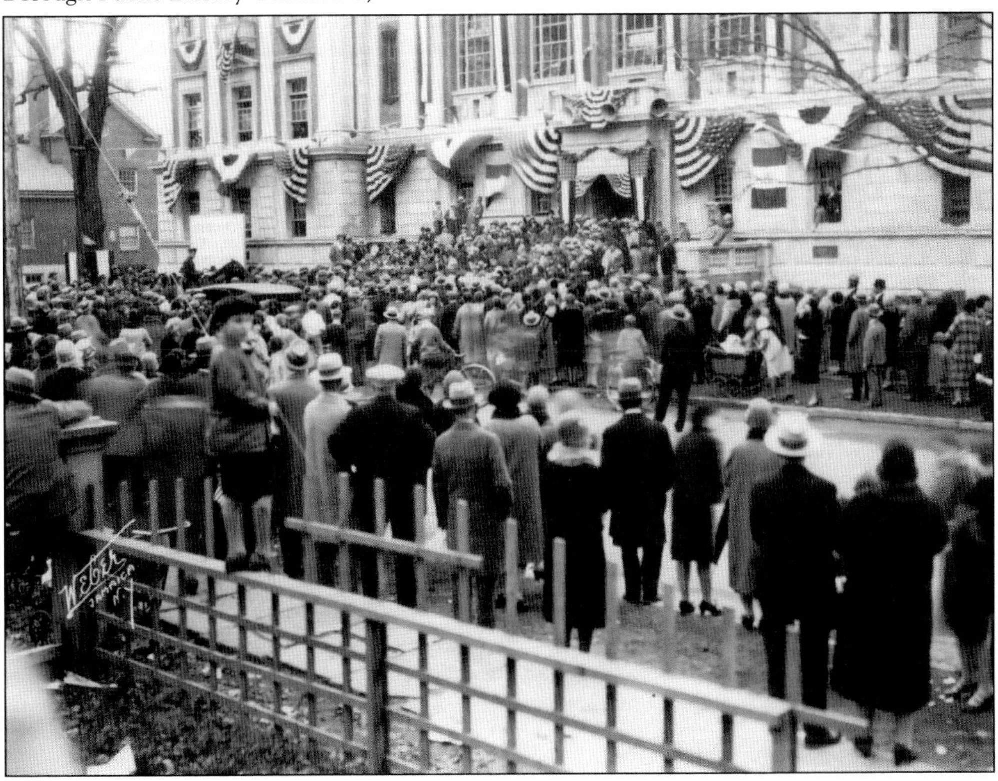

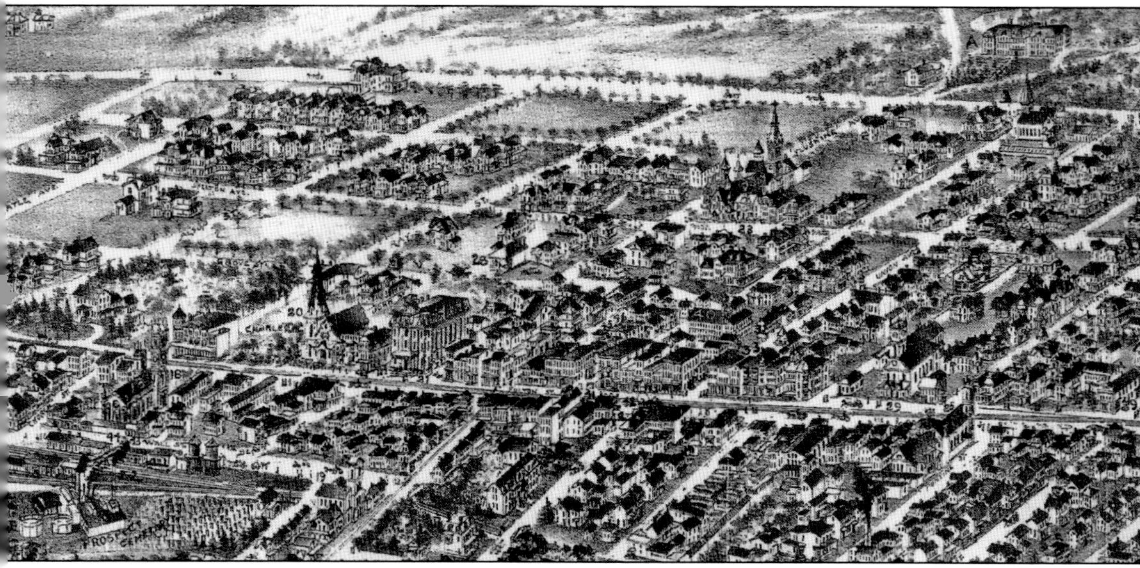

This is the heart of the Jamaica community in 1895. In the foreground is Jamaica Avenue, and above it is Hillside Avenue. At top right is the Jamaica State Normal School (label A). To the right is the first Jamaica High School, and next to it is St. Paul Church (No. 24). Starting at the left along Jamaica Avenue are the home of Rufus King, with circular drive; the Dutch Reformed Church across the street (No. 18); and Grace Episcopal Church (No. 20). The next structure is the town hall (No. 21) located at the corner of Flushing Avenue (Parsons Boulevard). Behind it is the Baptist church (No. 28). Farther back and to the right is St. Mary's German Catholic Church (No. 23). Back on Jamaica Avenue is the Presbyterian church (No. 29), and across the street is the Methodist church (No. 25). At the bottom left is Prospect Cemetery, and next to it is St. Monica's Catholic Church (No. 19).

Three

On the Streets
All Roads Lead to Jamaica

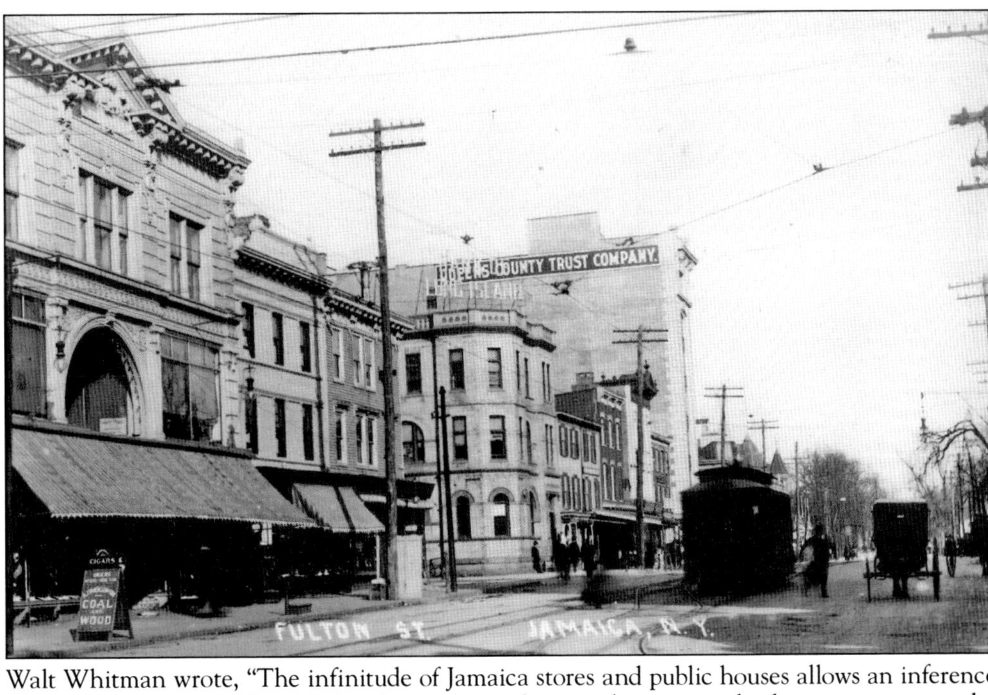

Walt Whitman wrote, "The infinitude of Jamaica stores and public houses allows an inference much which is the truth, viz.: that farmers, travelers, marketmen, and other passengers on the turnpike through the village give it all its trade and retail business." This view looks east on Fulton (Jamaica) Avenue. The Queens County Trust Company building is on the northwest corner of Jamaica Avenue and Union Avenue (162nd Street). (Bob Stonehill Collection.)

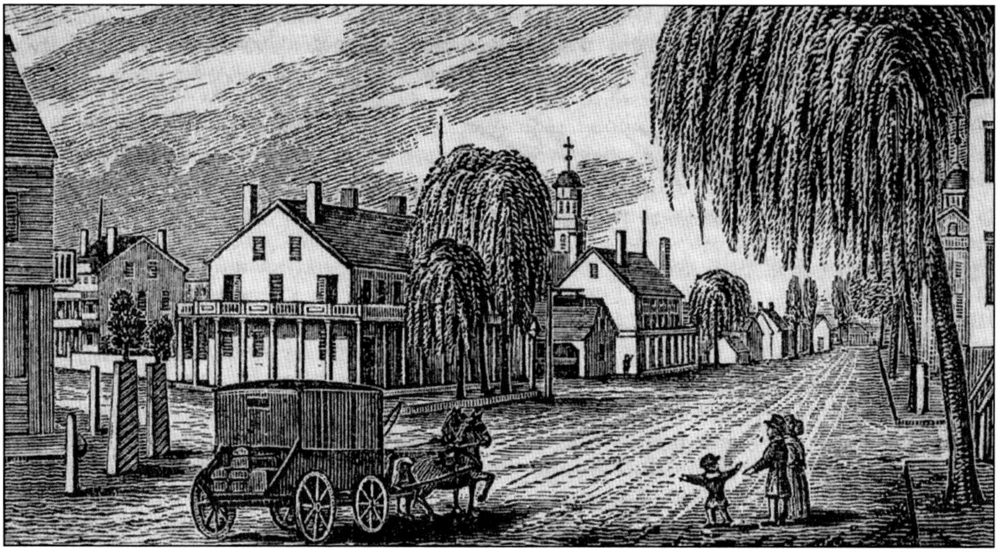

An 1841 engraving looks west on Jamaica Avenue and shows the Parsons Boulevard intersection at right. Behind the horse-drawn stagecoach is the Queens Head Tavern, where George Washington stayed in 1790. It features a wraparound porch. On the right, partially hidden by the tree, Grace Church was erected in 1822 and destroyed by fire in 1861. Across the road is the steeple of the Dutch Reform church erected in 1833 and lost to a fire in 1857.

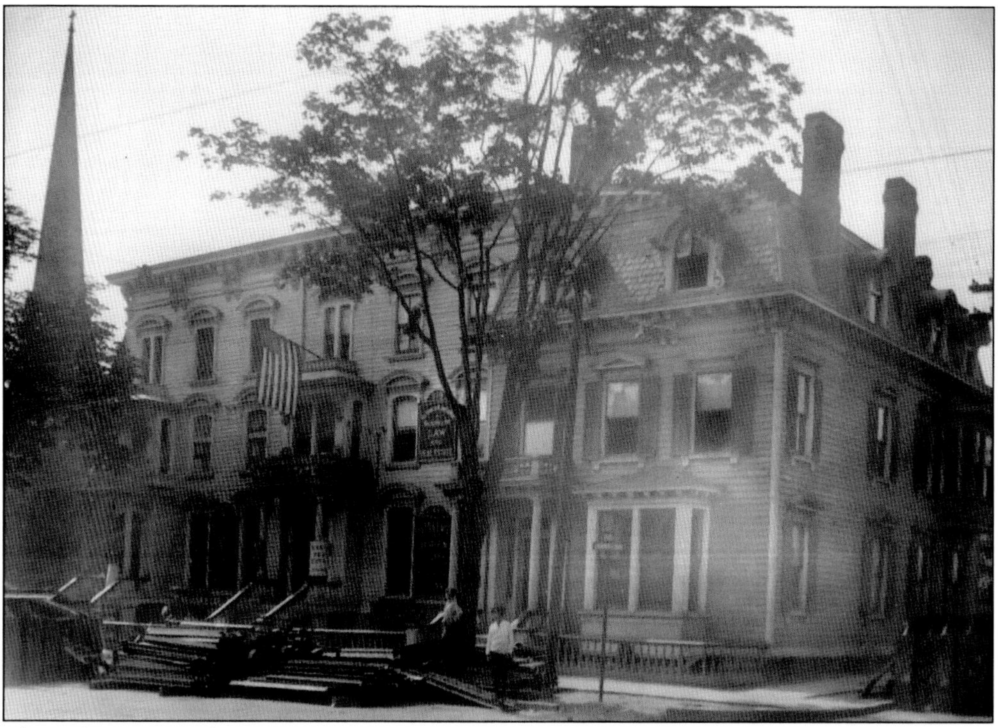

This is the same northwest corner of Jamaica Avenue and Parsons Boulevard in 1917. The sandstone steeple of Grace Church, erected in 1862, is visible at the left. Iron beams on the ground are part of the construction of the elevated train line along Jamaica Avenue that was completed in 1918 and demolished in 1977. (Archives at Queens Library, Frederick Weber Photographs.)

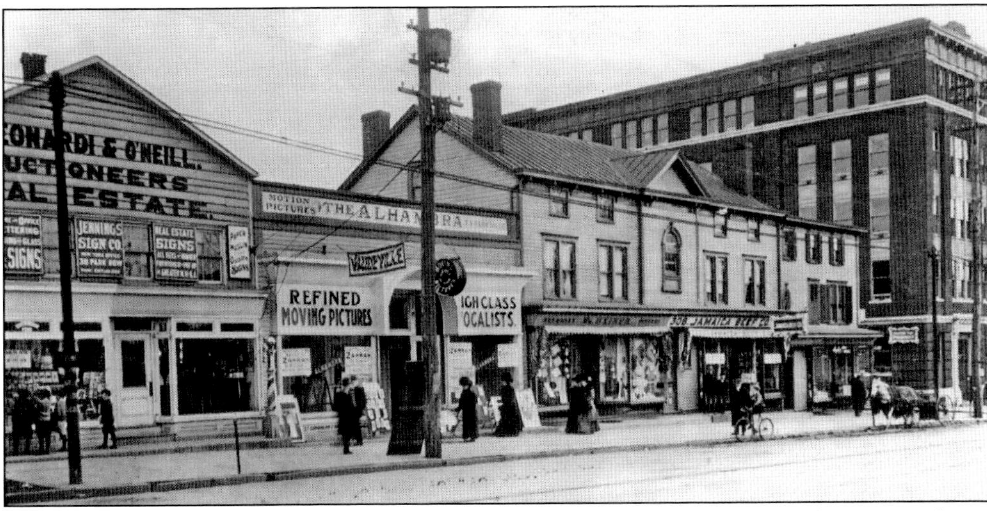

Here is the south side of Jamaica Avenue west of Parsons Boulevard. Various businesses shown are, from left to right, Leonardi & O'Neill Auctioneers/Real Estate, the Alhambra Motion Pictures and Vaudeville (with high-class vocalists and featuring Zahrah the Hypnotist), William Exiner Dry Goods and Notions, Jamaica Beef Company, and Weiss Central Pharmacy. The brick building is the Jamaica Post Office. The Joseph P. Addabbo Federal Building occupies this entire site today. (Q Gardens Gallery.)

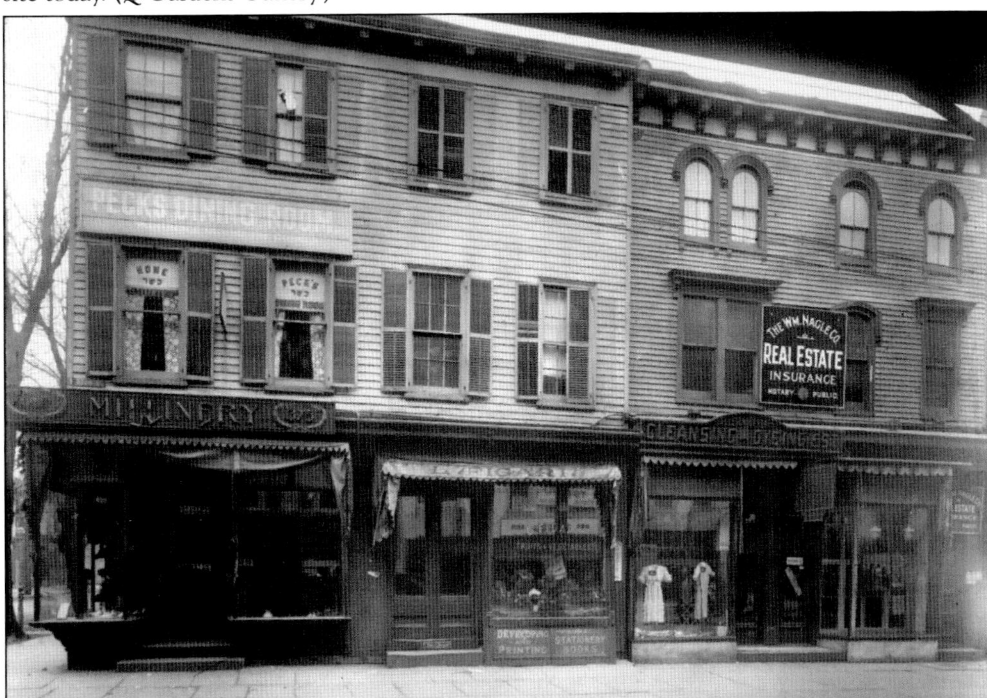

Various businesses shown on the northeast corner of Jamaica Avenue and Union Avenue (162nd Street) include, from left to right, Peck's Dining Room, A.E. Box Millinery, L. Figari Fruits and Vegetables, Eastern District Cleaning and Dyeing Company, and William Nagle Real Estate and Insurance. Peck's Dining Room features advertisements in Hebrew for kosher foods. (Archives at Queens Library, Frederick Weber Photographs.)

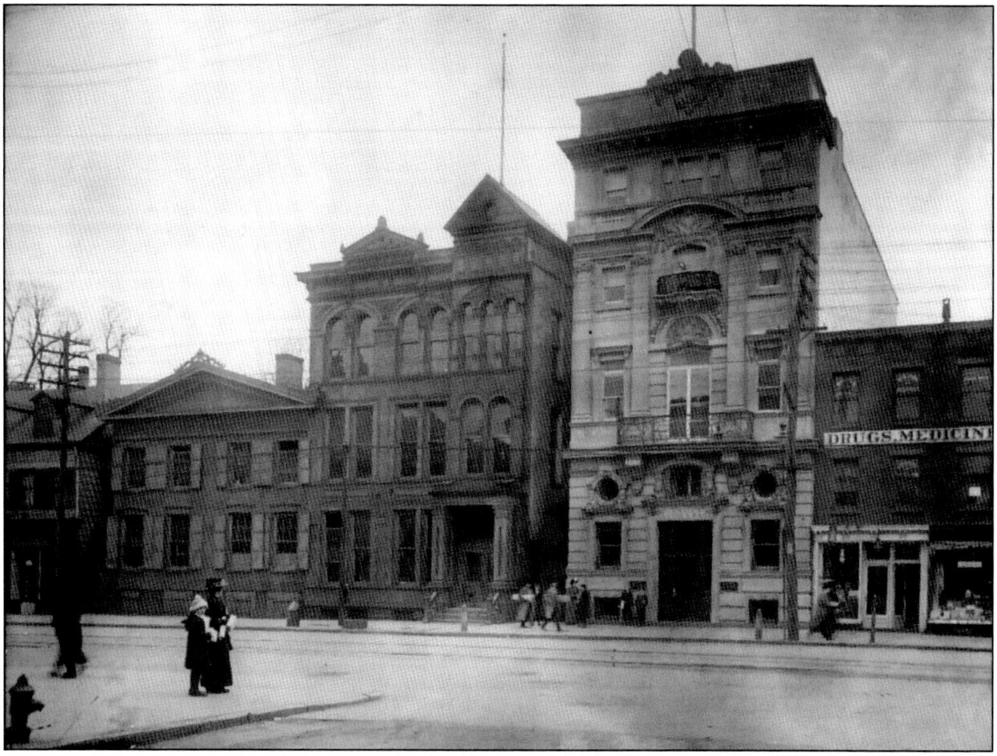

This view looks south from Herriman Avenue (161st Street) to Jamaica Avenue. The ornate stone building is the Jamaica Saving Bank. It is next to the County Clerk's Office–Borough of Queens. John Sutphin held the county clerk position for 30 years. Sutphin Boulevard was named in his honor after his 1907 death. The Register Building replaced the clerk's office building and today houses the Jamaica Center for Arts and Learning. (Archives at Queens Library, Frederick Weber Photographs.)

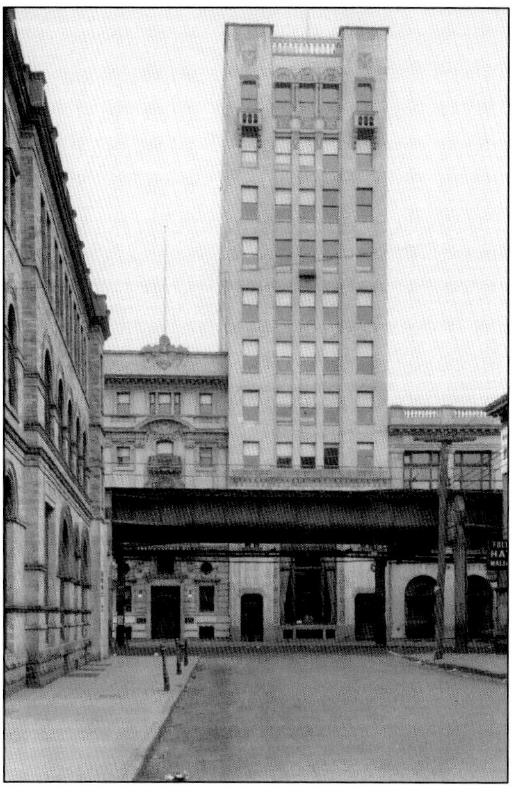

The 1928 photograph at left is the same location as above, showing elevated train tracks covering Jamaica Avenue. The Jamaica Savings Bank is the oldest banking institution in Jamaica and incorporated in 1866. It started with 15 customers who deposited $2,675. The ornate Beaux-Arts building was erected in 1898 and is today a city landmark. The taller building is the National Title Guaranty Company. (Archives at Queens Library, Frederick Weber Photographs.)

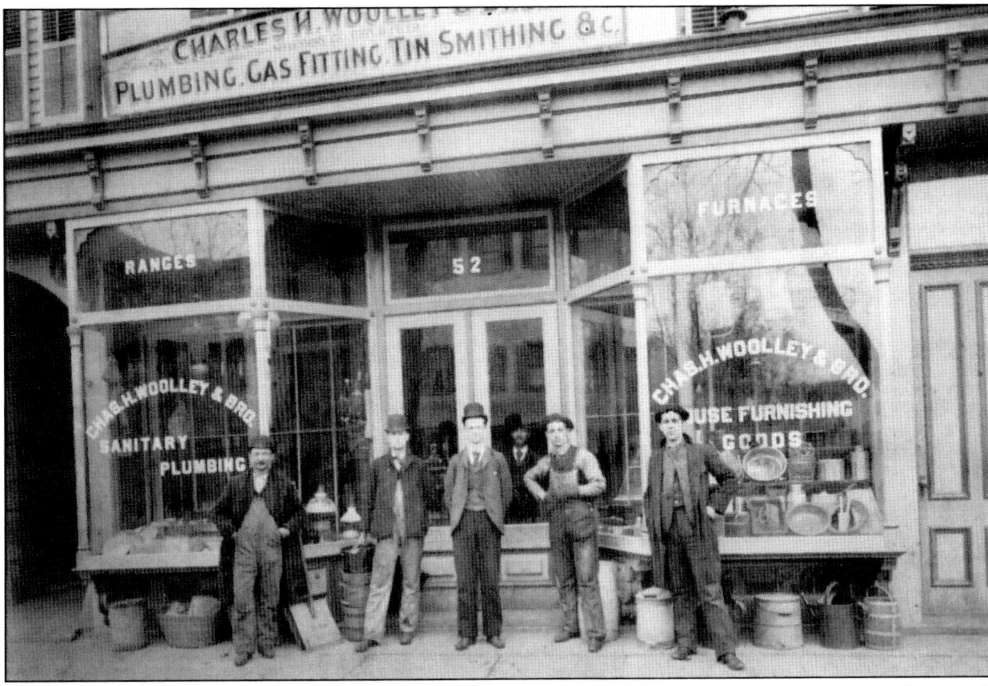

Opened in 1889 by brothers, the Charles and Samuel Woolley Plumbing store is on the south side of Jamaica Avenue between New York Boulevard (Guy Brewer) and Union Hall Street. An 1894 Woolley advertisement reads, "No man, who has had experience with defective steam, gas, water, or drain pipe, wants to have it repeated, for such things are always annoying, and in many cases dangerous." (Archives at Queens Library, George Winans Collection.)

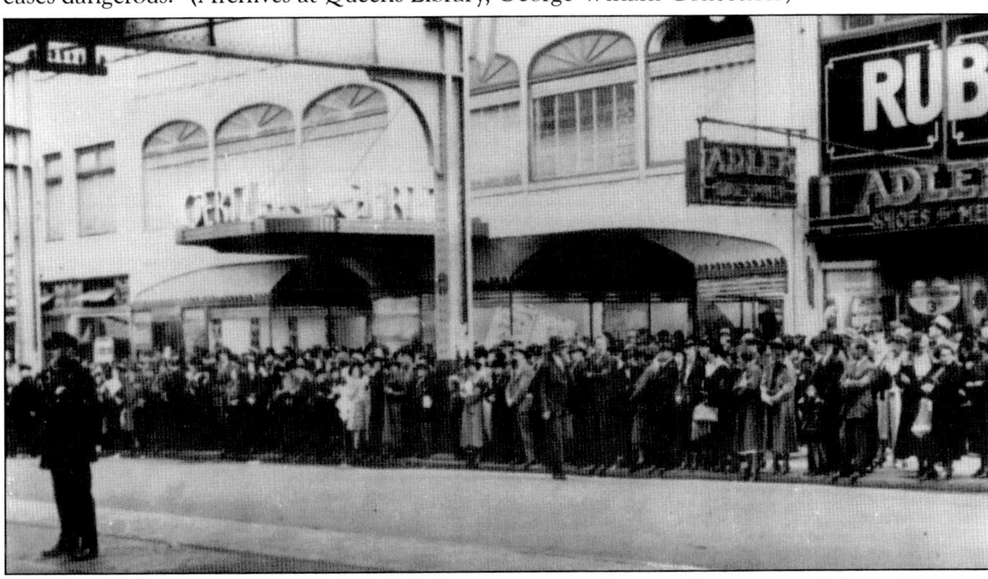

This is the opening of Gertz Department Store in 1935 at the same location as the Woolley store. The Gertz family came from Russia and founded a stationery store on Jamaica Avenue in 1918. Stanley Gertz, born in Jamaica in 1921, became a businessman and philanthropist working at the Jamaica flagship store. He was a founder and longtime director of the Greater Jamaica Development Corporation. (Archives at Queens Library, Frederick Weber Photographs.)

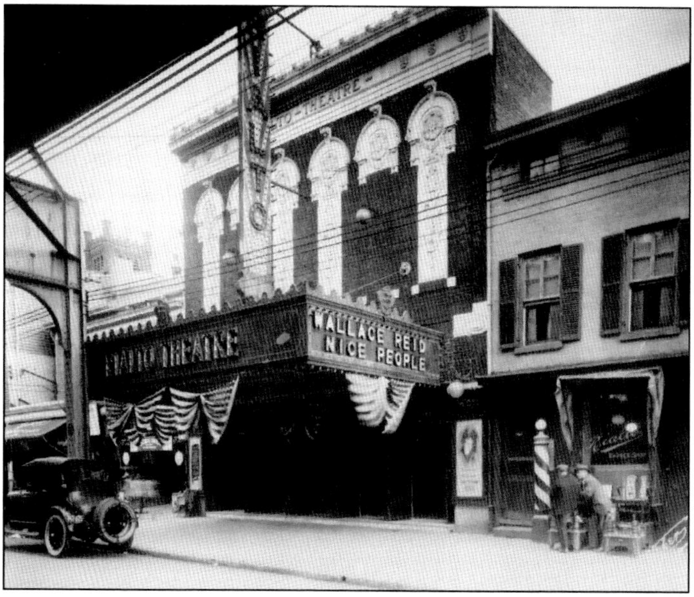

The Rialto Theater, located on the south side of Jamaica Avenue at 152nd Street, opened in 1918 and was later renamed the Savoy; the tower of the Dutch Reform Church is at the left. There were many theaters in Jamaica. Some are still standing and others have vanished—Jamaica (opened in 1913), Merrick (opened in 1921), Hillside (opened in 1926), Alden (opened in 1928), and Valencia (opened in 1929). (Archives at Queens Library, Frederick Weber Photographs.)

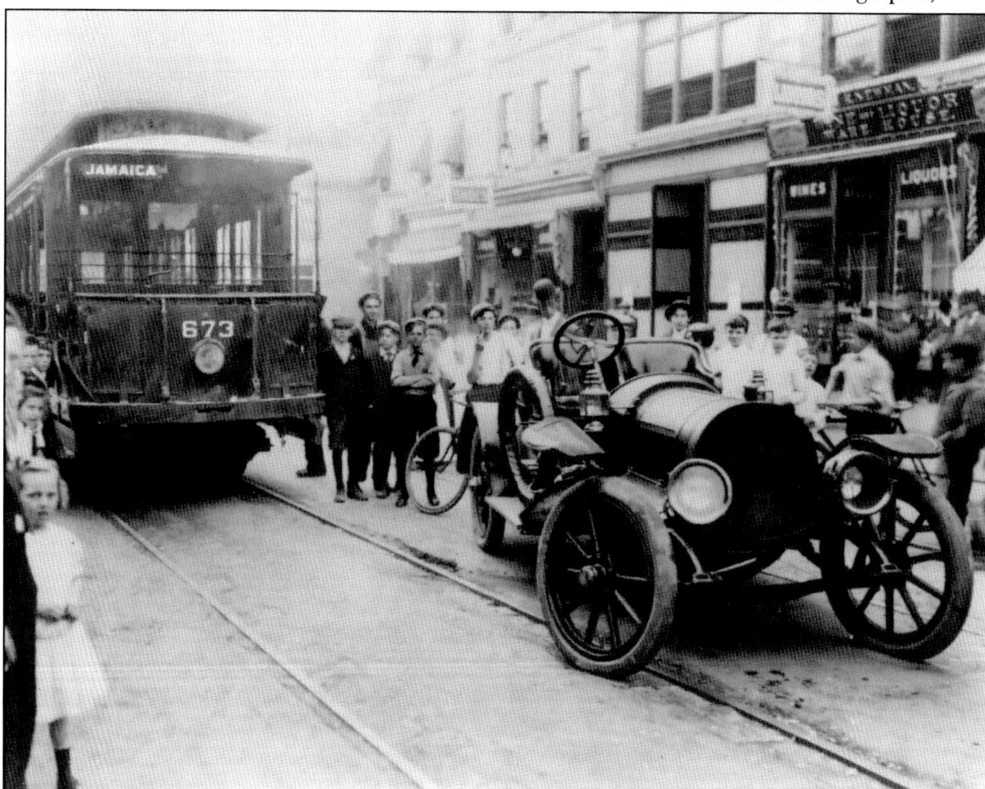

This is a 1910 photograph of an accident between a Jamaica railway car and automobile on Jamaica Avenue between Merrick Boulevard and 168th Street. According to the *New York Times* on October 14, 1907, "Squad of motor cycle policemen at Jamaica, looking for automobile speeders made six arrests. In two instances had to draw their revolvers to stop the speeding machines." (Archives at Queens Library, Frederick Weber Photographs.)

Four

Leaving an Impression
Making Jamaica Unique

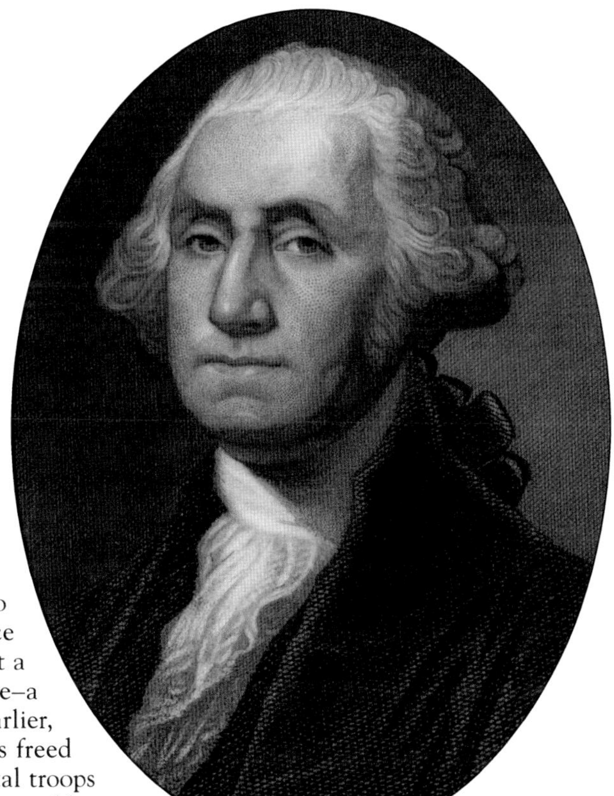

An entry in the diary of George Washington reads, "April 20, 1790 About 8 o'clock I crossed to Brooklyn and proceeded to Flat Bush–thence to Utrich–thence to Gravesend–thence through Jamaica where we lodged at a Tavern kept by one William Warne–a pretty good and decent house." Earlier, on December 8, 1783, Jamaica was freed from British occupation. Continental troops celebrated by displaying the 13 stripes on a liberty pole in front of the tavern.

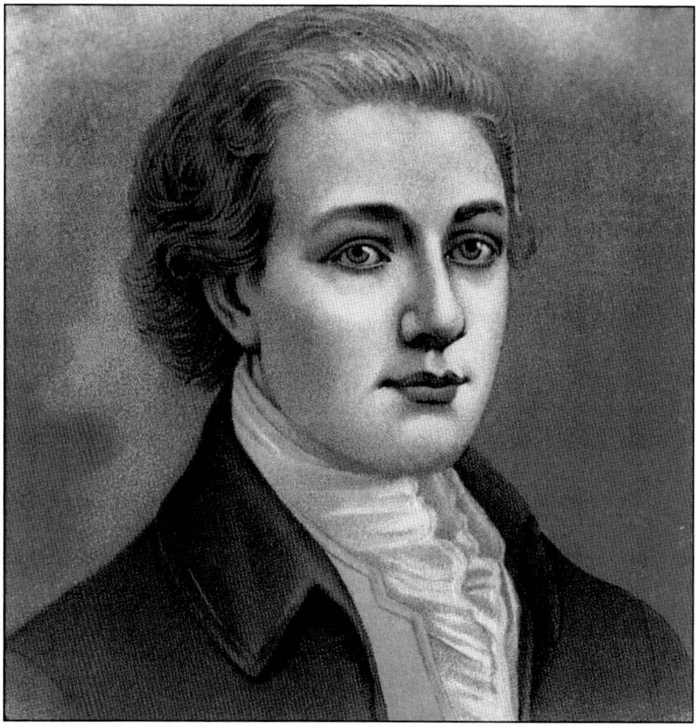

Marinus Willett, an outstanding American leader of the American Revolution, was born in Jamaica in 1740, the great-grandson of Thomas Willett, the first mayor of New York City. Marinus served in the militia during the French and Indian War, was a colonel in the Continental Army during the Revolutionary War, and a leader of the Sons of Liberty. He served as mayor of New York City from 1807 to 1808.

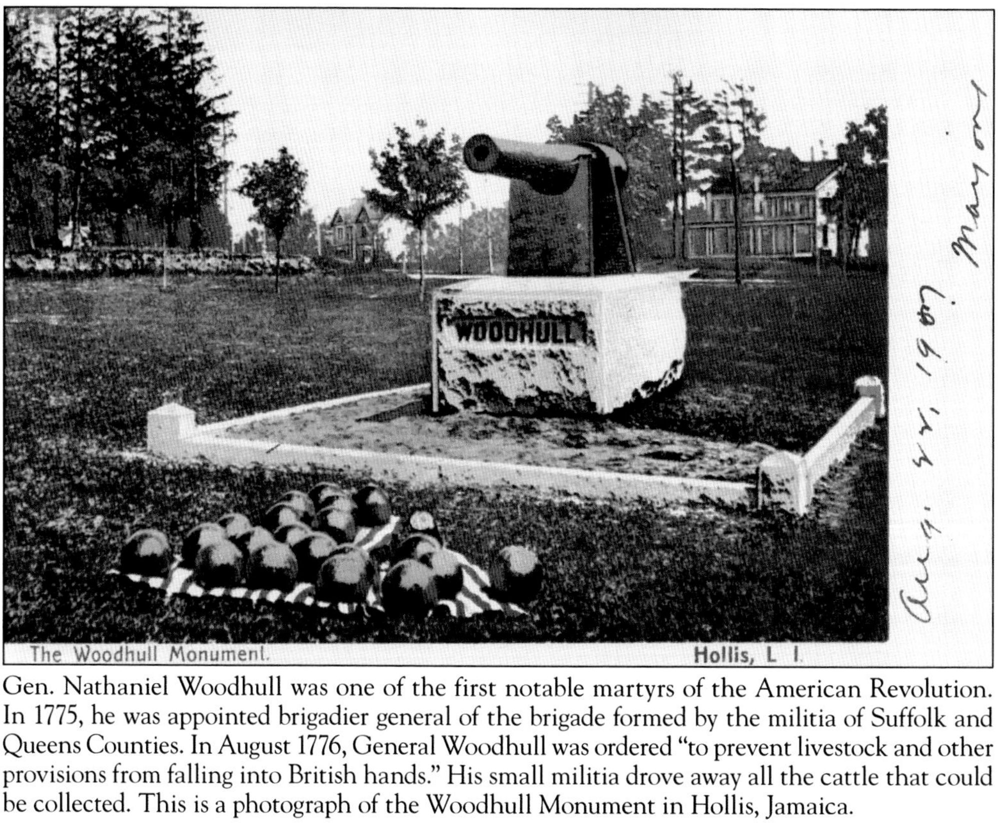

Gen. Nathaniel Woodhull was one of the first notable martyrs of the American Revolution. In 1775, he was appointed brigadier general of the brigade formed by the militia of Suffolk and Queens Counties. In August 1776, General Woodhull was ordered "to prevent livestock and other provisions from falling into British hands." His small militia drove away all the cattle that could be collected. This is a photograph of the Woodhull Monument in Hollis, Jamaica.

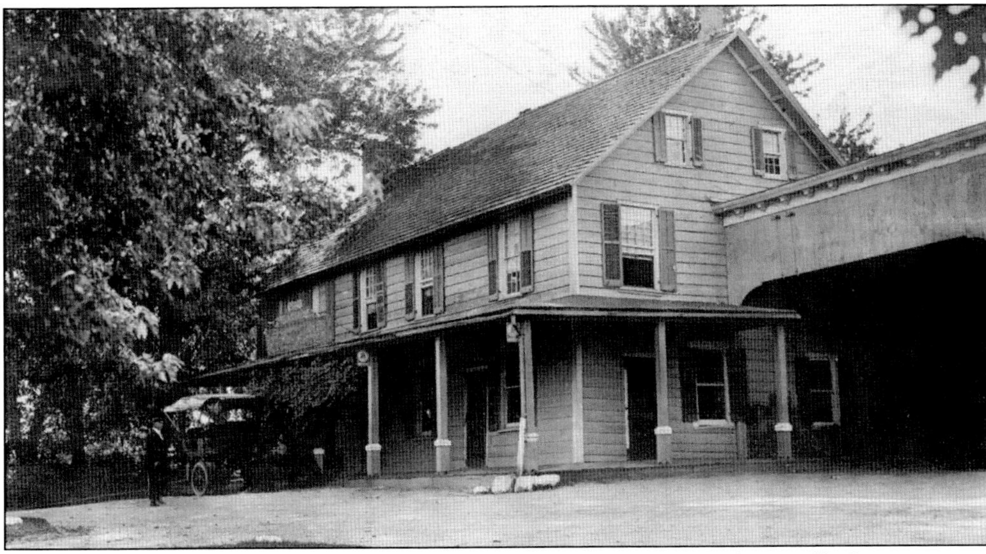

Awaiting orders at Carpenter's Tavern (Jamaica Avenue and 197th Street), Woodhull was captured by the British. Ordered to say "God save the King," he replied "God save us all" and was savagely attacked. Woodhull was taken to the old stone church in Jamaica, where his wounds were dressed. It was found necessary to amputate his arm. After this was done, infection set in, resulting in his death on the September 20, 1776.

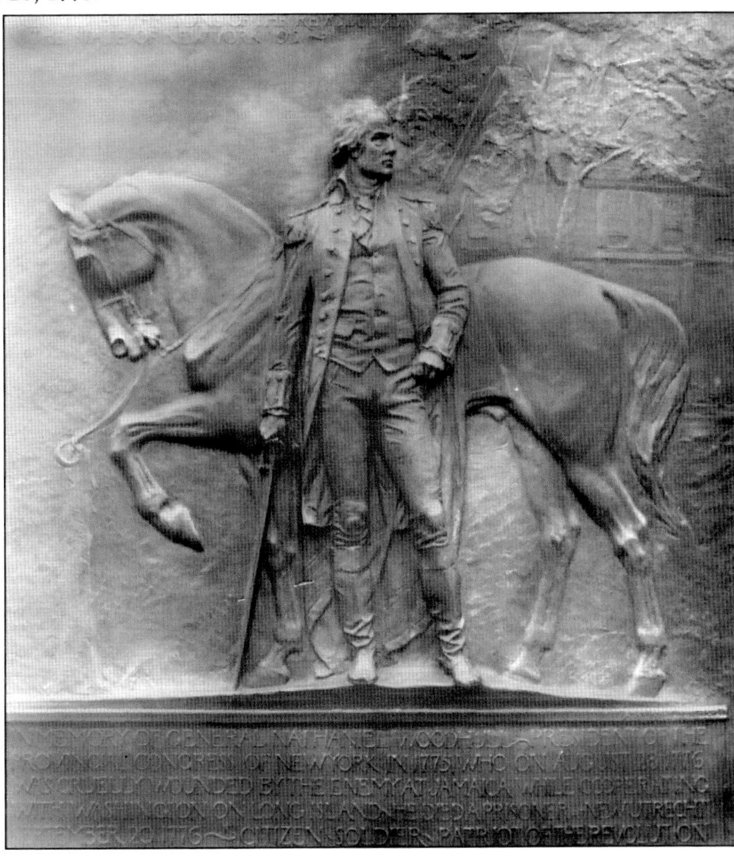

In 1912, a plaque was presented by the Sons of the Revolution at PS 35. The inscription reads, "In memory of Gen. Nathaniel Woodhull, who on August 28, 1776, was cruelly wounded by the enemy at Jamaica while cooperating with Washington on Long Island. He died a prisoner at New Utrecht, September 20, 1776, a citizen, soldier, patriot of the Revolution." (Archives at Queens Library, Frederick Weber Photographs.)

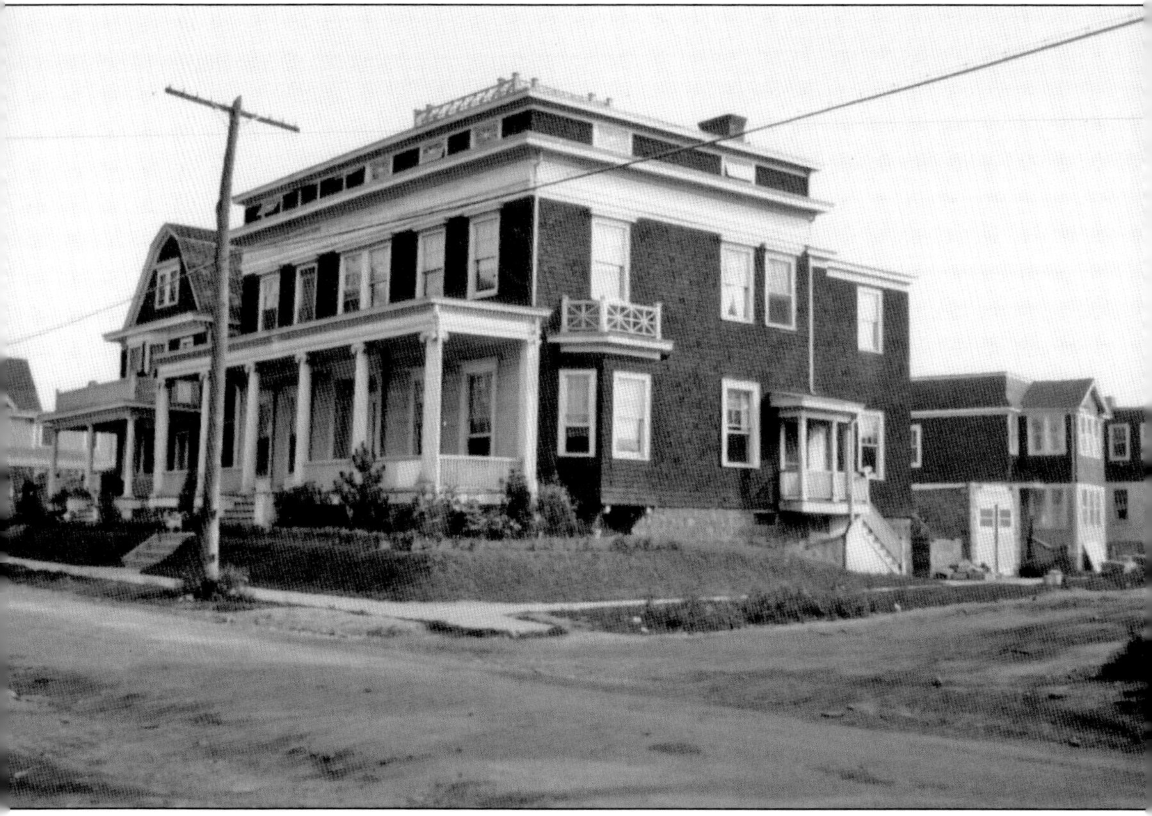

Rev. Abraham Keteltas was born in 1732. He moved to Jamaica in 1760 and purchased a farm. He could preach in three languages—French, Dutch, and English. According to the *Long Island Democrat* on February 17, 1885, "At the outbreak of the American Revolution he was a fiery patriot and proclaimed that he would shoulder his musket rather than pay the tea tax. He was a leading spirit at patriotic meetings stirring up the spirit of rebellion. He was elected a member of the Provincial Congress. Upon the British occupation of Long Island he was forced to flee leaving his property to the mercy of the enemy. His farm was stripped of everything that the soldiers needed and his 100 acres of woodland cut bare. His house was occupied by the British General Skinner." Keteltas returned home and died in 1798. The mansion house was accidently burned in 1799 but rebuilt. This photograph shows the Keteltas mansion located at the northwest corner of 144th Street and Eighty-ninth Avenue. (Archives at Queens Library, Eugene Armbruster Collection.)

Abigail Adams came to Jamaica to be with her daughter Abigail Smith and wrote, "Jamaica, Long Island, November 24, 1788. I find this place a very retired one, rural and delightful in the summer." Abigail was an early supporter of women's suffrage and an abolitionist. Local PS 131 was named the Abigail Adams School, and Eighty-fourth Avenue, the street in front of the school, was renamed Abigail Adams Avenue.

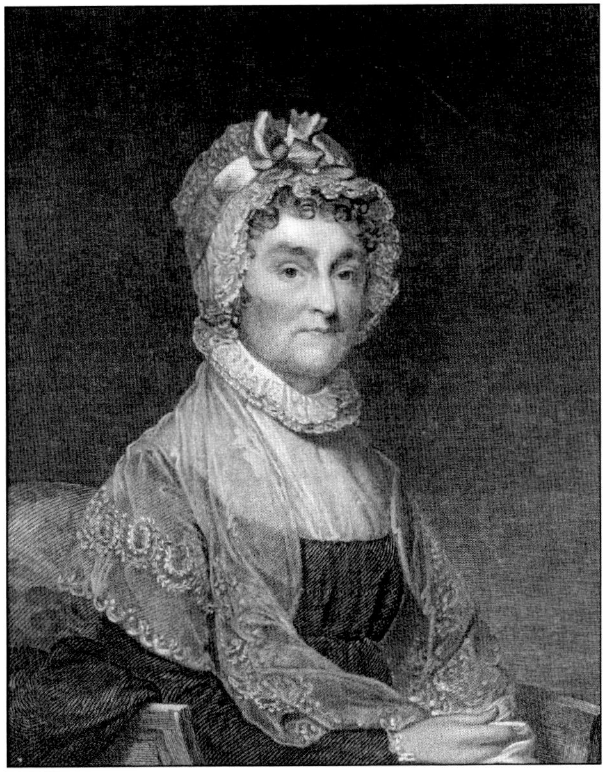

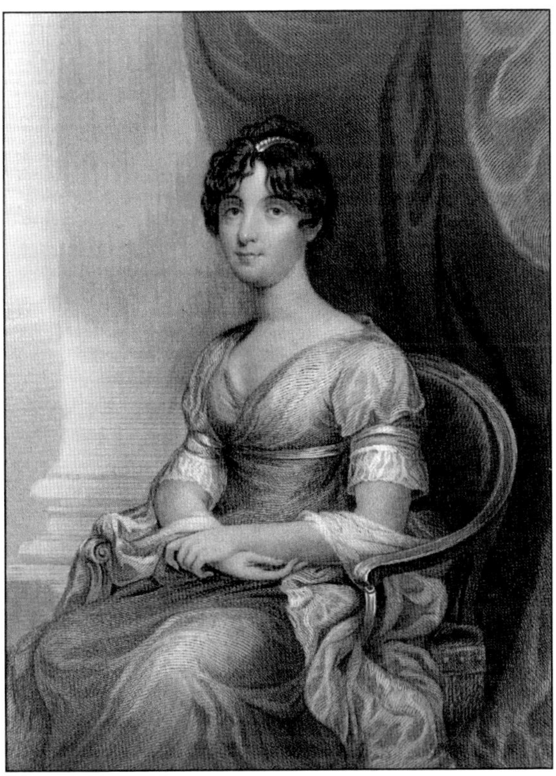

Mary Alsop King, born in New York in 1769, was the daughter of merchant John Alsop, a member of the Continental Congress from New York. She married Rufus King in 1786. She was a lady of remarkable beauty, with gentle and gracious manners and a well-cultivated mind. The latter years of her life were passed in Jamaica, Long Island, where she died in 1819. She is buried at the Grace Church cemetery.

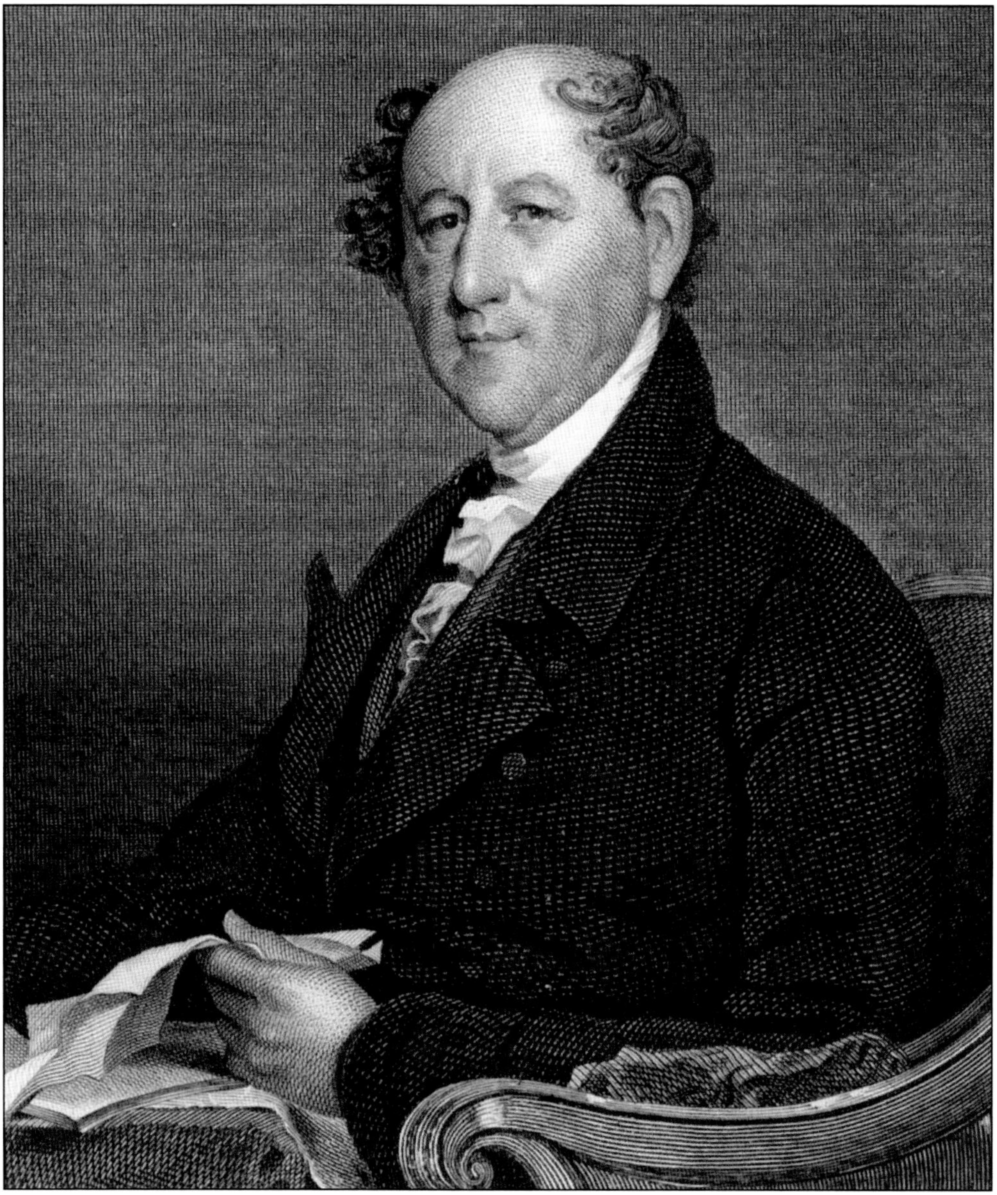

Born 1755, Rufus King graduated from Harvard, and he later served in the American Revolution. A lawyer, King entered politics, becoming a member of the Massachusetts Legislature and representative in the Confederation Congress. A delegate at the 1787 Constitutional Convention, he helped draft and signed the Constitution and was elected to the New York State Senate. From 1796 to 1803, under the administrations of George Washington, John Adams, and Thomas Jefferson, he was ambassador to England. King George III, sorry to see him leave said, "For your conduct here has been so entirely proper, both as it has regarded the interest of your own Country and of this, as to have given me perfect satisfaction." Running unsuccessfully for vice president in 1804 and 1808, he lost the 1816 presidential election to James Monroe. In the US Senate, King spoke against slavery: "I have yet to learn that one man can make a slave of another. If one man cannot do so, no number of individuals can have any better right to do it." These were radical words at the time, spoken 43 years before the Emancipation Proclamation.

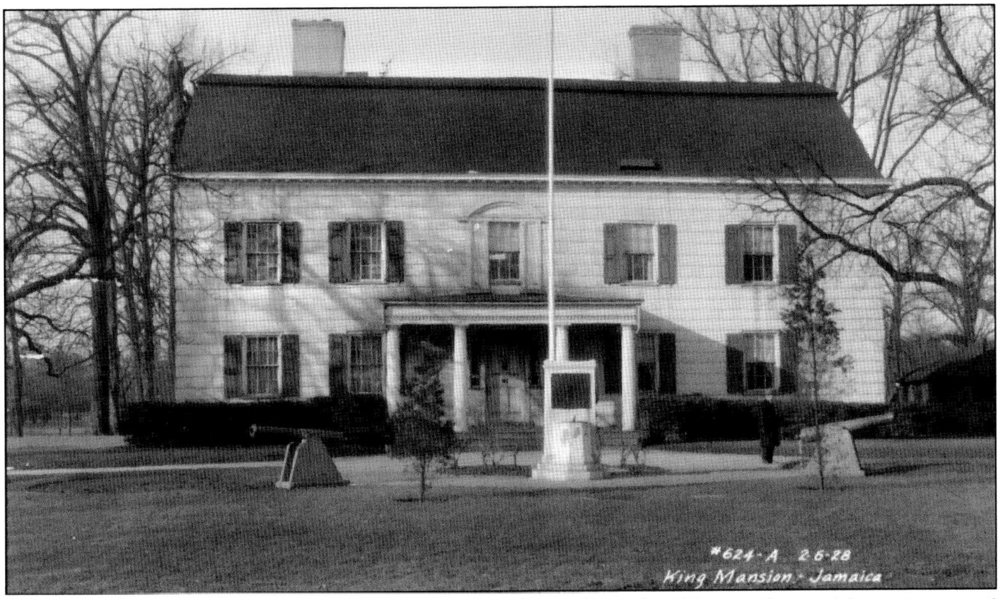

In 1806, the King family moved to Jamaica and purchased a 90-acre farm. Alterations and improvements were made to the house, including a library filled with books relating to the Americas. Rufus King embellished the farm with flowering shrubs and trees. Firs and pine were shipped from New Hampshire, believed to be among the first of their kind introduced into this part of Long Island. By 1817, he imported cattle of the North Devon breed. (Archives at Queens Library, Borough President of Queens Collection.)

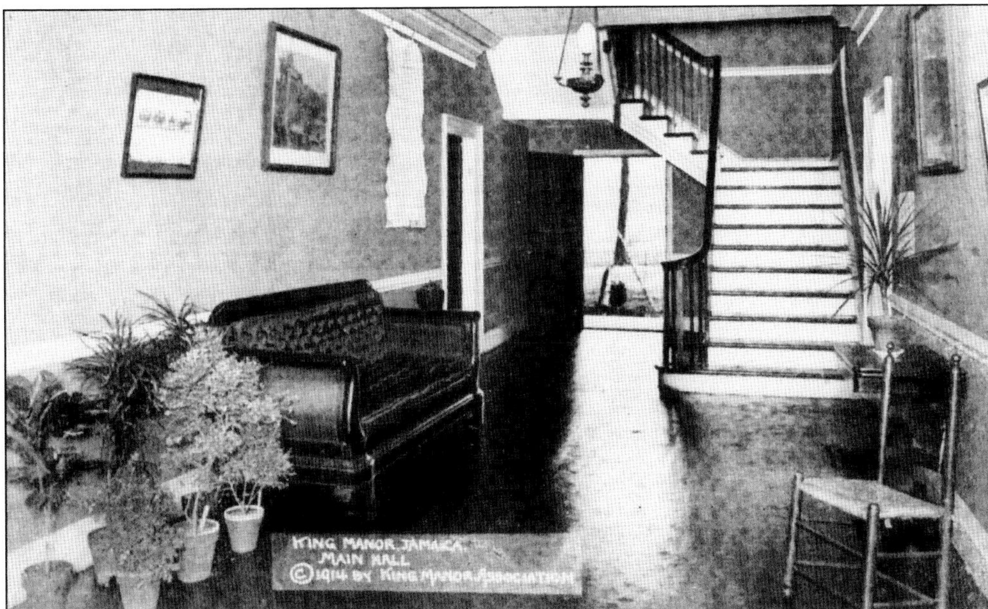

John Alsop King (1788–1867), son of Rufus King, served as New York governor from 1857 to 1859. He also served in the New York State Assembly and Senate and was the New York representative to Congress. King resided in the King family home at Jamaica until his death. This photograph shows the main entrance hall of the house. Among the many descendants of the King family are musician David Crosby and actress Jane Wyatt.

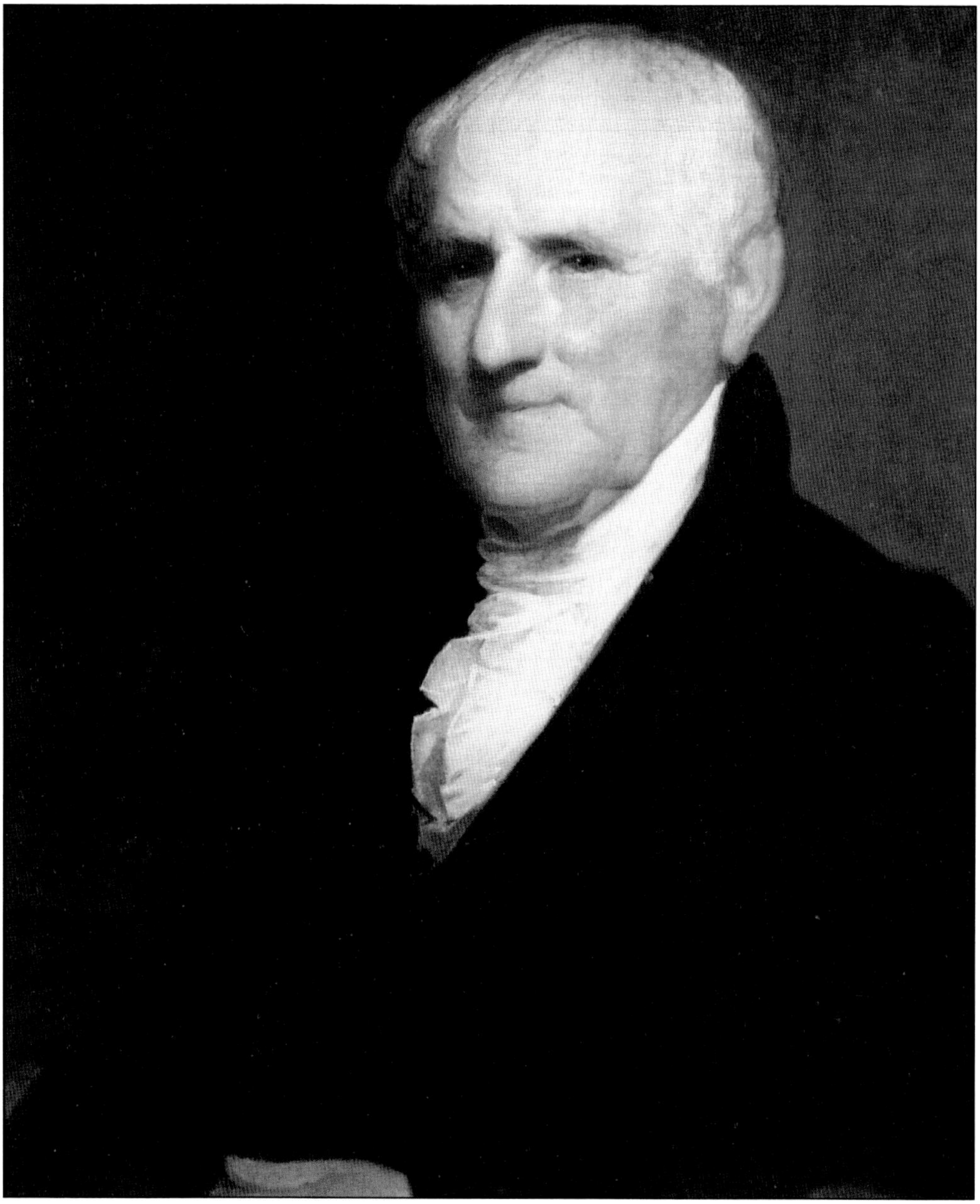

Egbert Benson was born in New York City on June 21, 1746. He was a Founding Father of the United States and graduated from King's College in 1765. He became distinguished for his eloquence to argue a case or cause in a court of law. Benson was appointed the first New York State attorney general and elected to the first state legislature. In 1788, he took the lead in the legislature, which ratified the US Constitution, and was a member of the Continental Congress from 1784 until 1788. Benson was judge of the Supreme Court of New York from 1794 until 1802 and also sat on the federal bench as a circuit judge. He was a member of Congress again from 1813 to 1815. Benson was also the first president of the New York Historical Society and author of *Vindication of the Captors of Major André* (1817) and a monograph entitled *Memoir on Dutch Names of Places* (1835). He died in Jamaica on August 24, 1833, and is buried at Prospect Cemetery. This portrait of Egbert Benson is by noted American artist Gilbert Stuart.

James Henry Hackett was a renowned actor born in New York City in 1800. He established a reputation as a player of eccentric character parts with great success. He performed in the United States and Britain, achieving a reputation in the works of Shakespeare, particularly the role of Falstaff. Hackett was a polished gentleman and a close friend of Washington Irving, James Fenimore Cooper, John Quincy Adams, and other notabilities.

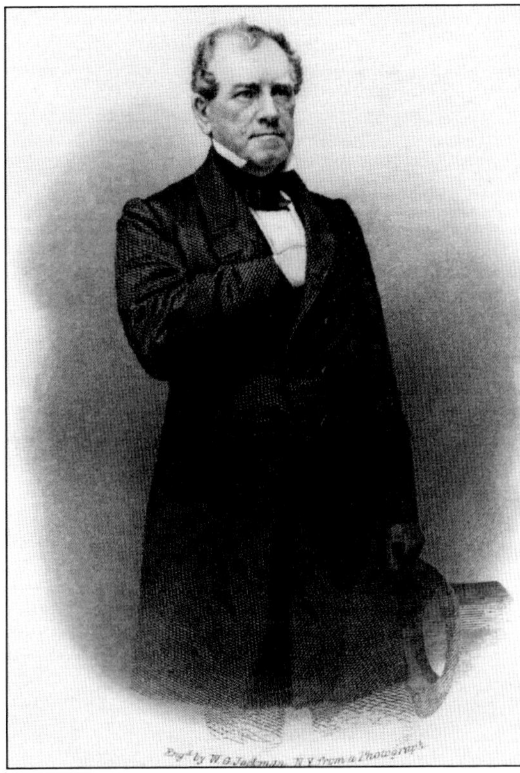

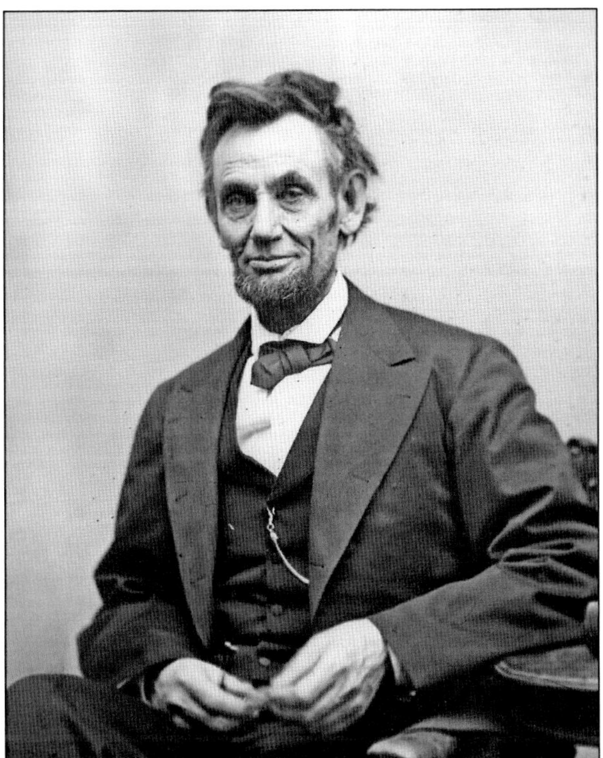

Abraham Lincoln saw *Henry IV* on March 13, 1863, when Hackett played Falstaff and wrote to him, "The first presentation of Falstaff I ever saw was yours here, last spring. Perhaps the best compliment I can pay is to say I am very anxious to see it again." They dined at the White House, discussing the Falstaff plays. Hackett died on December 28, 1871, and is buried in Jamaica's Prospect Cemetery.

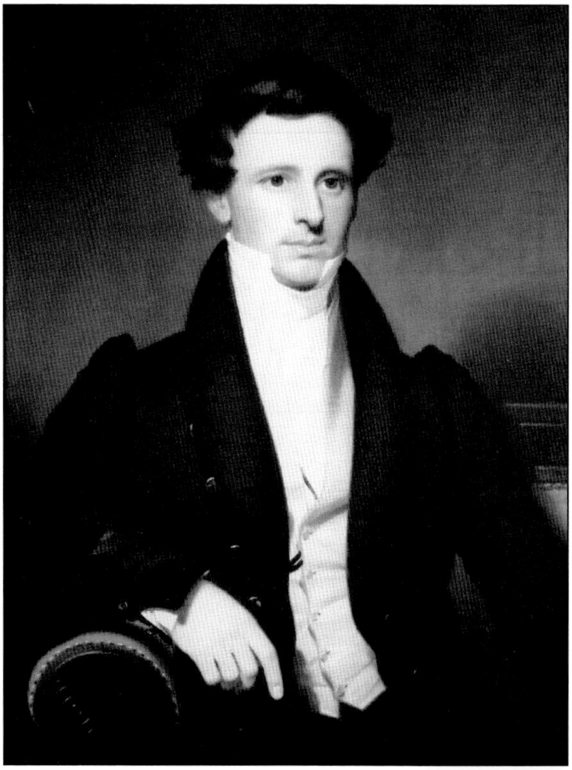

Nicholas Ludlum was born in Jamaica in 1799 and ran a successful hardware business in New York City. According to the *Long Island Farmer* on December 29, 1868, "We notice the death of Mr. Nicholas Ludlum, of New York City. Our citizens have evidence of the good deeds of Mr. Ludlum, who has expended a large sum in building the Chapel at the Prospect Cemetery, in this village, and otherwise improving the grounds."

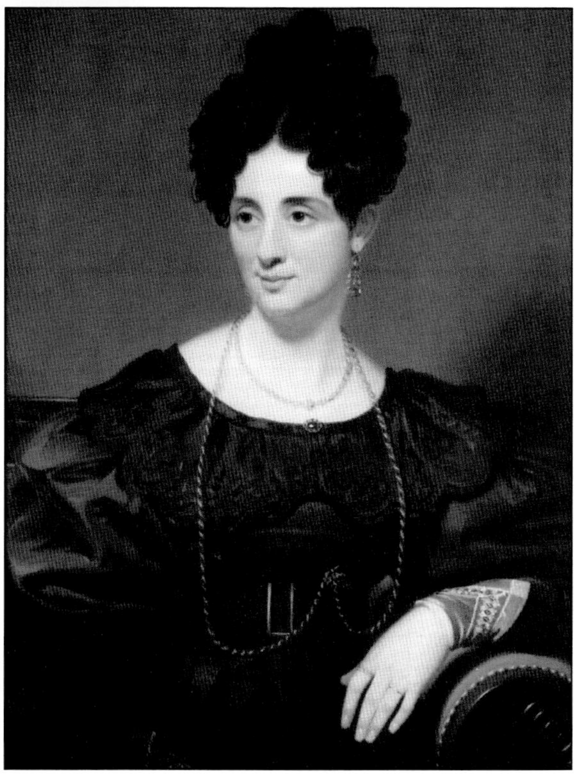

Sarah Birdsall Ludlum was the wife of Nicholas Ludlum. The 1857 Chapel of the Sisters at Prospect Cemetery (page 30) was built in memory of their daughters Cornelia Maria, Mary Cecelia, and Mary. A fourth daughter, Adelia, would go on to marry Sen. James Otis of New York. (Ludlum family; photograph by Larry Racioppo.)

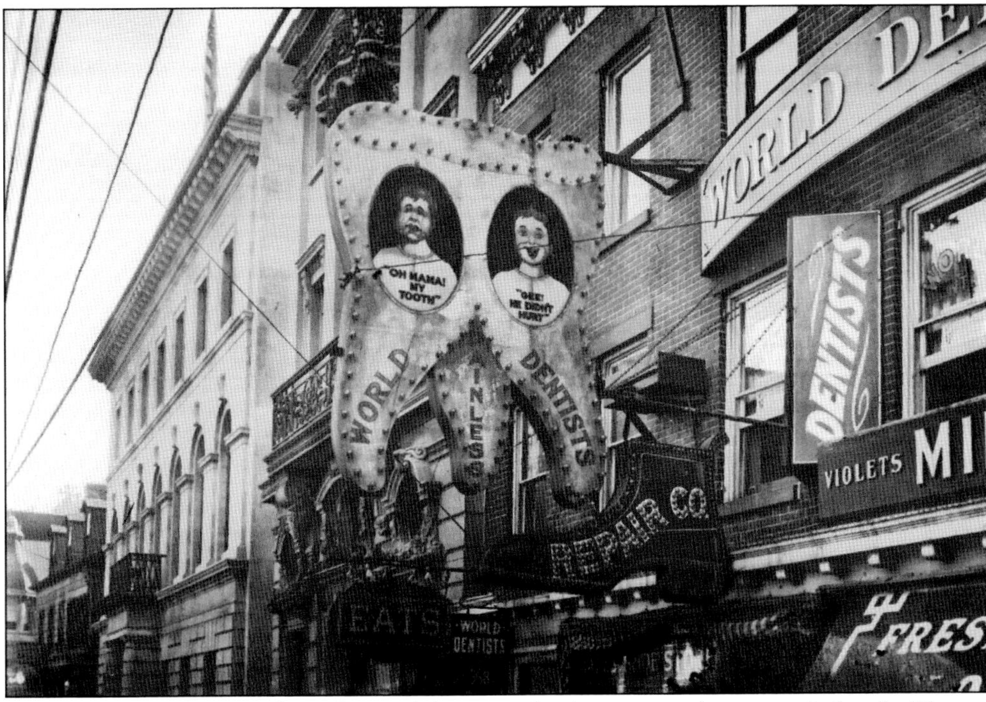

Robert Woofendale, an early professional dentist in the American colonies, studied under Thomas Berdmore, dentist to King George III. Woofendale's 1766 *New York Mercury* advertisement says that he will "perform all operations upon the teeth sockets, gums and palate, likewise fixes artificial teeth, so as to escape discernment." Retiring to Jamaica, Woofendale died in 1828 and is buried at Grace Cemetery. This photograph shows Jamaica Avenue and 160th Street with a dental advertisement. (Archives at Queens Library, Frederick Weber Photographs.)

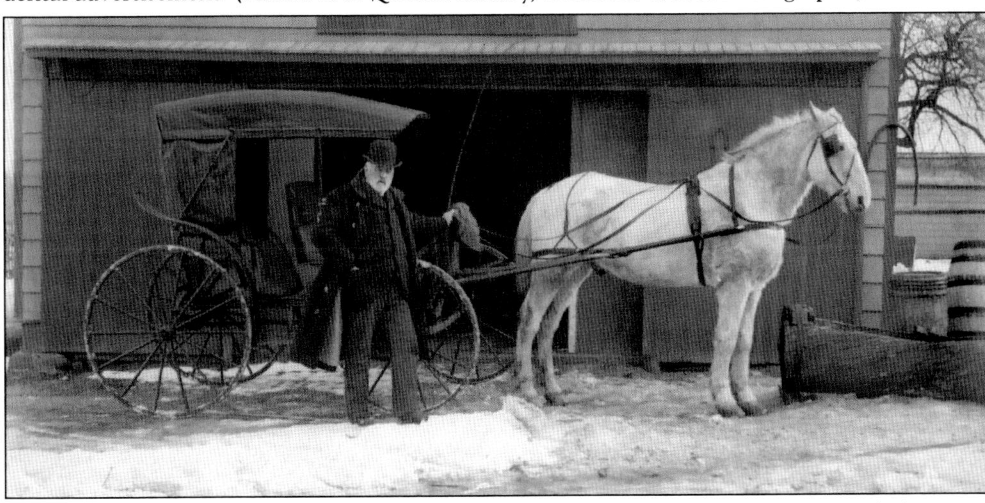

The *Roswell American Newspaper 1870 Directory* listing of Jamaica newspapers includes "*Long Island Farmer*; Republican; eight pages, subscription $2.50, established 1819; Horace W. Love, editor; Charles Welling, publisher. *Long Island Democrat*; Democratic; four pages, subscription $2; established 1835; J.J. Brenton, editor and publisher and *Jamaica Standard*; Democratic; four pages; subscription $2.50; established 1868; John O'Donnell Jr. editor and proprietor." This 1890 photograph shows O'Donnell of the *Standard*. (Archives at Queens Library, Portraits Collection.)

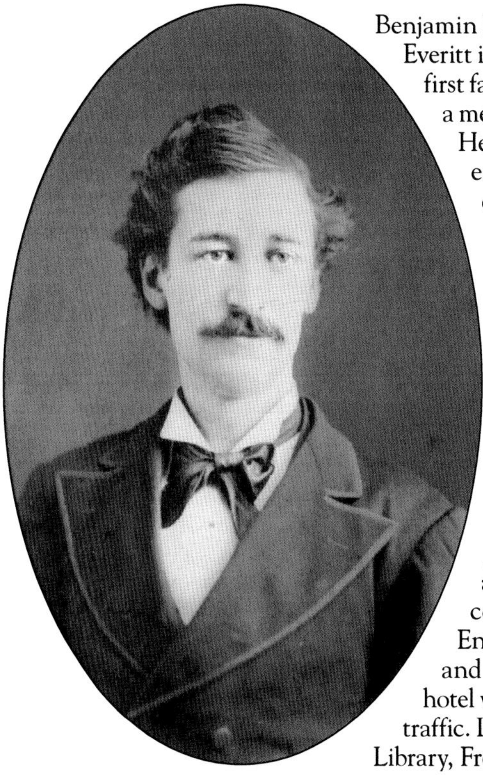

Benjamin F. Everitt was born in Jamaica in 1848. The name Everitt is among the earliest on Long Island and among the first families of Queens County. In 1868, Everitt became a member of the office of the county clerk for 10 years. He then became manager of the family undertaking establishment. In 1883, Everitt was chosen coroner of Queens County and served until 1895. (Archives at Queens Library, Portraits Collection.)

John Distler, a prominent Jamaica citizen, served as an alderman and as fire marshal with the fire company named in his honor. He owned the West End Hotel, located at the corner of Jamaica Avenue and Van Wyck Avenue. Today, the location of this hotel would be in the center of the Van Wyck Expressway traffic. Distler died on April 22, 1910. (Archives at Queens Library, Frederick Weber Photographs.)

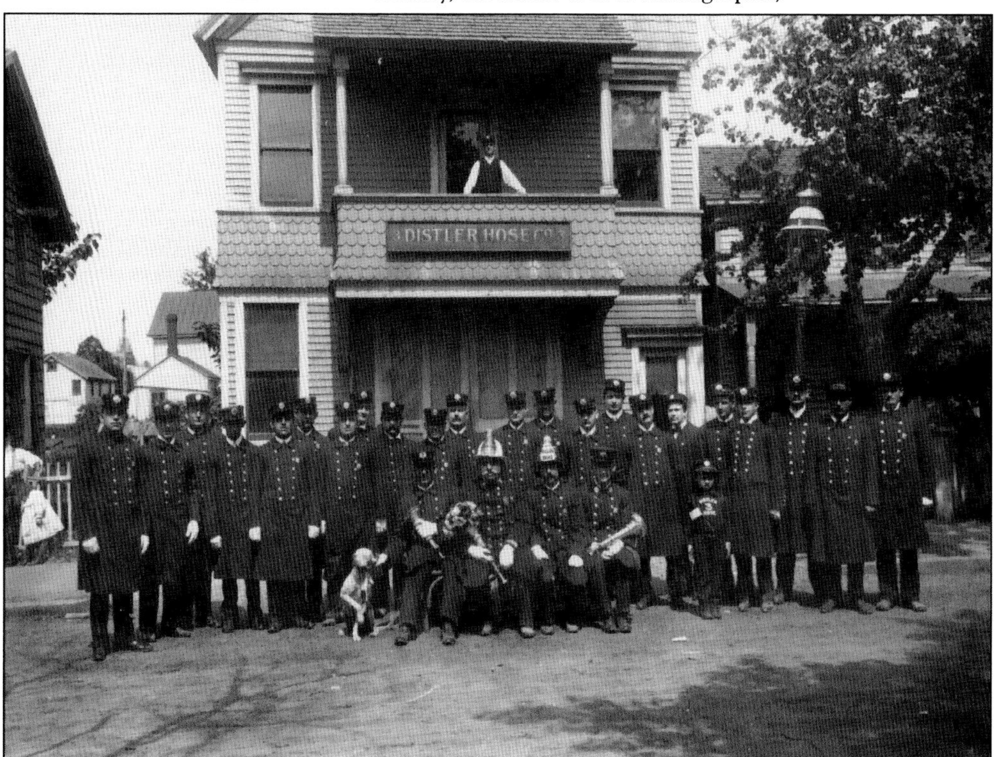

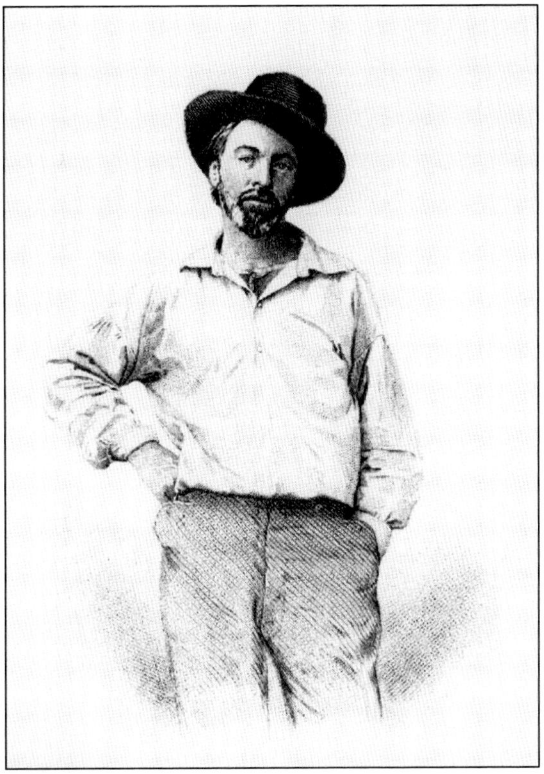

Walt Whitman (1819–1892) was a poet, essayist, journalist, and humanist. James Brenton, who established the weekly newspaper *Long Island Democrat* in Jamaica, printed two of Whitman's early prose pieces and a poem, "Our Future Lot." He hired Whitman as a typesetter in 1839, and Whitman boarded in the Brenton home. After he left, Whitman continued to write for Brenton through 1841, publishing several poems and a series of short articles.

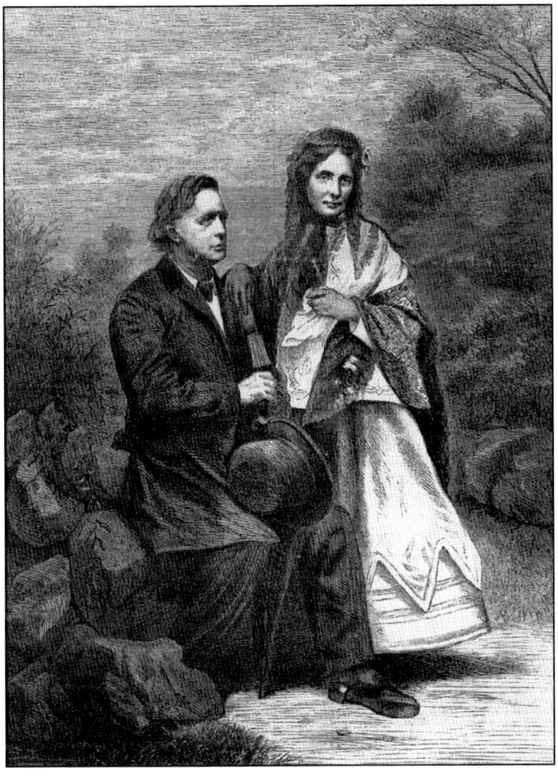

Rev. Henry Ward Beecher, a prominent clergyman, social reformer, abolitionist, and speaker poses with sister Harriet Beecher Stowe, author of *Uncle Tom's Cabin*. In 1885, he gave a lecture on "The Reign of the Common People" at the town hall. "Clear in his statement, pointed in his illustrations, original in his thoughts and style of argument, he held the close attention of his audience," said the *Long Island Democrat* on February 3, 1885.

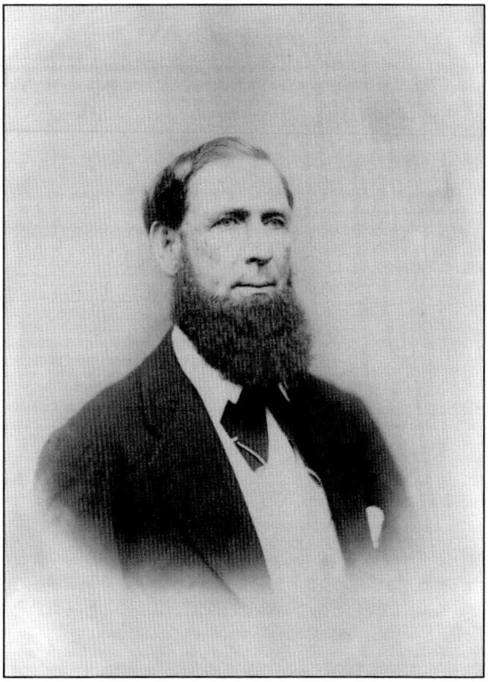

William Durland's Long Island ancestry dates back to the 1600s. He was a farmer, owned a grocery store and a riding stable, and was elected sheriff of Queens County from 1864 to 1866, with his son George serving as undersheriff. George would succeed his father as sheriff from 1866 to 1869. (Archives at Queens Library, Portraits Collection.)

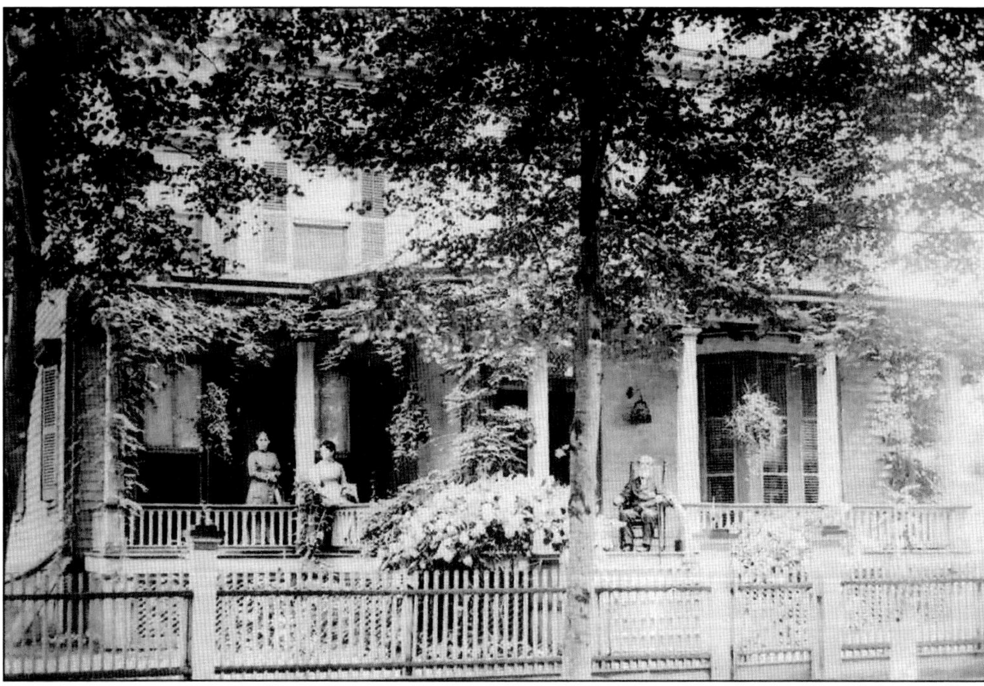

William Durland sits on the porch of his Jamaica home located at 22 Flushing Avenue (Parsons Boulevard) with daughters Hester and Sarah. His son William established the Durland's Riding Academy at Sixty-sixth Street and Central Park West, where the Vanderbilts, Roosevelts, and Astors boarded their horses. Today, the building is registered with the New York City Historical and Landmarks Preservation Societies and is now ABC Studios, with the original facade still intact.

Candace Wheeler was the most important textile and interior designer of the 19th century. Wheeler professionalized the role of women in decorative design by founding the Society of Decorative Art in New York and the Women's Exchange. She worked with the Tiffany Company, producing designs for the White House and the home of Mark Twain (pictured here). Wheeler developed Associated Artists, an all-female design firm in New York.

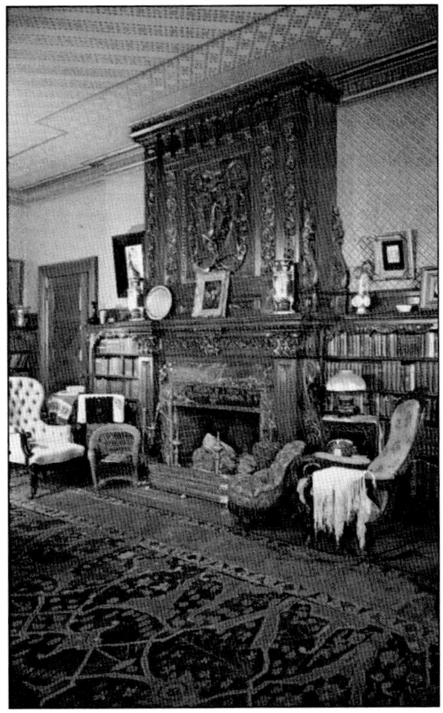

Candace's daughter Dora Wheeler Keith was born in Jamaica and educated at the Art Students League. She won awards at the Pan-American Exposition in New York in 1886, as well as the Louis Prang Prize for greeting card designs. At the 1893 Chicago's World Fair, she helped to decorate the Women's Building. This portrait of Dora was painted by William Merritt Chase. Candace died in 1923 and is buried in Prospect Cemetery.

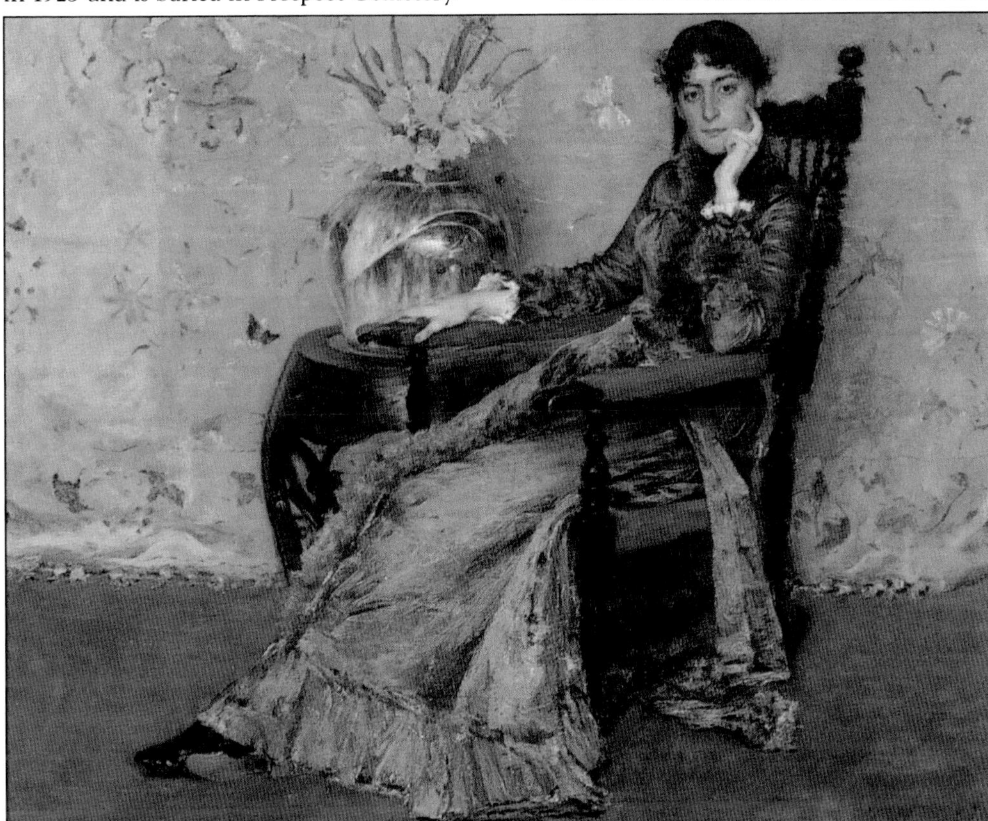

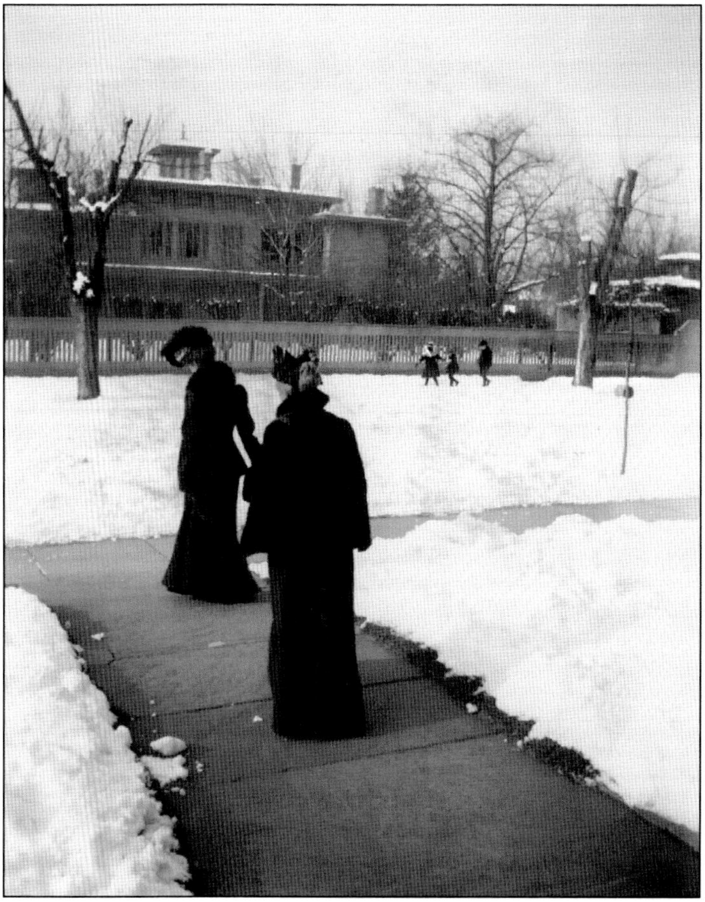

Ex-governor Richard C. McCormick lived at 88 Herriman Avenue (161st Street), Jamaica (pictured). "He was appointed Governor of the Arizona Territory by President Andrew Johnson, and at once set about placing the people in a better condition for defending themselves against the hostile Apaches," reported *The New York Times* on June 3, 1901. (Archives at Queens Library, George Winans Collection.)

As reported in the *Long Island Democrat* on October 13, 1868, "General Tom Thumb and his beautiful wife Lavinia will appear one day only at Union Hall Academy, Jamaica on October 15. Three years in Europe where they delighted all the Kings, Queens, Emperors and Five Million citizens of the Old World. They are the most astonishing and delightful Wonders of the Age! A beautiful and symmetrical couple in miniature." Tom is pictured with P.T. Barnum.

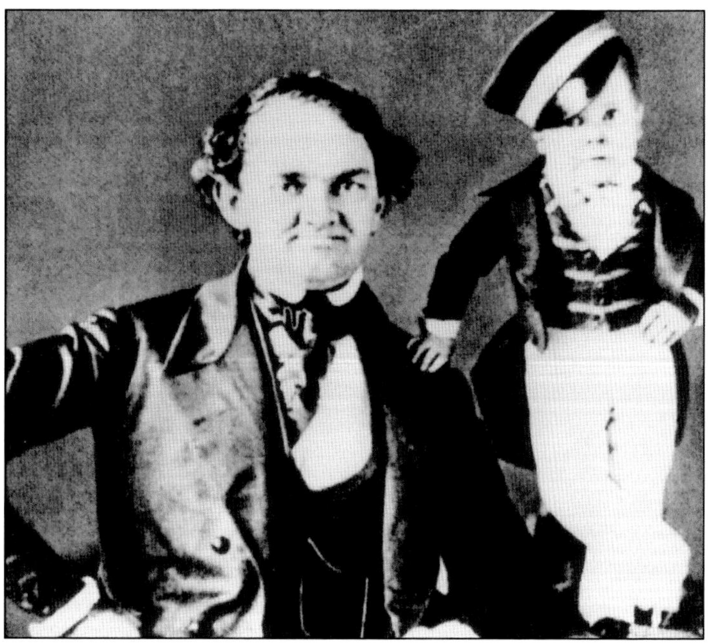

Born in 1866, Theodore Frederick Archer was a prosperous real estate developer and auctioneer in Jamaica. His father started the business in 1872 with the help of his two sons, Theodore and James, and it was called T.F. Archer & Sons. Theodore later became chief of the Jamaica Fire Department. He married Jennie Wilkinson and had six children. (Archives at Queens Library, Portraits Collection.)

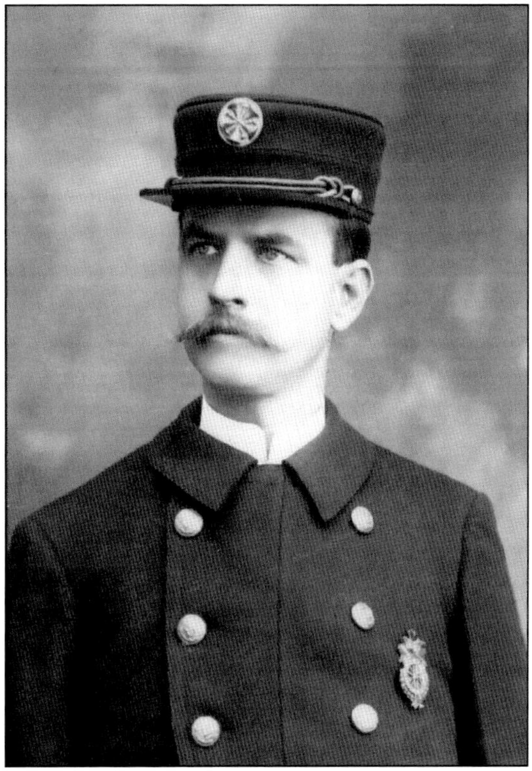

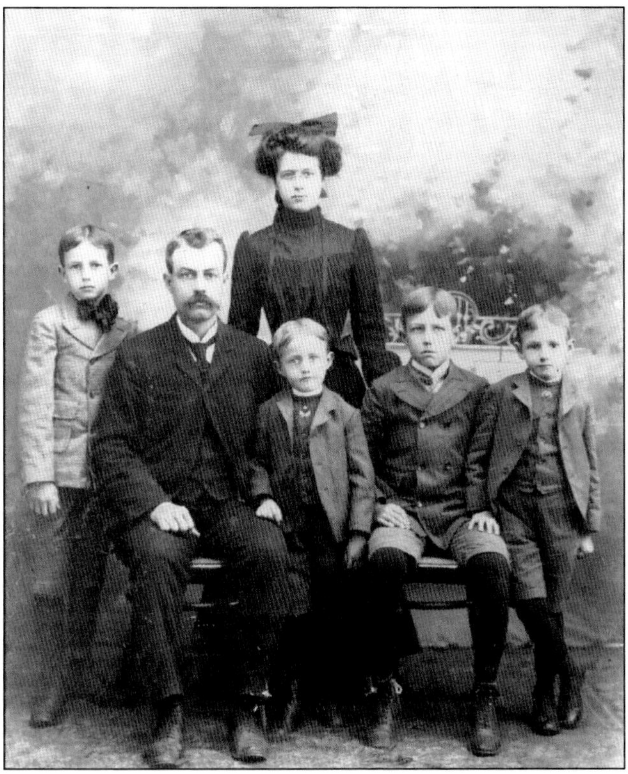

James Cornish Archer, born in 1862, began to assist his father in business at the age of 12 and developed an aptitude for the work, becoming his father's right-hand man. This family portrait shows, from left to right, James Jr., James, Marjorie, John Wesley, Elmer Young, and Alvin. Archer Avenue was named in honor of the Archer family. (Archives at Queens Library, Portraits Collection.)

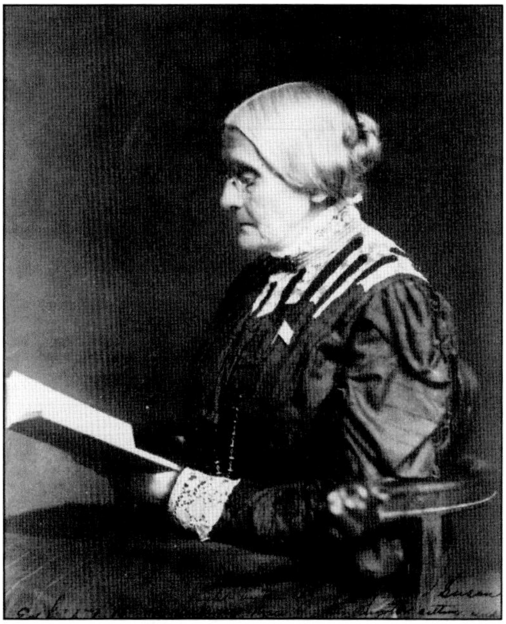

"The Woman Suffrage New York State Constitutional Convention will be held at the Town Hall on March 1 and 2. The leading speakers will be Susan B. Anthony, Rev. Anna Shaw and Miss Carrie Lane Chapman. The object of the event is to discuss the advisability of amending the constitution of the State so as to enfranchise women citizens," reported the *Long Island Democrat* on February 27, 1894.

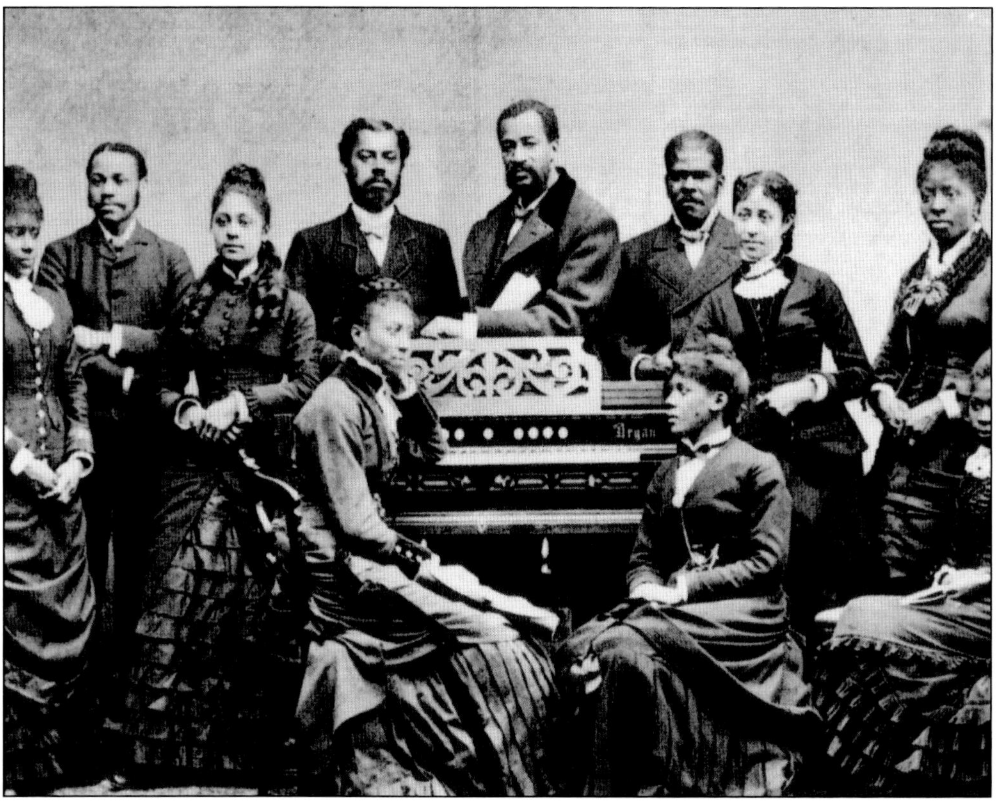

"The Texas Jubilee Singers," declared a writer for the *Long Island Democrat* on May 5, 1885, "will give one of their enjoyable concerts at the Jamaica Town Hall. The company is an excellent one. These singers are the same troupe that visited Jamaica, and gave such general satisfaction. Go hear them again!" Pictured here are the Fiske Jubilee Singers.

Jacob Riis was a celebrated American reformer, journalist, author, and photographer. On March 7, 1888, he gave an illustrated lecture, "The Outcasts of New York—Riches and Misery; Splendor and Squalor—The Other Half; How it lives and dies in New York," at the Jamaica Town Hall. "The lecture and exhibition of Mr. Jacob Riis was very well attended and proved exceedingly interesting," reported the *Long Island Democrat* on March 13, 1888.

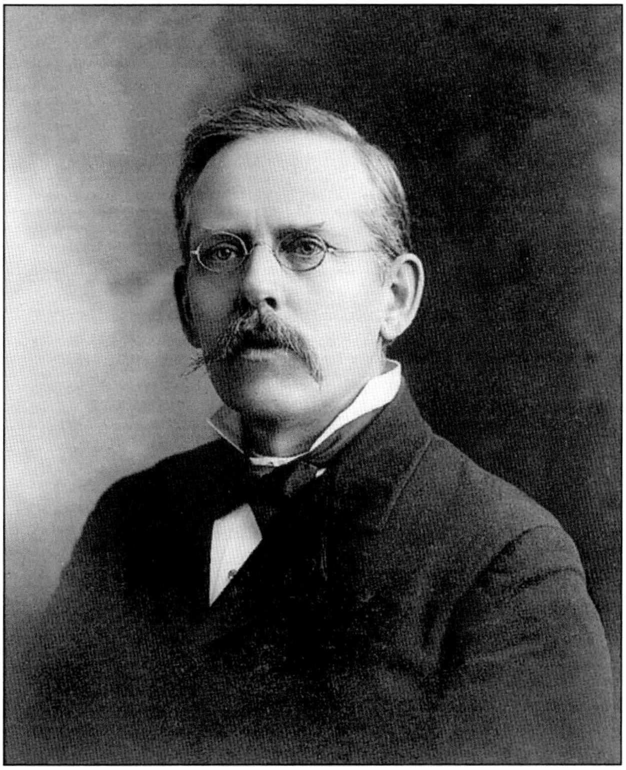

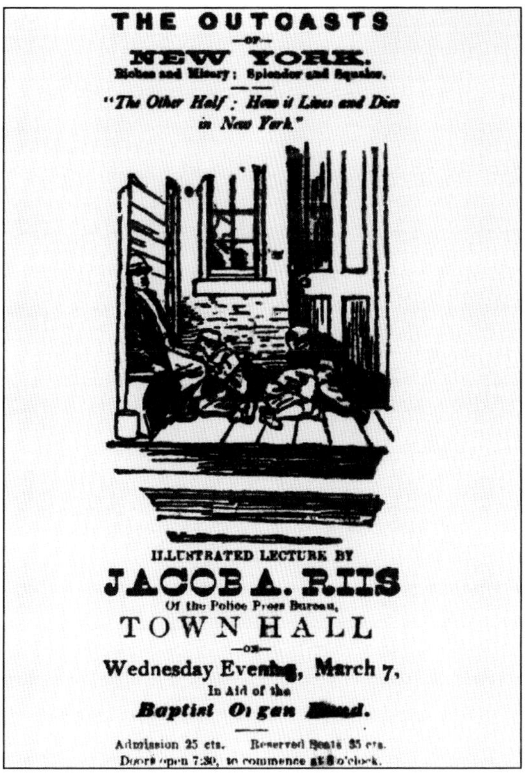

"Riis is a terse and graphic speaker, and pathos and mirth were mingled in a very pleasant manner, in his running comments on the scenes shown by calcium light on canvass. He gave a startling exhibition of the abodes of poverty and vice in New York City, and well calculated to draw the attention of well disposed persons to the condition of the poor," reported the *Long Island Democrat* on March 13, 1888.

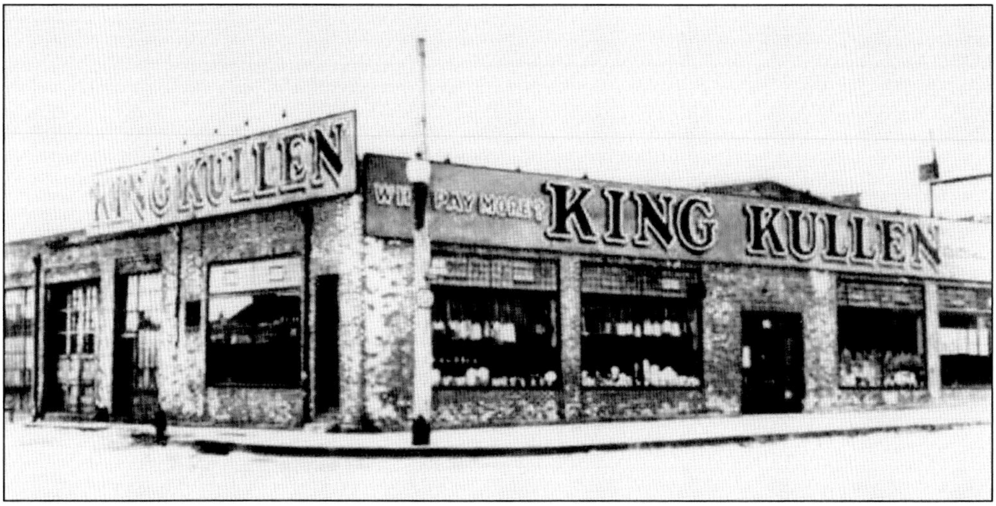

Michael J. Cullen, known as "King Kullen," was the founder and head of the King Kullen supermarkets. Cullen leased a vacant garage on Jamaica Avenue in Queens, just a few blocks from a busy shopping district, and on August 4, 1930, opened the doors to America's first supermarket, King Kullen Grocery Company. The Smithsonian Institution recognizes King Kullen as America's first supermarket.

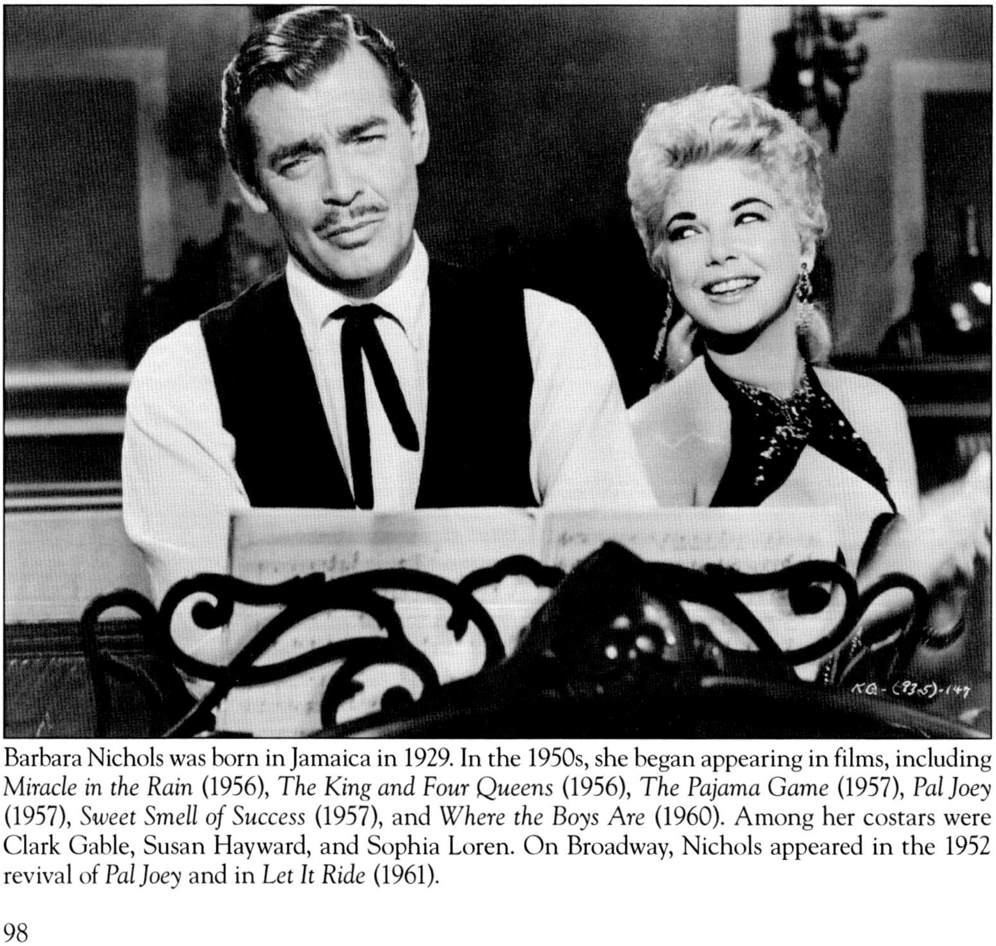

Barbara Nichols was born in Jamaica in 1929. In the 1950s, she began appearing in films, including *Miracle in the Rain* (1956), *The King and Four Queens* (1956), *The Pajama Game* (1957), *Pal Joey* (1957), *Sweet Smell of Success* (1957), and *Where the Boys Are* (1960). Among her costars were Clark Gable, Susan Hayward, and Sophia Loren. On Broadway, Nichols appeared in the 1952 revival of *Pal Joey* and in *Let It Ride* (1961).

Bob Beamon was born in Jamaica in 1946. When attending Jamaica High School, he was discovered by renowned track coach Larry Ellis. At the 1968 Summer Olympics, Beamon set a world record for the long jump of 8.90 meters (29 feet, 2.5 inches). The record stood for 23 years and was named by *Sports Illustrated* magazine as one of the five greatest sports moments of the 20th century.

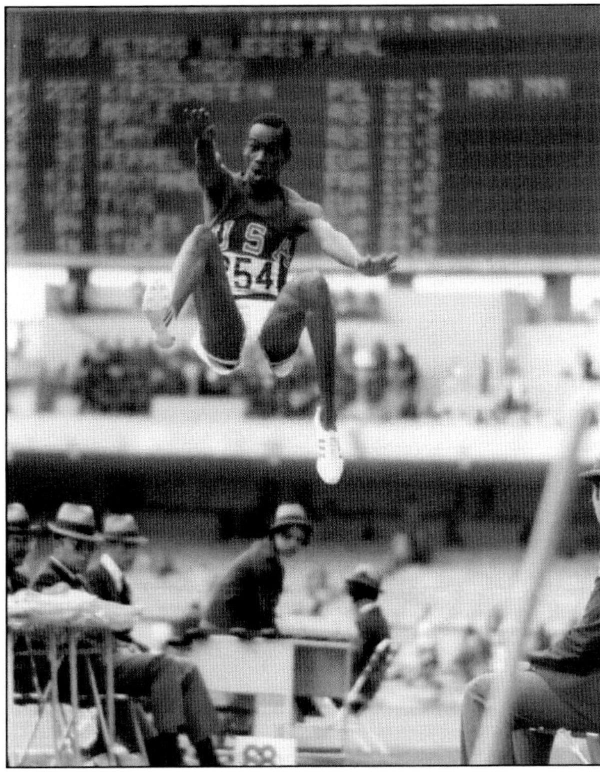

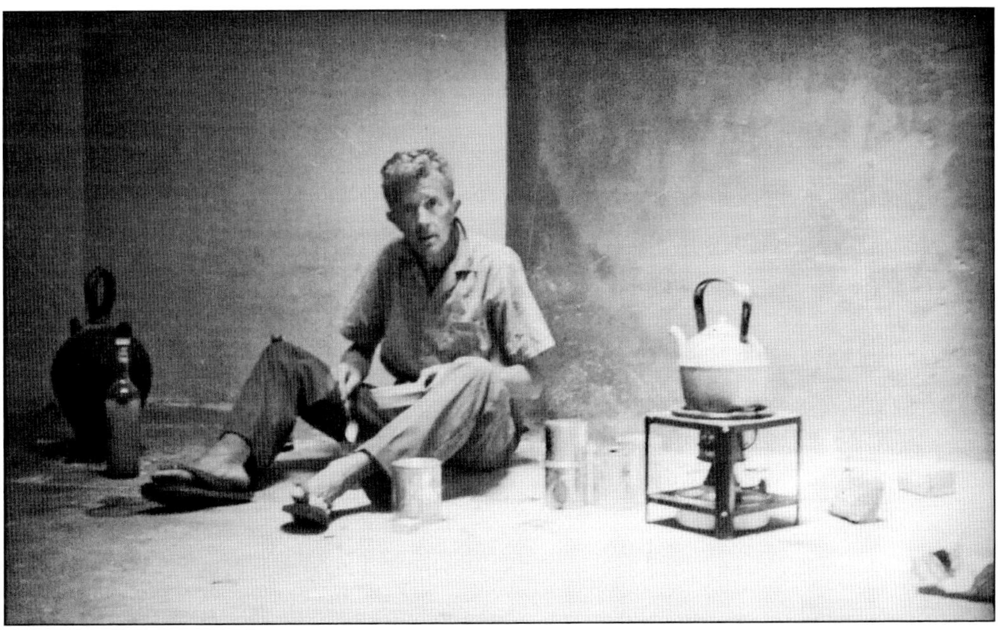

Paul Bowles (1910–1999), an expatriate writer, composer, author, and traveler, was born in Jamaica. He studied music with Aaron Copland and wrote music for various theatrical productions, as well as other compositions. Bowles achieved critical and popular success with the publication in 1949 of his first novel, *The Sheltering Sky*, made into a film by Bernardo Bertolucci in 1990. In 1947, Bowles moved to Tangier, Morocco, with his wife and remained there for 52 years.

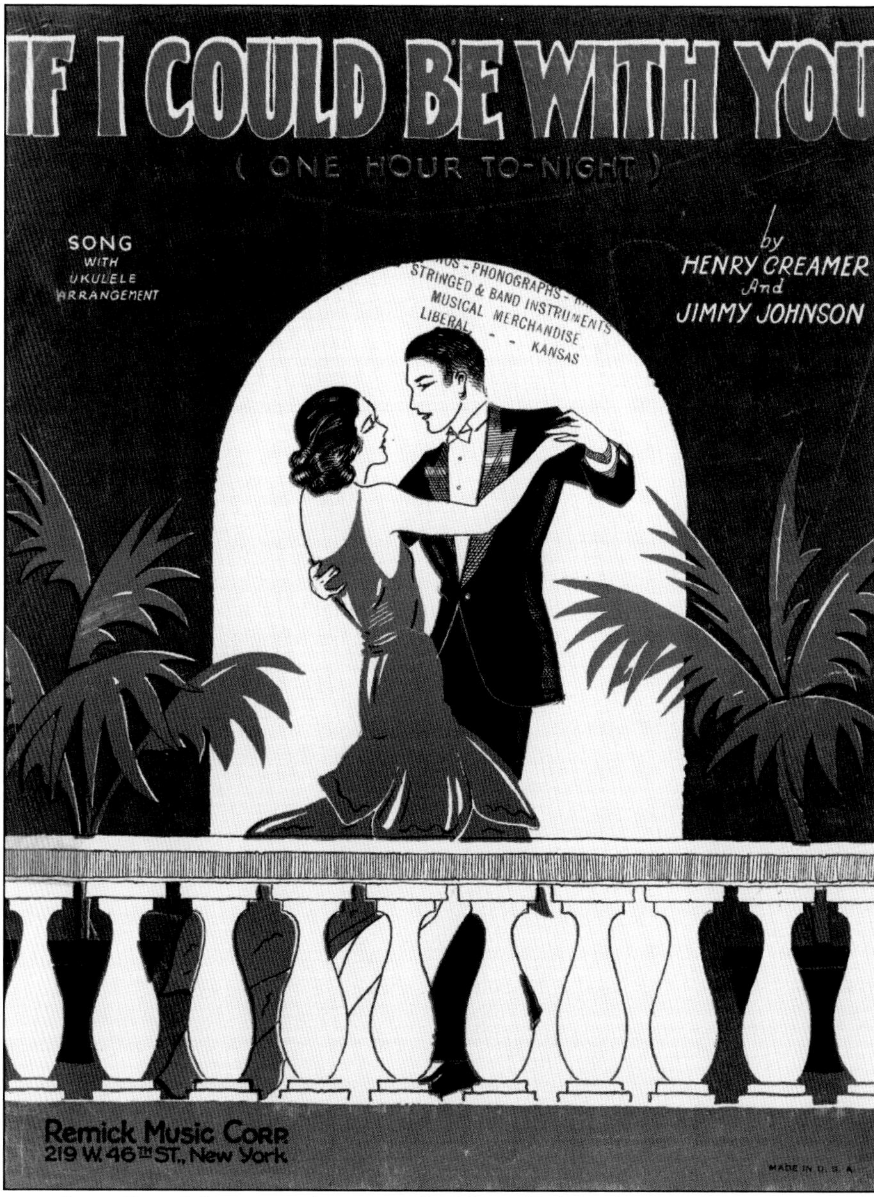

Jazz pianist James Price Johnson was known as the "Grandfather of Hot Piano." He emerged during the transitional period between ragtime—a music performed strictly from written scores—and the improvisatory and rhythmically more relaxed foundations of shout piano, or what became known as stride piano. Bringing together elements of ragtime, blues, African American religious music, and classical themes, Johnson originated a piano style that dominated New York City's African American musical world during the early decades of the 20th century. He died in 1955 in Jamaica. There have been many other musical legends with connections to Jamaica: Count Basie, Brook Benton, James Brown, Miles Davis, John Coltrane, Eddie "Lockjaw" Davis, Mercer Ellington, Ella Fitzgerald, Milt Hilton, Lena Horne, Illinois Jacquet, William Grant Still, Bill Kenny, Robert Taylor, Clarence Williams, Eva Taylor, Eileen Jackson Southern, Thomas "Fats" Waller, Frank Wess, Bart Williams, Earl Bostic, Wild Bill Davis, Slam Stewart, Cootie Williams, Oliver Nelson, James "Osie" Johnson, Rose Murphy, and Lester Young.

Five

Jamaica's Offspring
Dearest Treasures

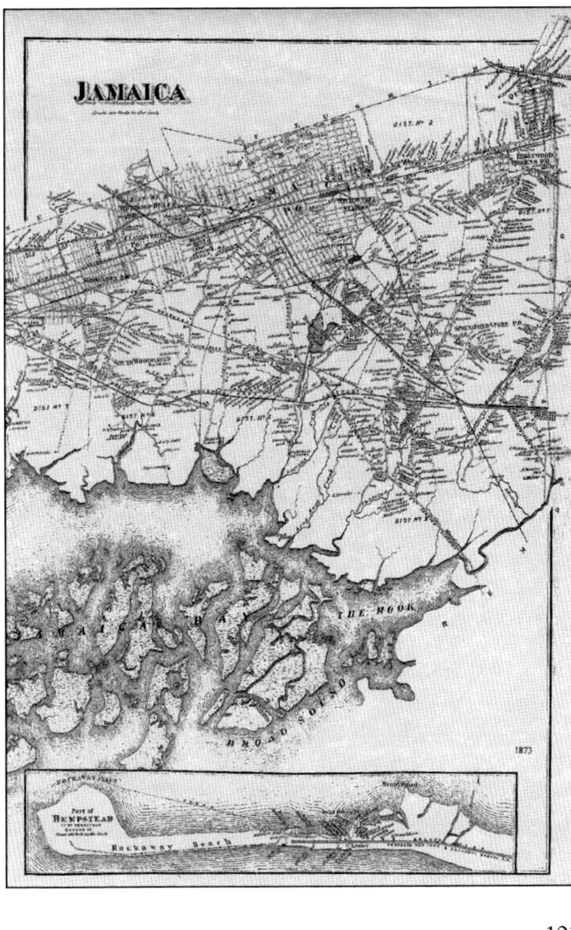

In 1683, the British divided the province of New York into counties, one of which was Queens. The Jamaica territory included the lands to the Nassau border on the east and the Brooklyn border on the west, extending north to present-day Union Turnpike and south to Jamaica Bay. Many towns developed over the centuries. Some flourished, while others have vanished. All towns within the territory have a zip code beginning with 114.

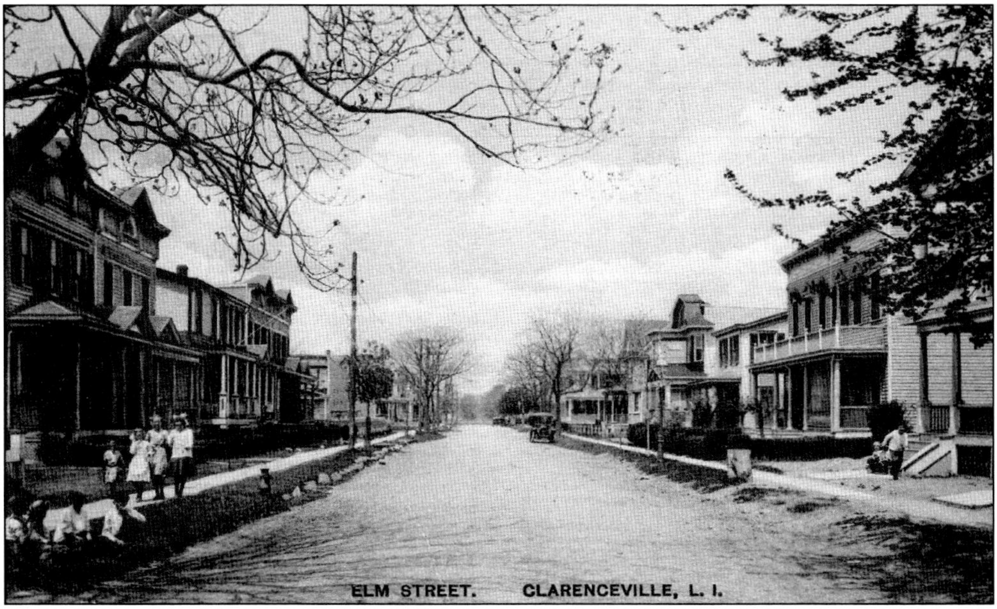

Clarenceville, a farming community founded in 1852 on Jamaica Avenue and Greenwood Avenue (111th Street), was named for Clarence Miliken, the son of an original settler. According to the *Brooklyn Eagle* on November 2, 1852, "This village is finely located on a lovely plain, free from swamps and rough or mountain land. The title of the property is perfect, having been in one family for nearly 200 years." Clarenceville is now a part of Richmond Hill.

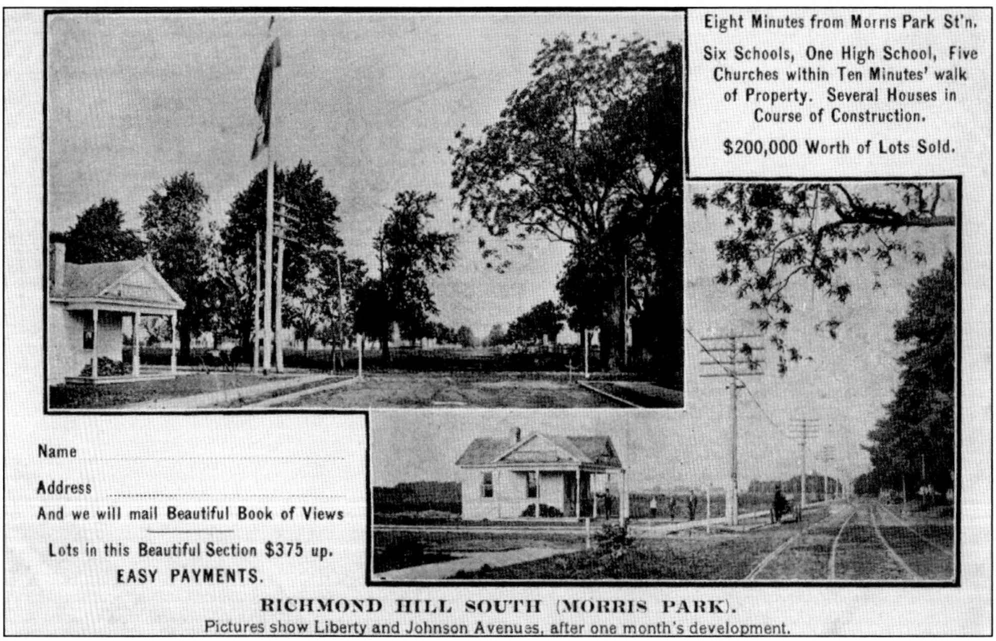

Morris Park was developed west of Jamaica by Frederick Dunton in 1885. The April 21, 1885, *Long Island Democrat* reported, " 'Morris Park,' exclaimed the conductor on the Brooklyn train, as the train neared the new station. The passengers strained their eyes to see the novelty, when the conductor informed them that 'the Park had not got erected yet.' Four houses are being erected there however." It is now part of Richmond Hill.

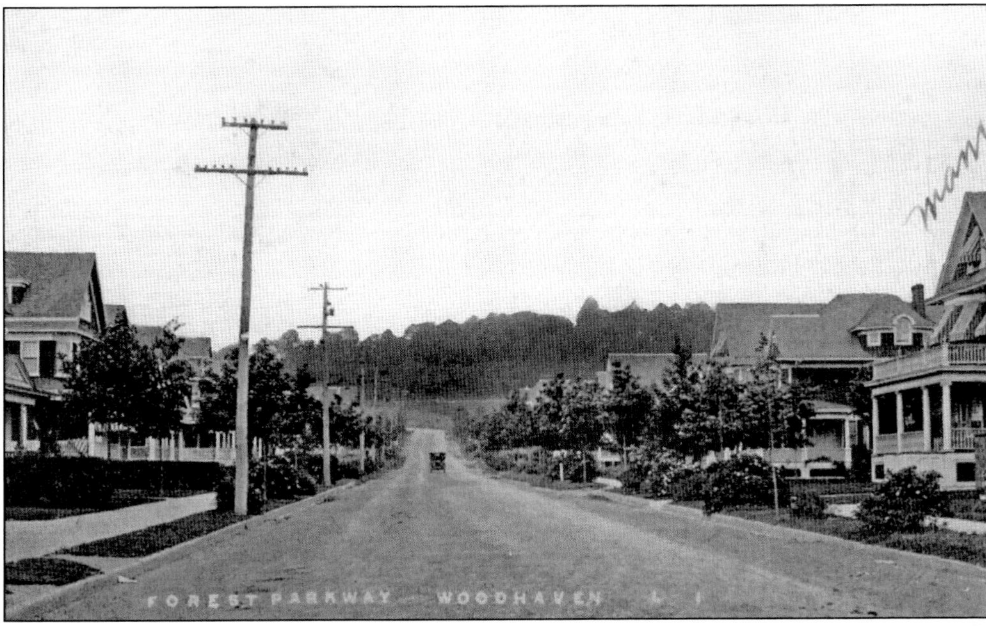

Woodhaven became the site of two racetracks—the Union Course (1821) and the Centerville (1825). Union Course was a nationally famous track situated in the area now bounded by Seventy-eighth Street, Eighty-second Street, Jamaica Avenue, and Atlantic Avenue. Match races between horses from the South against those from the North drew crowds as high as 70,000. Pictured here is Forest Parkway, looking north to Forest Park.

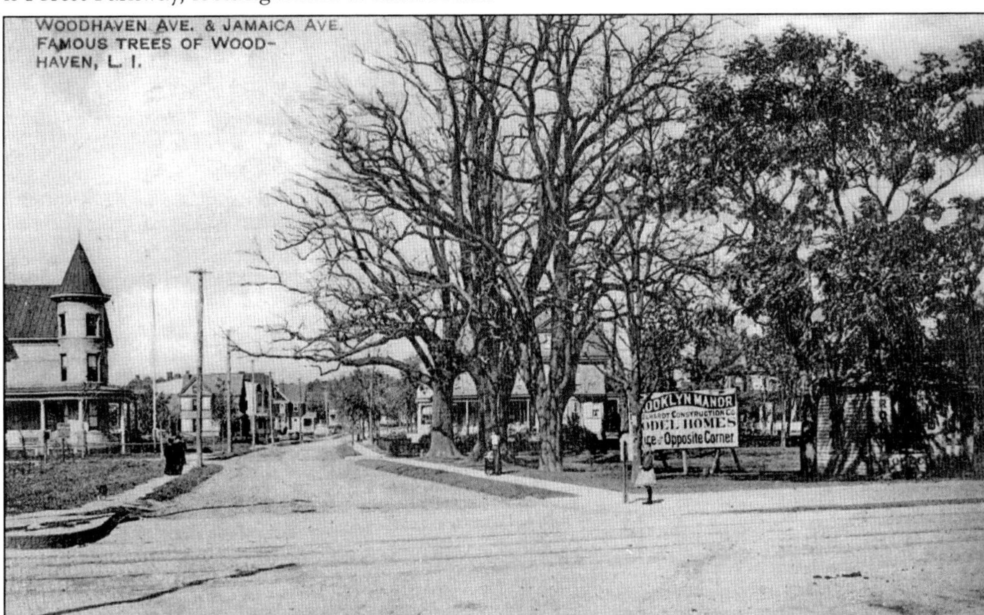

John R. Pitkin developed the eastern area as a workers' village called Woodville (1835). In 1853, residents petitioned for a local post office. To avoid confusion with a Woodville located upstate, the residents agreed to change the name to Woodhaven. Picture here is Woodhaven Avenue (Boulevard) at Jamaica Avenue, looking north. Today, this single dirt street is a busy eight-lane boulevard. The Woodhaven zip code is 11421.

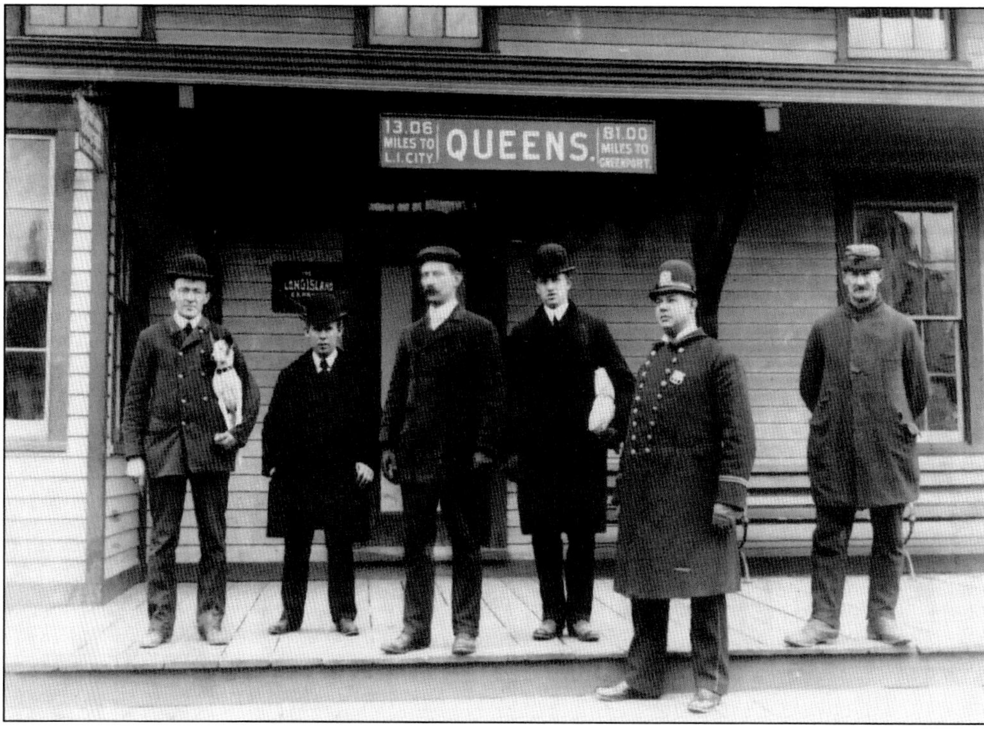

Queens Village's history goes back to 1824, when Thomas Brush established a blacksmith shop in the area. He prospered and built several other shops and a factory, and the community soon became known as Brushville. In 1834, the railroad arrived. The first station in the area was called Flushing Avenue in 1837, Delancy Avenue in 1838, and Brushville in 1842. In 1856, residents changed the name to Queens. (Bob Stonehill Collection.)

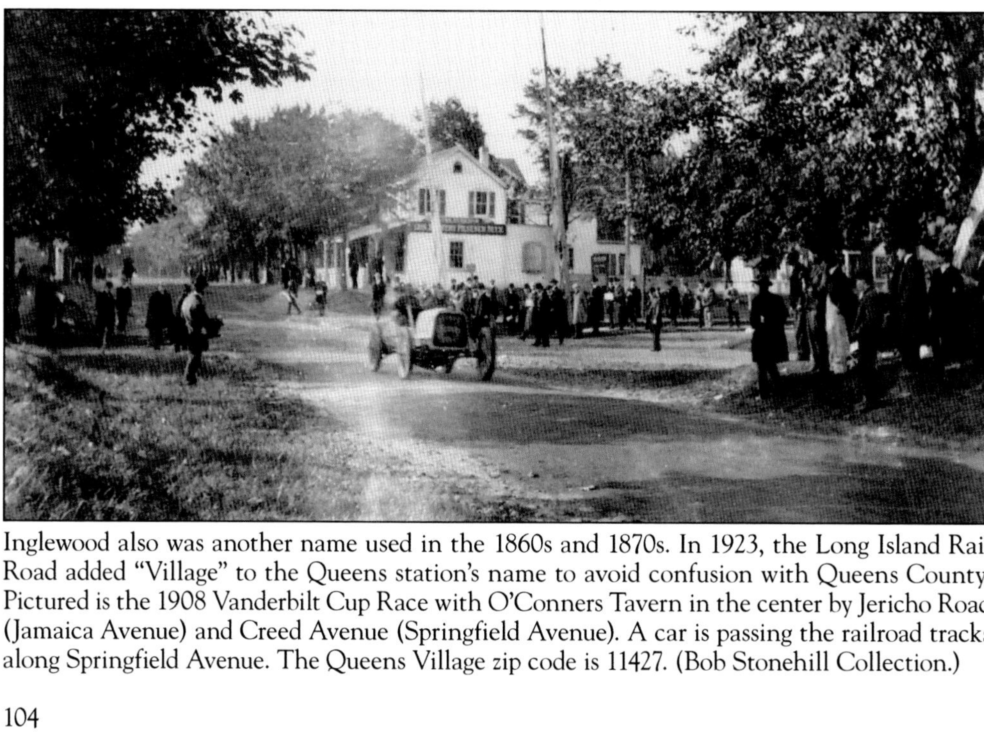

Inglewood also was another name used in the 1860s and 1870s. In 1923, the Long Island Rail Road added "Village" to the Queens station's name to avoid confusion with Queens County. Pictured is the 1908 Vanderbilt Cup Race with O'Conners Tavern in the center by Jericho Road (Jamaica Avenue) and Creed Avenue (Springfield Avenue). A car is passing the railroad tracks along Springfield Avenue. The Queens Village zip code is 11427. (Bob Stonehill Collection.)

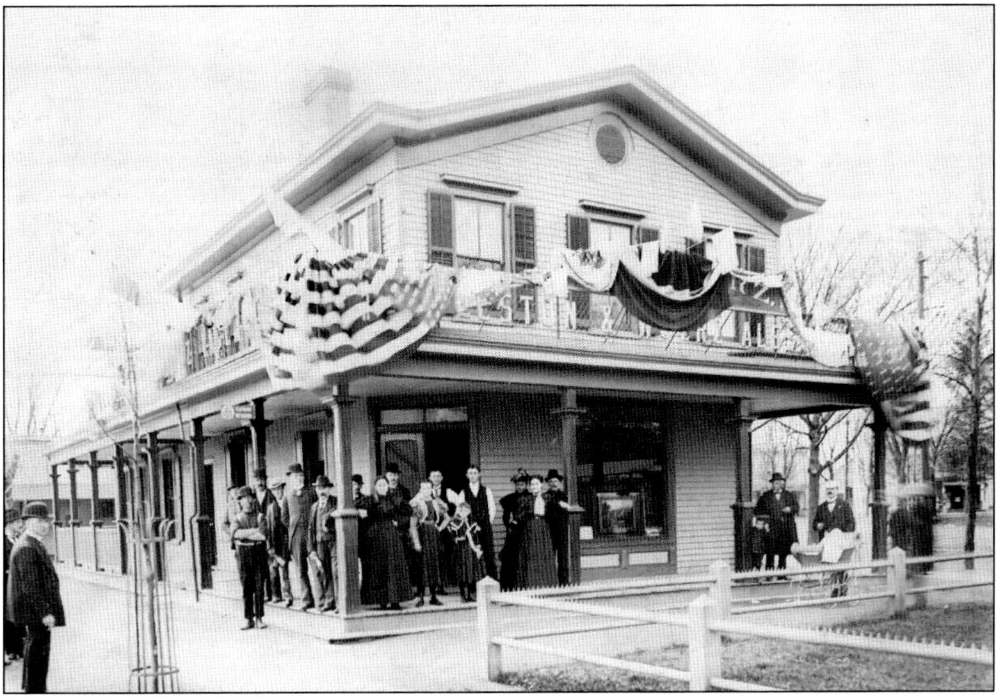

Richmond Hill was created in 1868 when Albon Platt Man bought the Lefferts and Welling farms, with a partner, landscape architect Edward Richmond, who laid out the community. Van Wicklen's grocery store (shown) opened in 1868, later to become the famed Triangle Hofbrau. The main junction was the intersection of Myrtle, Jamaica, and Lefferts Avenues. After the Richmond Hill passenger depot was built, the community developed rapidly.

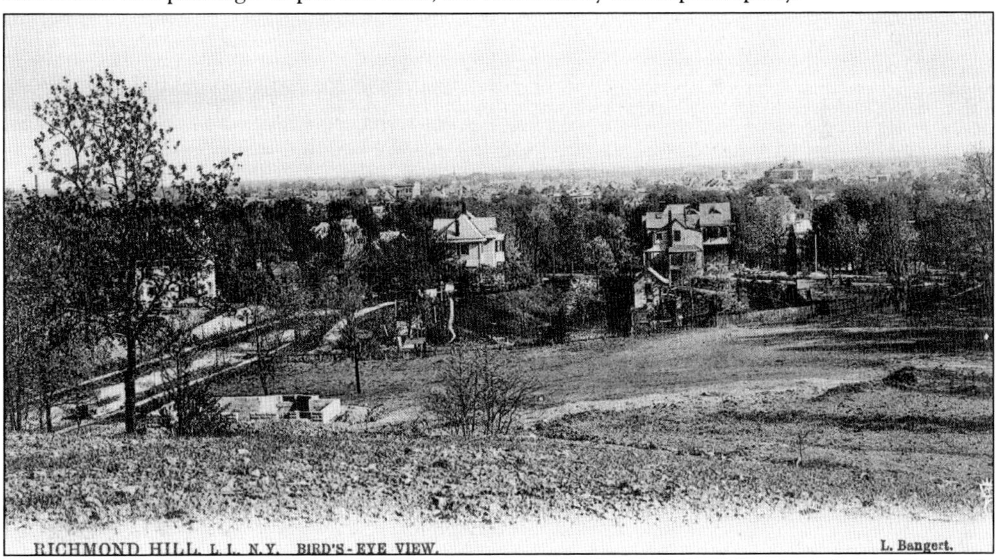

An 1870 advertisement described Richmond Hill as "perfectly healthy." "Residents have full benefit of ocean breezes, cooler in the summer and mildest in winter. All the upland on a gentle ridge, with a southern slope affording beautiful sites that overlooked the ocean. Some 4,000 shade and ornamental trees were planted." It was one of the earliest planned residential communities on Long Island. The Richmond Hill zip code is 11418.

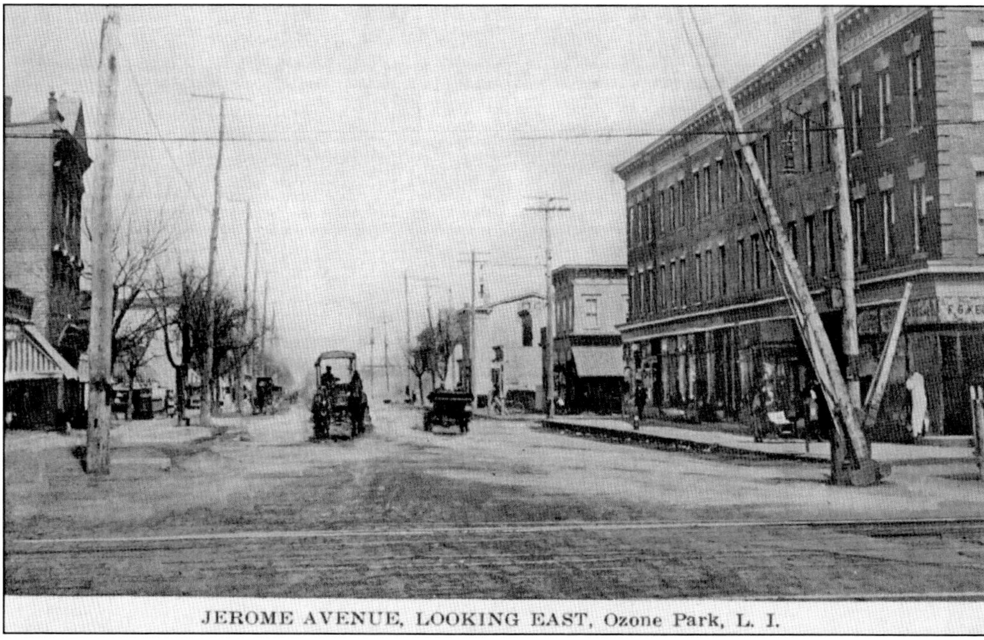

Ozone Park was created and settled in 1882. The name Ozone Park was selected to enhance buyers with the idea of refreshing breezes blowing in from the Atlantic Ocean to a parklike community. Two partners, Benjamin W. Hitchcock and Charles C. Denton, began carving farmland into building lots.

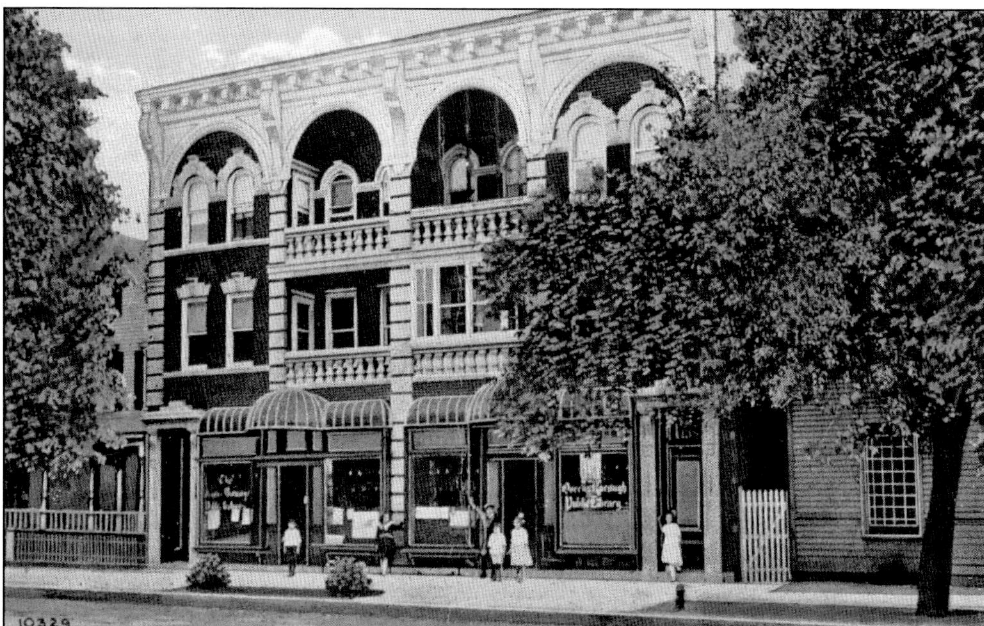

Housing first developed after the Long Island Rail Road began service through the area in 1880 as part of its route from Long Island City to Howard Beach. Railroad transportation helped in the development of the neighborhood—allowing people to get into the city easily and increasing its popularity among families looking to move to the suburb. The Ozone Park zip codes are 11416 and 11417, and South Ozone Park's is 11420.

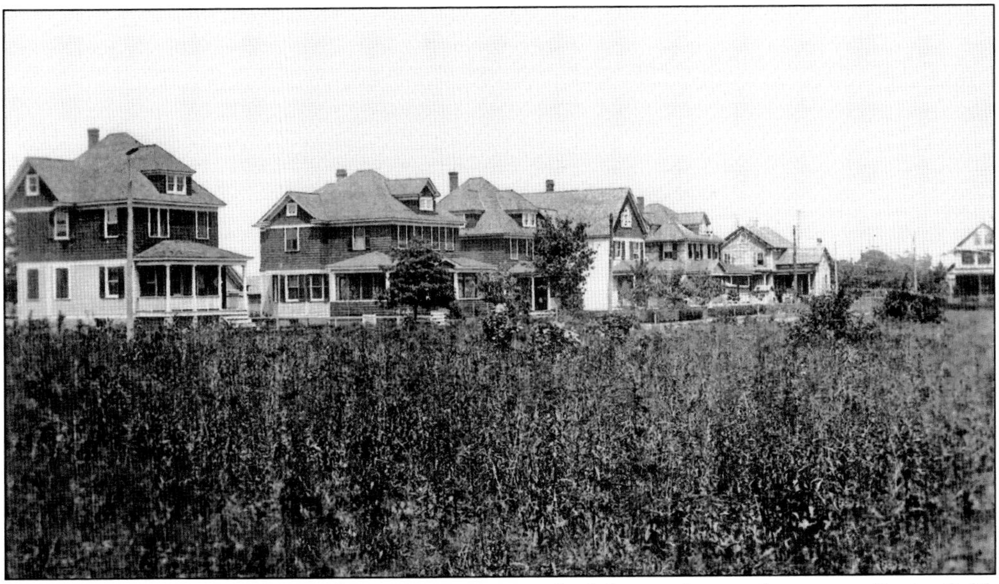

Rosedale in the colonial period was the eastern end of the settlement known as Springfield, named for the abundant amount of freshwater. Rosedale was originally called Foster's Meadows, after John Foster, an early British settler. There was a Foster Meadow's LIRR station in the late 1800s. This photograph from 1910 shows 246th Street. (Q Gardens Gallery.)

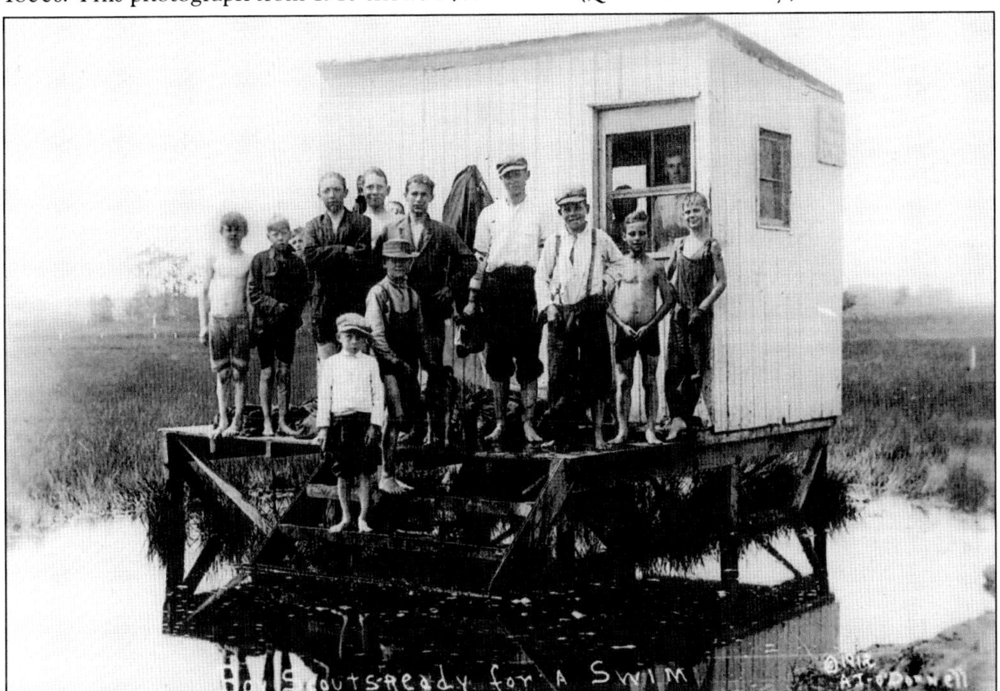

The only road through the meadows was known as Old Foster's Meadow Road until it was renamed Brookville Boulevard in the 1920s. Rosedale community was established in 1888. In 1894, the area was divided into building lots and the present name was established, but the area remained farmland until the mid-1930s. Seen here, Boy Scouts take a swim in the creek at Rosedale in 1912. The Rosedale zip code is 11422. (Bob Stonehill Collection.)

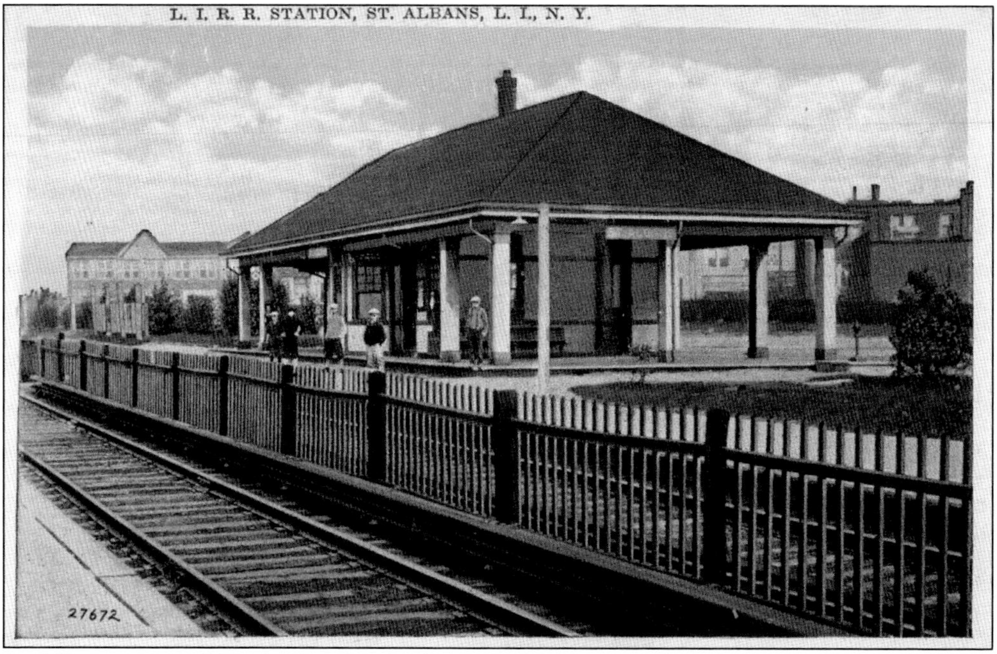

St. Albans remained farmland and forest for most of the 1700s and 1800s. In 1899, a post office was designated St. Albans, after the English town named for St. Alban, the first Christian martyred in England. The name was already used in 1894 for the local school district in Queens. There was also a road called St. Albans Avenue, and the LIRR St. Albans station had opened in 1898.

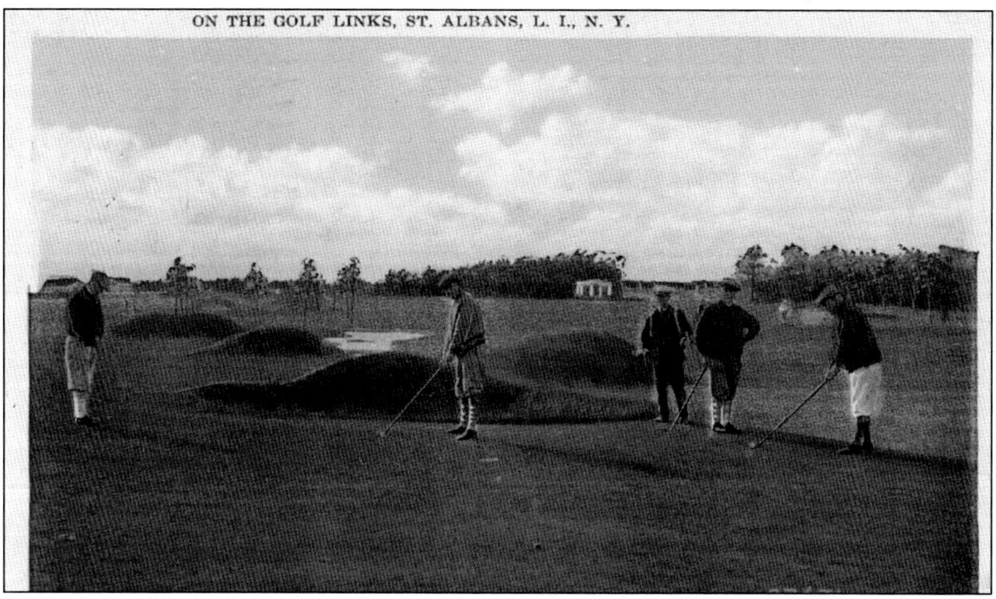

In 1915, St. Albans Golf Course attracted rich and famous golfers, including baseball star Babe Ruth. The Depression forced the golf course owners to sell, but plans for private development dissolved. In 1942, the land was seized by the federal government, which built the St. Albans Naval Hospital, with 3,000 beds and 76 wards, in 1943. It was turned over to the Veterans Administration in 1974 and is now the Veterans Administration St. Albans Primary and Extended Care Facility. The St. Albans zip code is 11412.

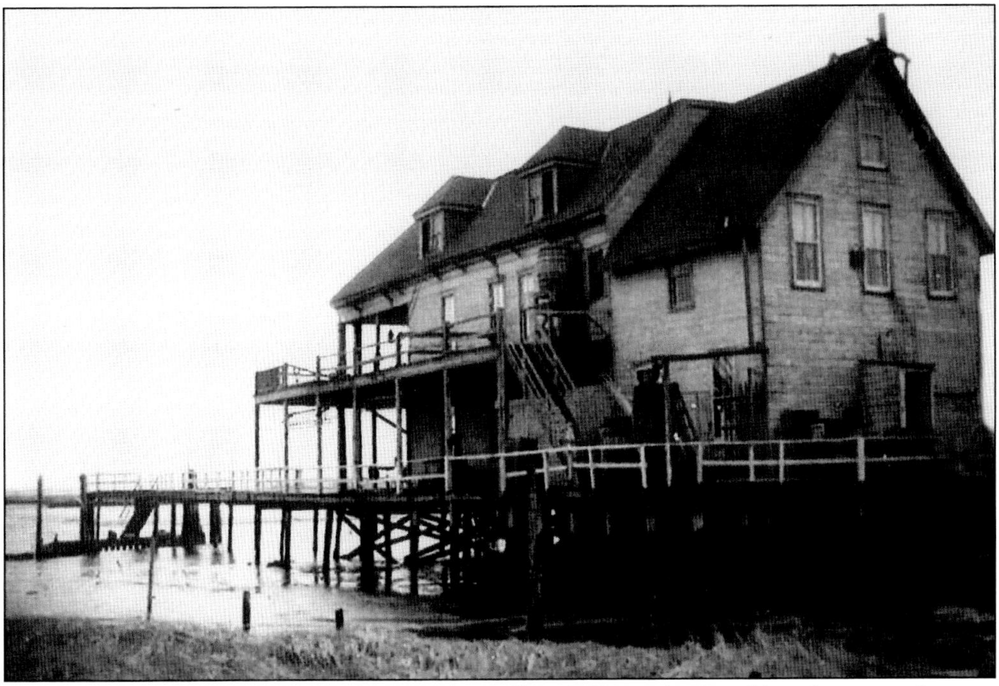

Howard Beach was established in the 1890s by William J. Howard, a Brooklyn glove manufacturer who operated a 150-acre goat farm. In 1897, he bought land and filled it in, building 18 cottages and opening and operating a hotel until fire destroyed it in 1907. In 1909, Howard formed the Howard Estates Development Company. By 1914, the company had dredged and filled the land, accumulating 500 acres. This photograph shows a hotel. (Q Gardens Gallery.)

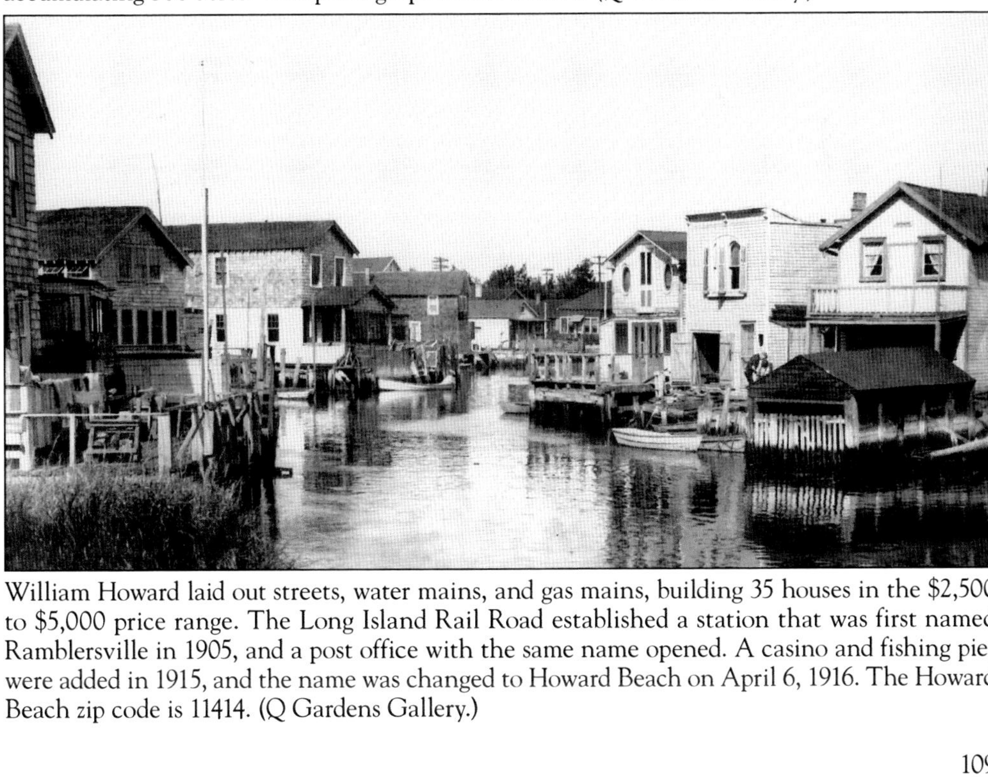

William Howard laid out streets, water mains, and gas mains, building 35 houses in the $2,500 to $5,000 price range. The Long Island Rail Road established a station that was first named Ramblersville in 1905, and a post office with the same name opened. A casino and fishing pier were added in 1915, and the name was changed to Howard Beach on April 6, 1916. The Howard Beach zip code is 11414. (Q Gardens Gallery.)

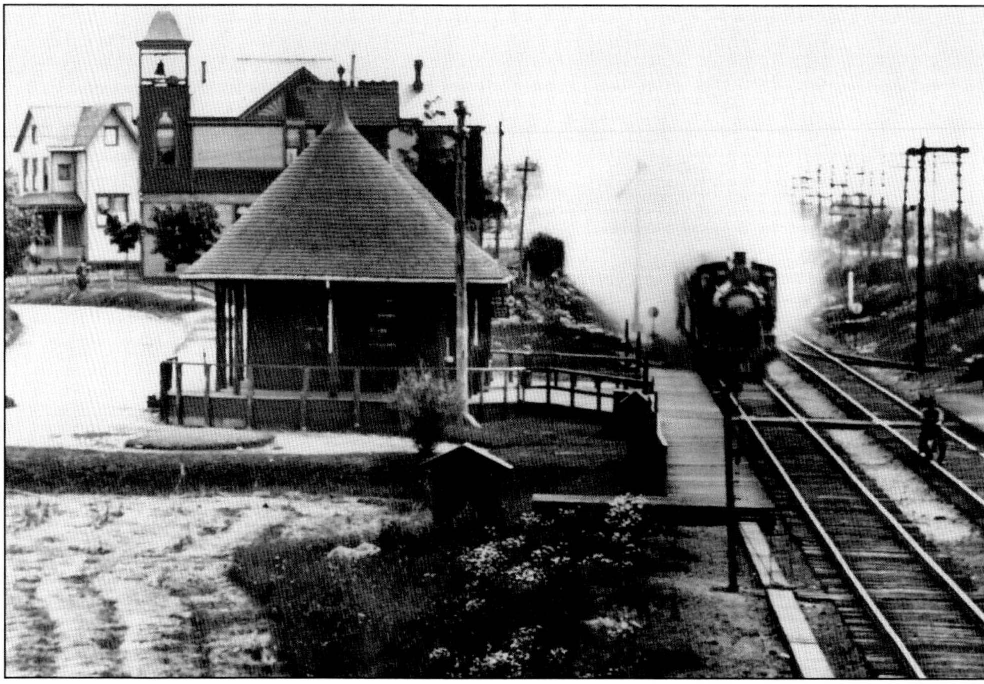

Hollis was developed by Frederick Dunton. In 1885, he and partners purchased two farms and laid out the settlements of Hollis and Holliswood. By the early 1900s, there were 130 houses near the Hollis train station. Here, a train approaches the Hollis Station in 1900. The Hollis schoolhouse is seen in the background. Dunton gave the streets of Holliswood Latin or Spanish names, such as Rio, Como, Marengo, and so forth.

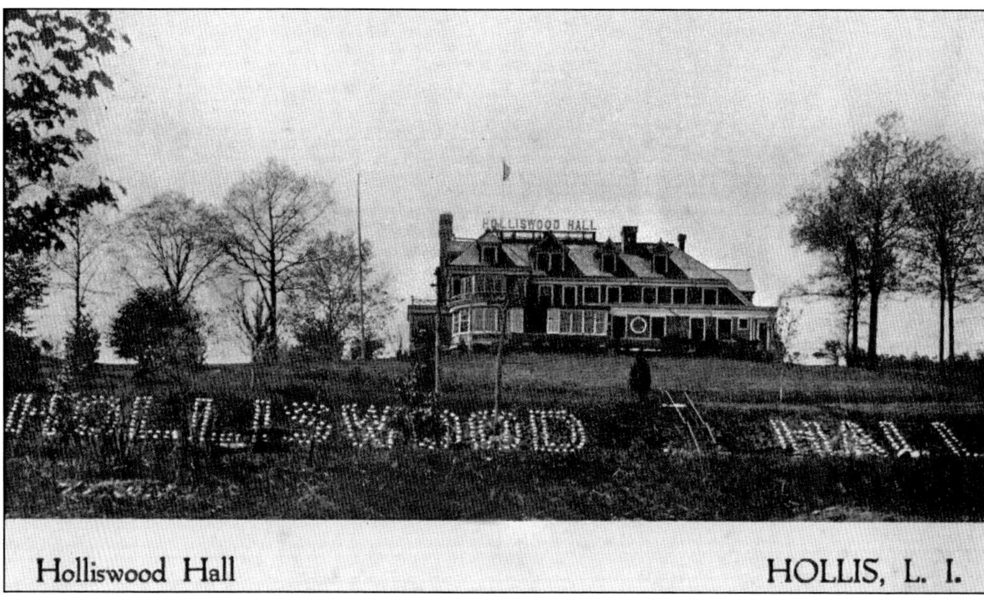

On the southern edge of Holliswood on Dunton Avenue, Frederick Dunton built a large and beautiful mansion called Holliswood Hall, with views all the way to the ocean. After Dunton's death, it was sold and became Brown's Chop House restaurant, reported to have been a speakeasy during Prohibition and torn down in 1949.

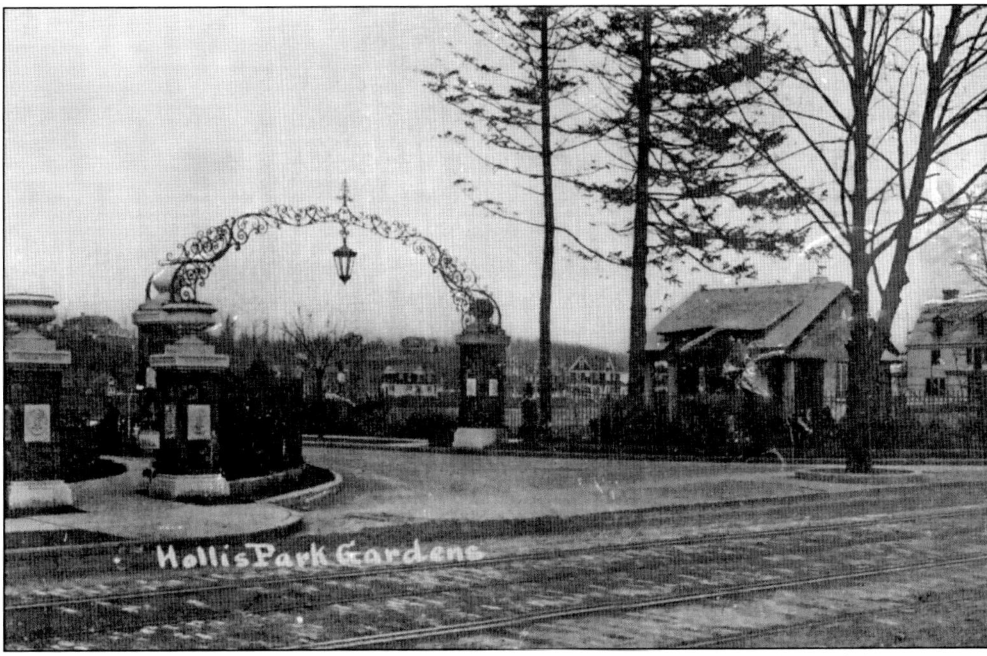

In 1906, a new development was established called Hollis Park Gardens, located from 191st to 195th Streets. It would cater to affluent residents, and nicer houses were built. A number of the elaborate masonry pillars seen in this vintage photograph and bearing the monograms of the development are still standing today, but the decorative ironwork has all disappeared.

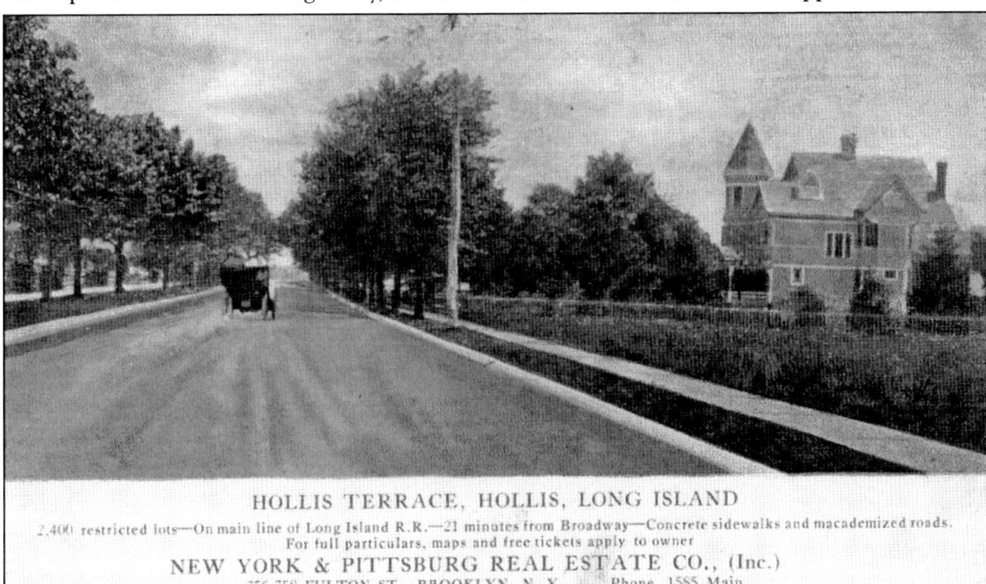

Hollis Terrace was developed in 1906 by the 104th Avenue area. According to a May 13, 1906, advertisement, "Hollis Terrace 21 minutes from Manhattan—The Greatest Development in New York City. Third rail electric trains, steam trains and trolleys in operation. All city conveniences, water, gas, electric lights, police and fire protection. Cement sidewalks guaranteed. All the comforts of the city combined with the pleasures of the country." The Hollis zip codes are 11423 and 11427.

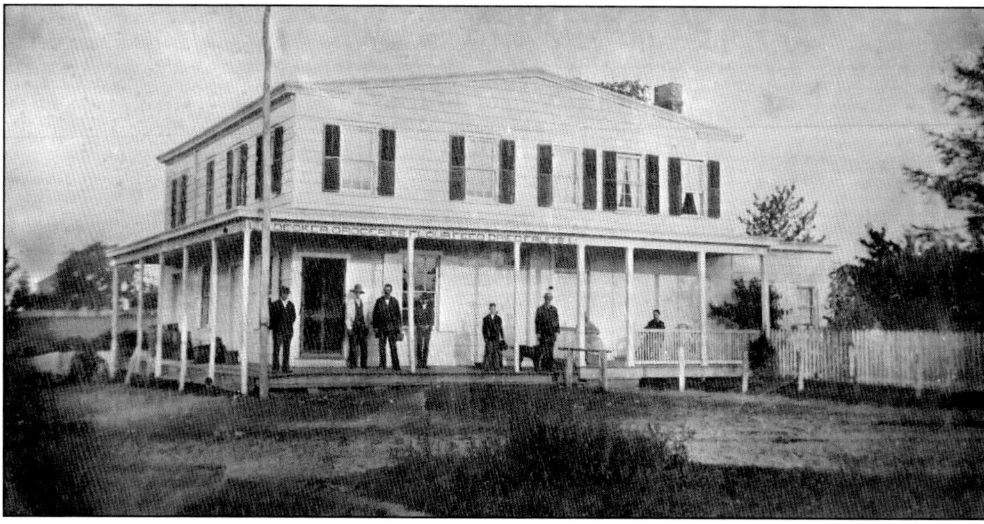

Springfield was settled by 1660 and was once dominated by farmland. Dutch and English farm families—such as the Higbies, Hendricksons, Nostrands, Bedells, and Baylises—moved to the community, which was originally located along Springfield Boulevard south of the Long Island Rail Road. Springfield Cemetery was established as early as 1670. Pictured here is the L. Decker General Store at the northwest corner of Springfield Avenue (Boulevard) and Merrick Road (Boulevard).

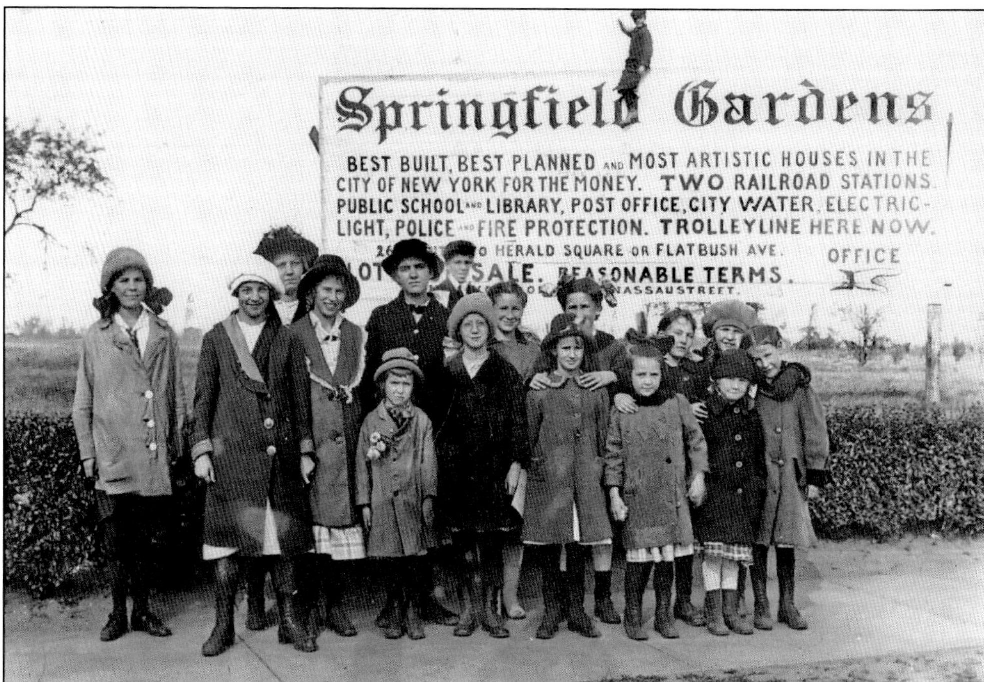

In the early 1900s, farms gave way to residential development, and hundreds of houses were built between 1920 and 1930. In 1927, the name was changed to the more elegant Springfield Gardens. In 1932, construction of the Springfield Boulevard sewer destroyed the natural pond and its feeder system. The city filled in the pond to create Springfield Park. The Springfield Gardens zip code is 11434. (Bob Stonehill Collection.)

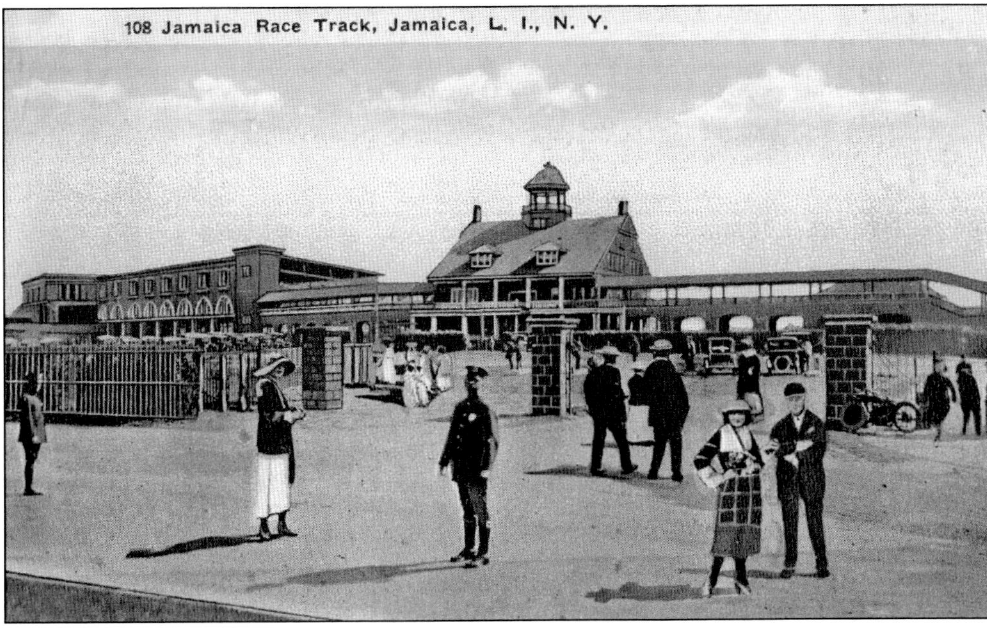

Rochdale Village is the former site of the Metropolitan Jockey Club (later Jamaica Race Track). Its opening on April 27, 1903, was attended by Lillian Russell, Diamond Jim Brady, and John W. "Bet-a-Million" Gates. This and the Queens County Jockey Club (Aqueduct) provided convenient outlets for sportsmen and their money. The Jamaica racetrack was shut down in 1959 and demolished.

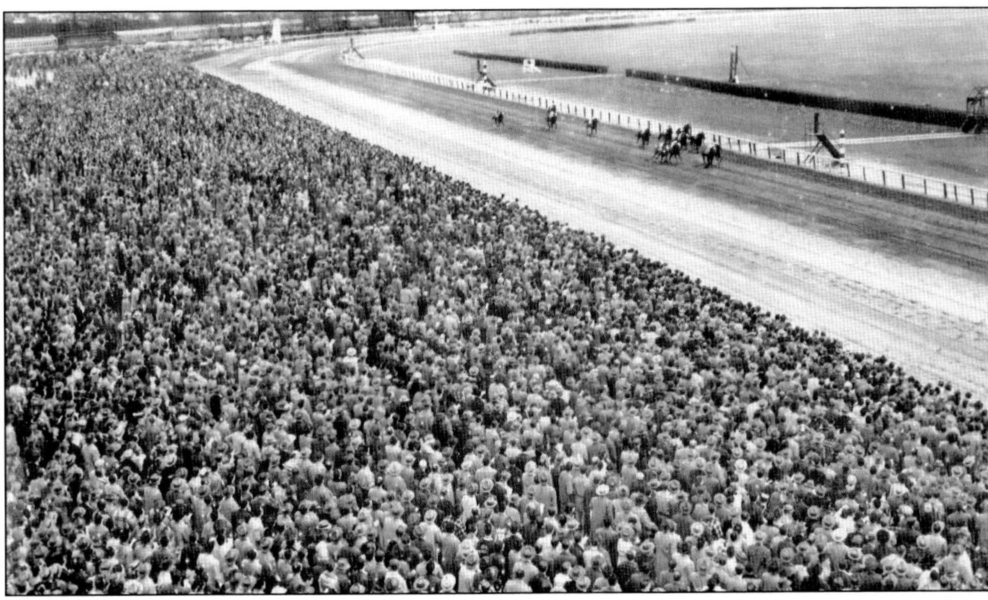

A residential cooperative designed by architect Herman Jessor and called Rochdale Village, after the English town of Rochdale, was built on the racetrack property. When opened, it was the largest private cooperative housing complex in the world. The architect's concept was an attractive community covering 122 blocks that would provide the residents with a parklike setting and facilities of suburbia within the limits of the urban Jamaica area. The Rochdale Village zip code is 11434.

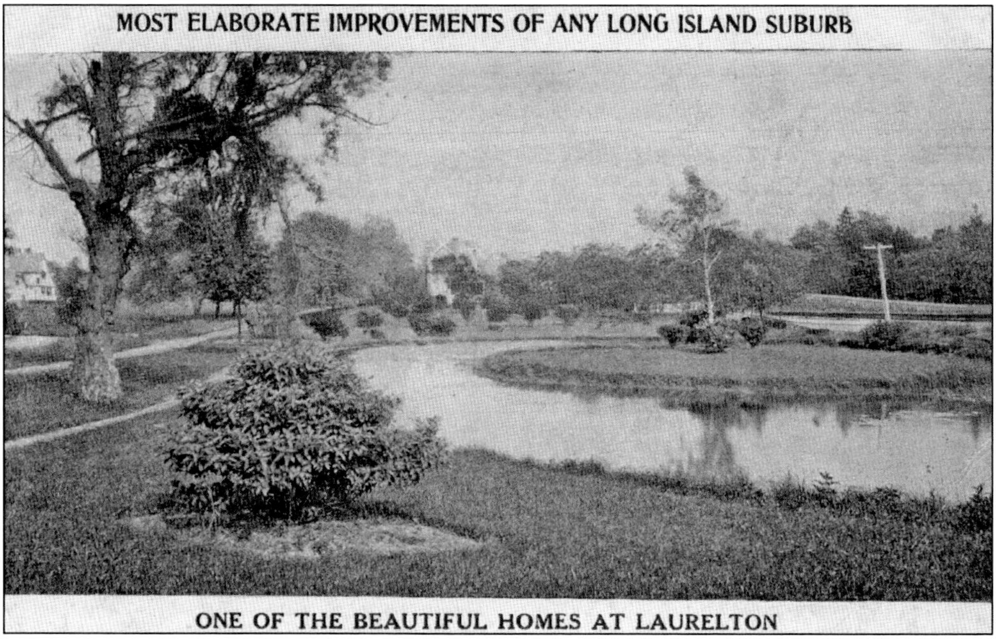

Laurelton was founded in 1905 by the Laurelton Land Company, which purchased several farms in the area and developed these properties the following year. Laurelton was created as a residential area for immigrant families in the 1920s and 1930s. It was modeled after an English village, with stately Tudor-style homes, both attached and detached.

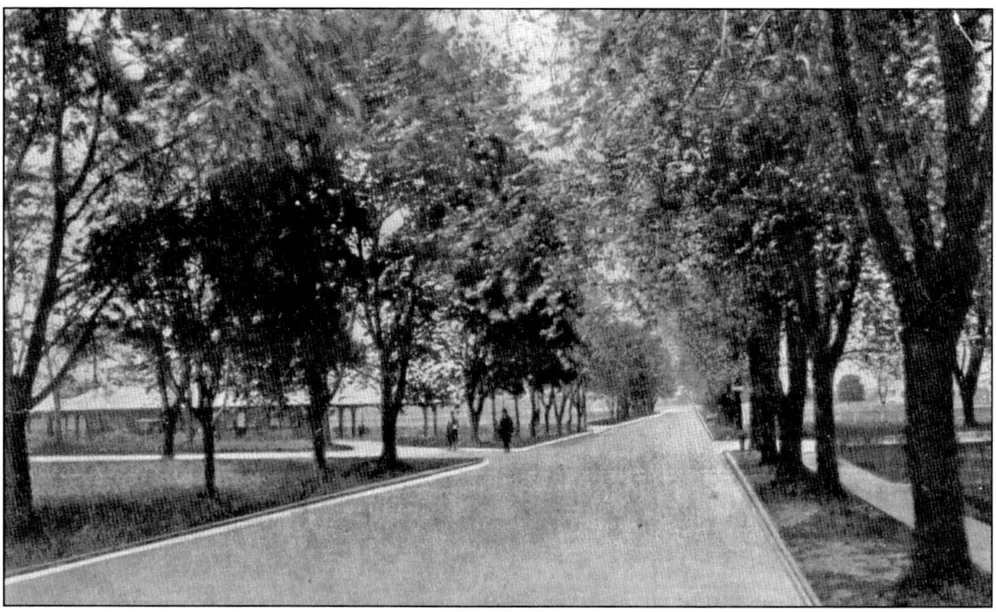

The area derives its name from the Laurelton station on the Long Island Rail Road, which was named for the laurels that grew there over 100 years ago. There are co-ops in converted garden apartment complexes and some new construction with more modern designs but no high-rise buildings, which has enabled Laurelton to keep its small-town feel. The Laurelton zip code is 11413.

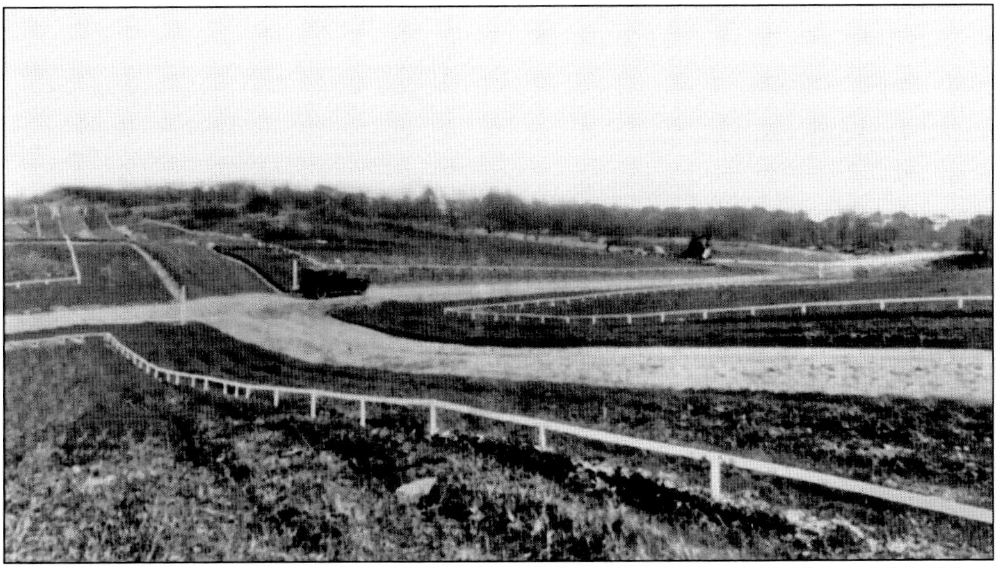

Briarwood is named for Herbert O'Brien's Briarwood Land Company, which started building houses in 1905. The company went bankrupt, leaving the area largely empty until the 1920s. The United Nations and New York Life Insurance Company constructed housing here in the 1940s. Diplomat Ralph Bunche and feminist writer Betty Friedan lived there. This photograph shows the intersection of Smedley Street and Hoover Avenue. (Q Gardens Gallery.)

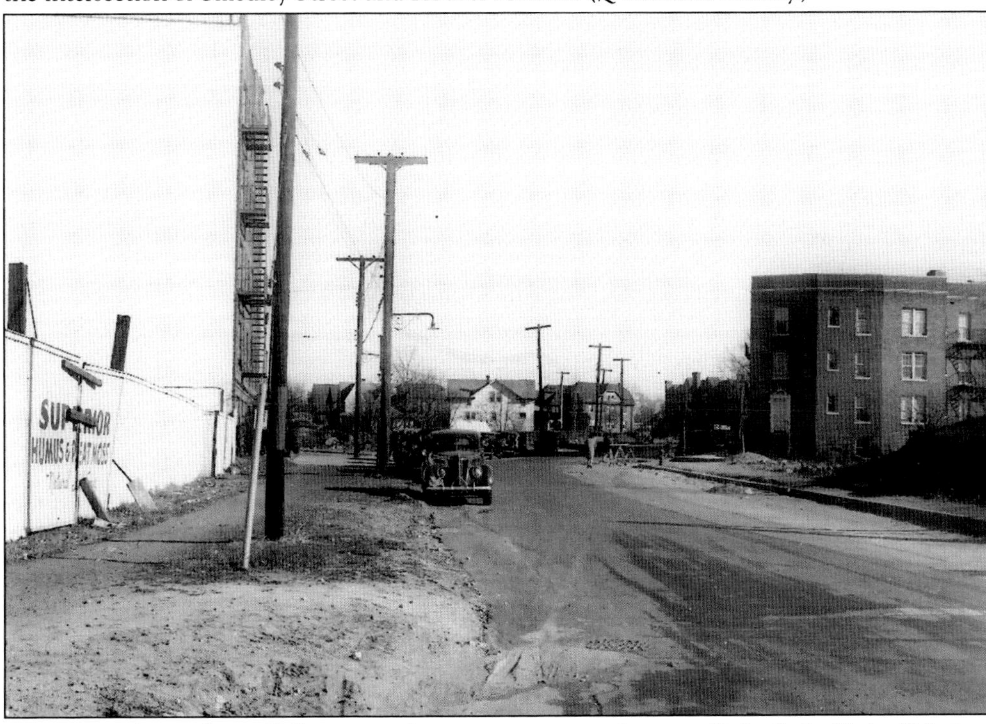

In Briarwood is Parkway Village, a garden apartment complex initially built for United Nations employees. It lent the area a very international flavor, with families from all over the world living there and attending the local public schools. This photograph shows the intersection of Queens Boulevard and Eighty-fourth Drive. The Briarwood zip code is 11435. (Q Gardens Gallery.)

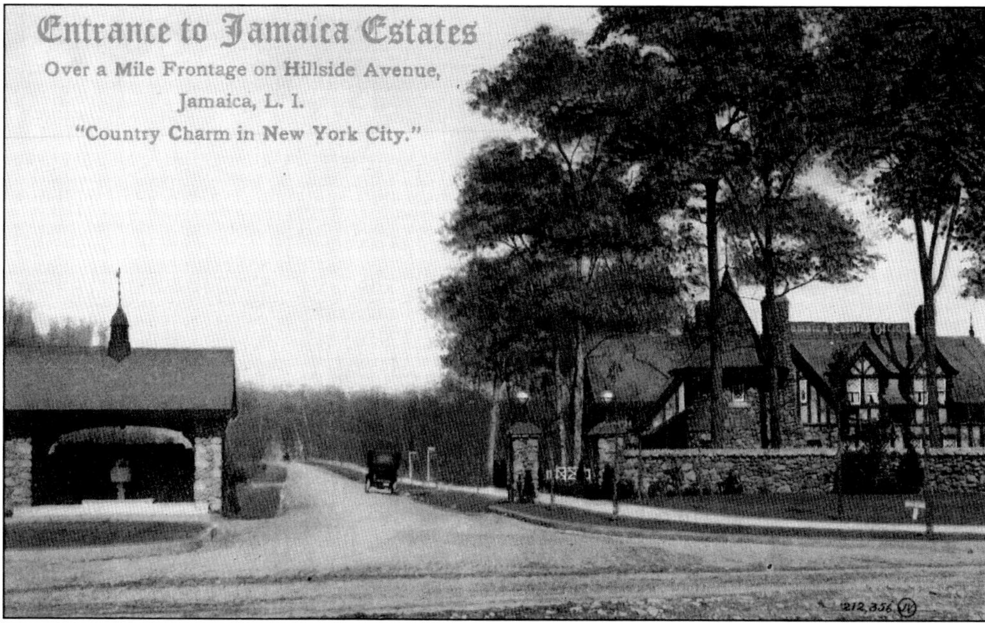

Jamaica Estates was founded in 1907 by real estate developers and speculators Ernestus Gulick and Felix Isman, who purchased 500 acres on the terminal moraine north of Jamaica. Their purpose was to erect an affluent resort with an English flavor. Celebrated architect John Petit designed an imposing entrance with an Elizabethan-style lodge and gateway. The lodge was razed, but the gatehouse survives and contains the World War II Memorial.

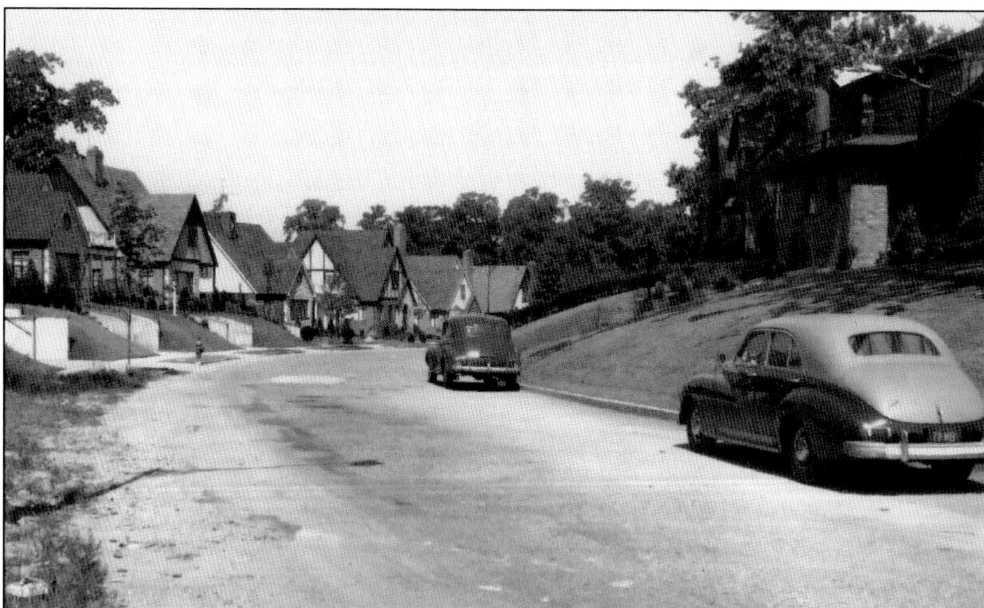

Early partners in the Jamaica Estates Corporation included Lt. Gov. Timothy Woodruff and New York City engineer and contractor Michael J. Degnon. The street system, with Midland Parkway as its centerpiece, was designed by well-known landscape architect Charles W. Leavitt. Jamaica Estates is distinguished for its Tudor-style homes and impressive landscaping. The Jamaica Estates zip code is 11432. (Q Gardens Gallery.)

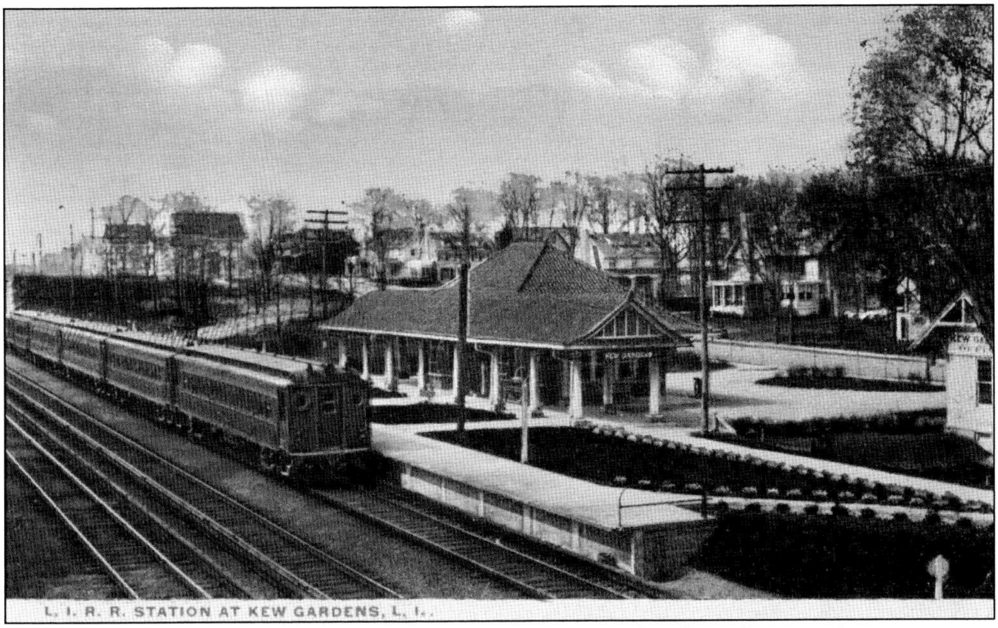

The Kew Gardens area served as a playground for Richmond Hill residents, with swimming in Crystal Lake's glacial pond, picnicking in the fields, or hiking in the forests. In 1875, Maple Grove Cemetery was opened, and in the 1890s, the Man family started a golf course. In 1908, Alrick Man, son of Richmond Hill founder Albon Man, established Kew Gardens. Crystal Lake was drained and is now the site of the Kew Gardens station.

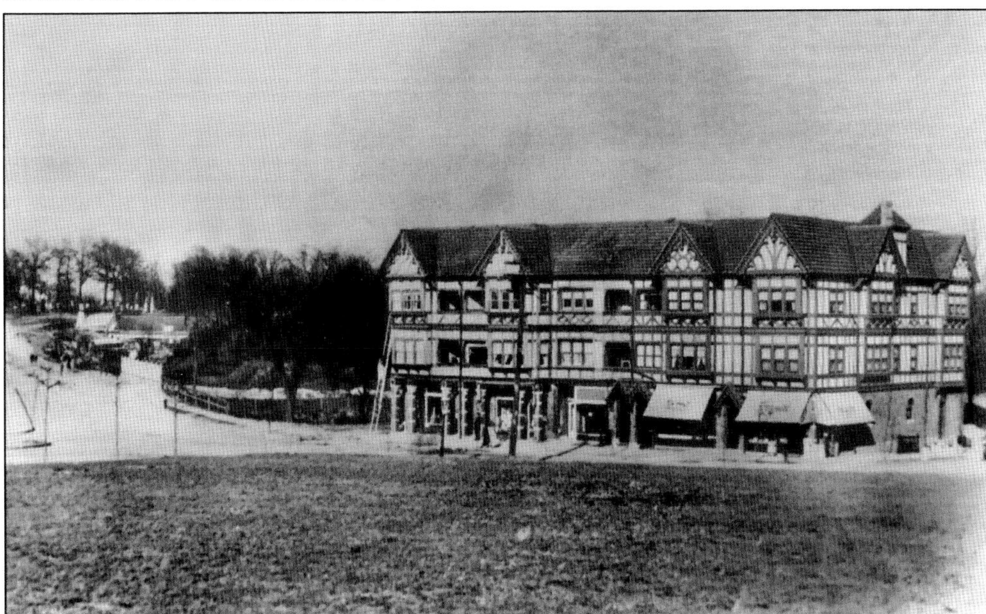

Alrick Man called it Kew and then Kew Gardens after the well-known botanical gardens in England, and the neighborhood was developed with an English favor. A clubhouse was built in 1916. In 1920, the Kew Gardens Inn opened for residential guests, who paid $40 a week for a room and bath and meals. Elegant one-family houses were built in the 1920s, as were apartment buildings. The Kew Gardens zip code is 11415.

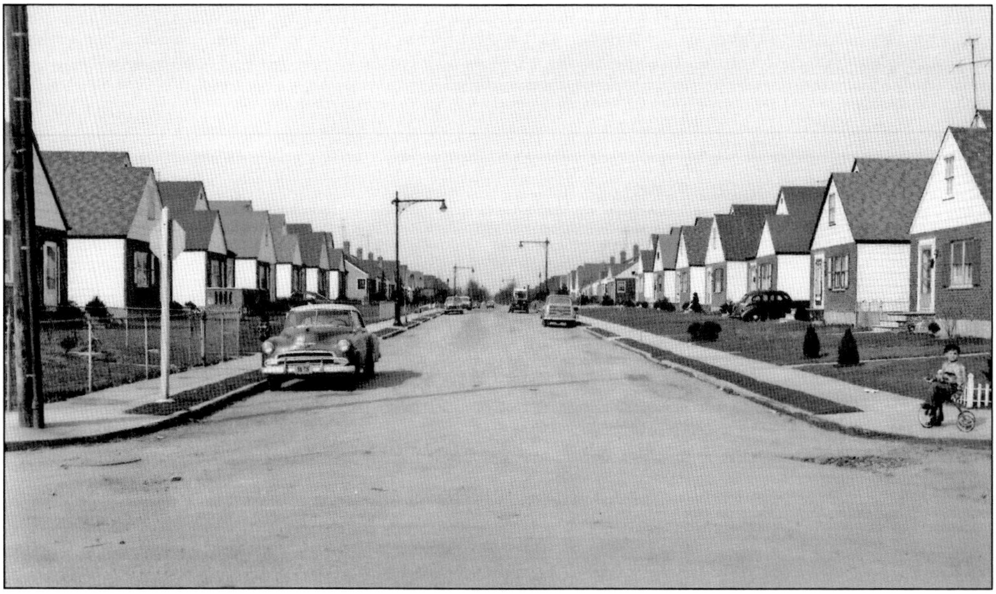

Cambria Heights, a farming community supplying produce to Brooklyn and Manhattan, was developed in 1923 on 163 acres of land bought by real estate agent Oliver B. LaFreniere. The name Cambria Heights was coined from the Cambria Title Savings and Trust Company, a bank based in Cambria County, Pennsylvania, that financed early housing developments aimed at working families. The "Heights" was added because of the area's high elevation. This photograph shows 230th Street. (Q Gardens Gallery.)

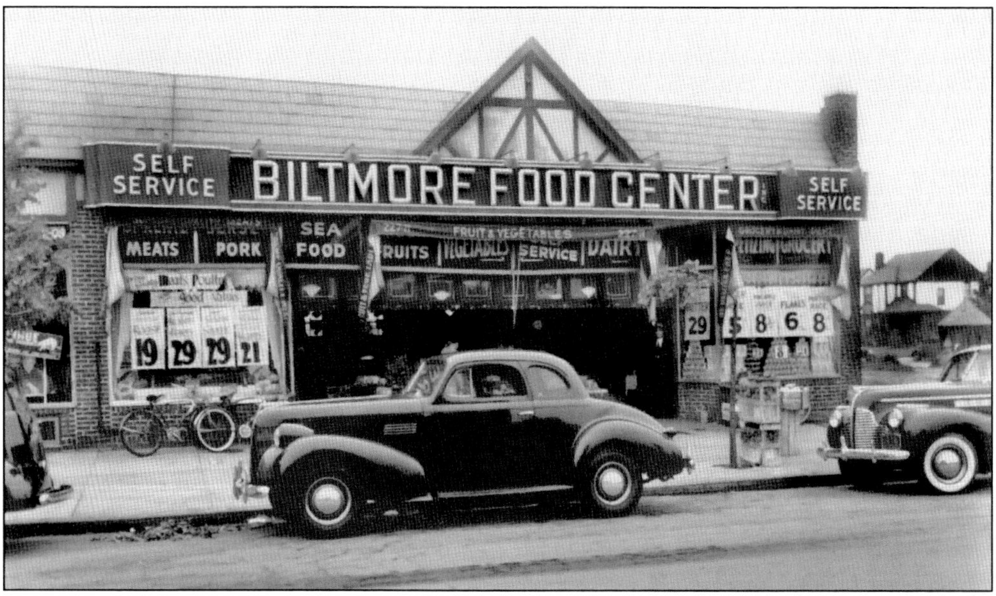

Cambria Heights was developed in the late 1920s as part of a housing boom that offered city dwellers an escape to the suburbs, which was made newly accessible with the opening of the Cross Island Parkway and expanded railroad service on the Long Island Rail Road. First populated by Jewish, German, Irish, and Italian residents, the community became a predominantly black community after the 1960s. This photograph shows Linden Boulevard. The Cambria Heights zip code is 11411. (Q Gardens Gallery.)

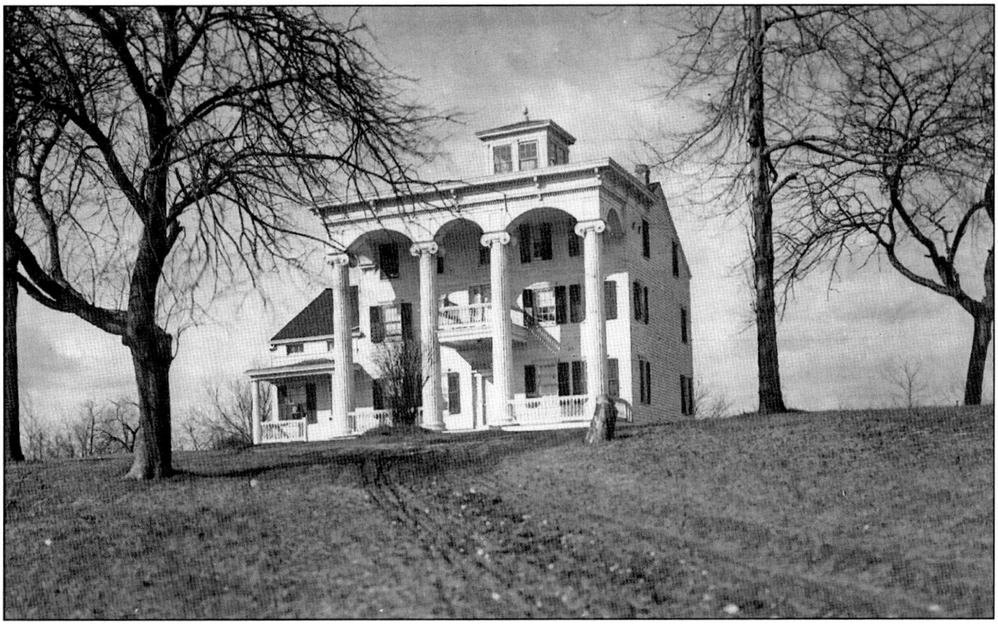

Jamaica Hills encompasses an area of about 65 blocks. This photograph shows the Clark Estates, sold in 1925, and the present site of Jamaica High School. The centerpiece is Captain Tilly Park, with Goose Pond at the center. The Tilly family once owned the land, and when their son was killed in the Philippines in 1899, it was renamed in his honor. (Archives at Queens Library, Frederick Weber Photographs.)

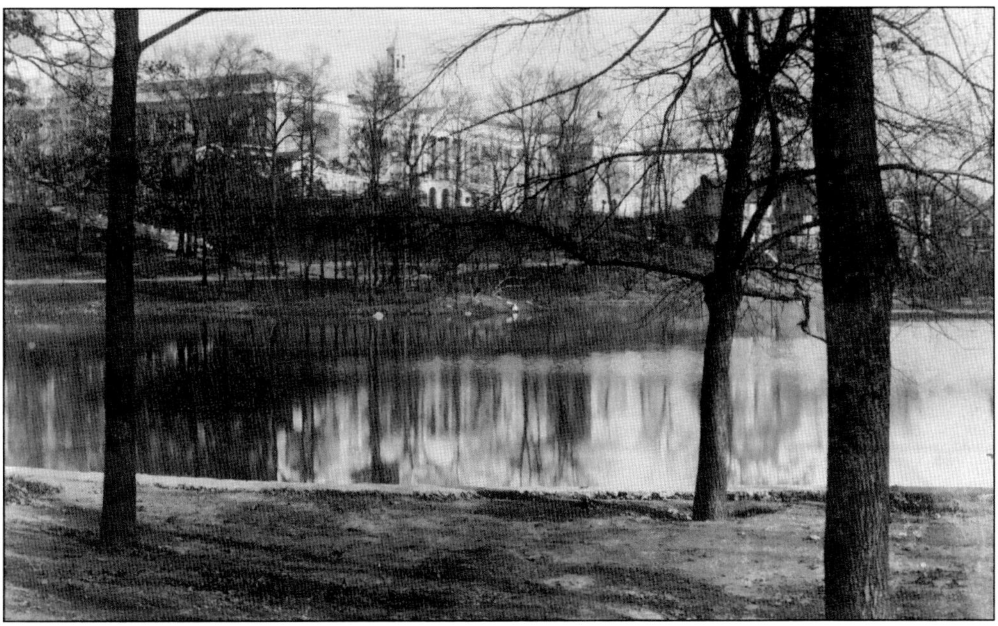

The Highland Park Society, a group of Jamaica landowners raising ducks and geese at the pond, owned the acreage. In 1908, they deeded the property to New York City for $1. The park was also called Highland Park and Upland Park. In 1941, Capt. George H. Tilly Camp No. 66 erected a monument dedicated to the heroes of the Spanish-American War from Jamaica. The building shown is Jamaica High School. The Jamaica Hills zip code is 11432.

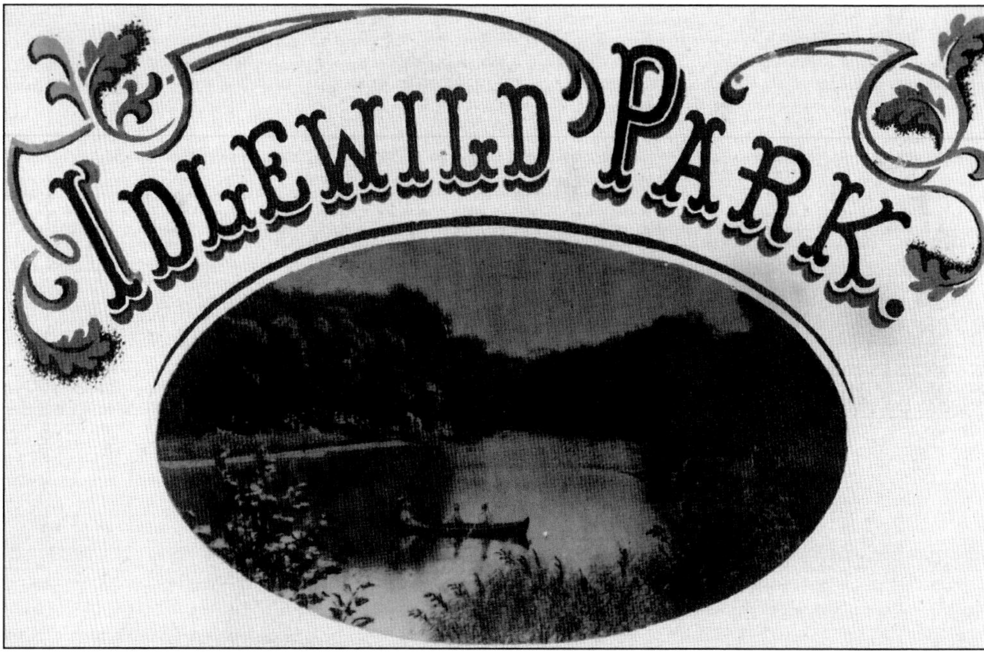

Idlewild was a countryside area south of Jamaica by Jamaica Bay. The name derives from a description of the land's character—peaceful but savage. In the 1920s, Idlewild Golf Course was built with a community of homes erected around it. The golf course was displaced by the Maj. Gen. Alexander E. Anderson Airport in 1943; Anderson had commanded a Federalized National Guard unit. With the urging of New York mayor Fiorello LaGuardia, the airport was renamed, and more well-known as, Idlewild.

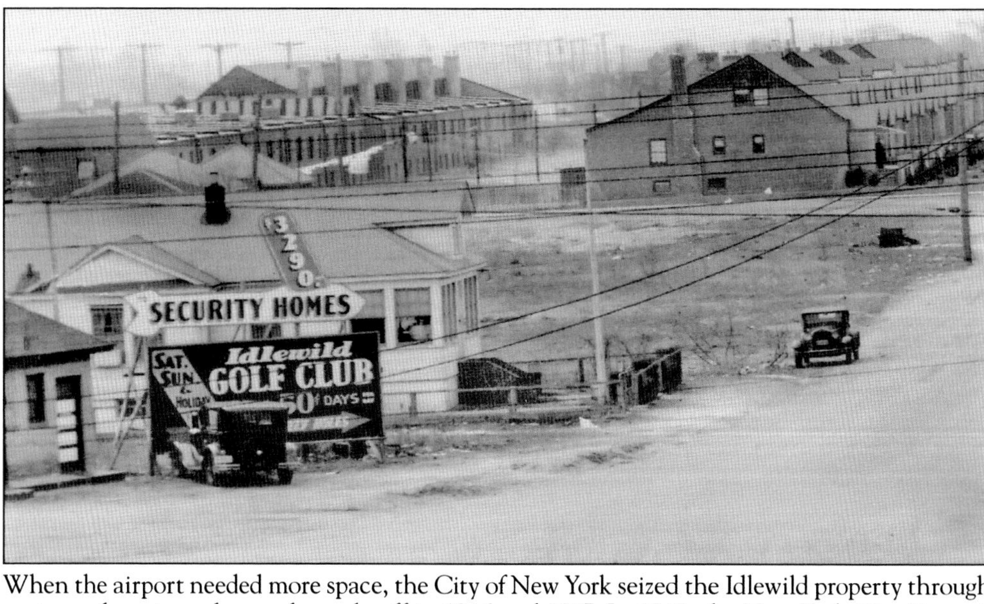

When the airport needed more space, the City of New York seized the Idlewild property through eminent domain and moved people off in 1946 and 1947. In 1948, the New York City Council changed the name to New York International Airport, Anderson Field, but the name Idlewild was commonly used. It was renamed John F. Kennedy (JFK) International Airport on December 24, 1963, one month after his assassination. The JFK zip code is 11430. (Q Gardens Gallery.)

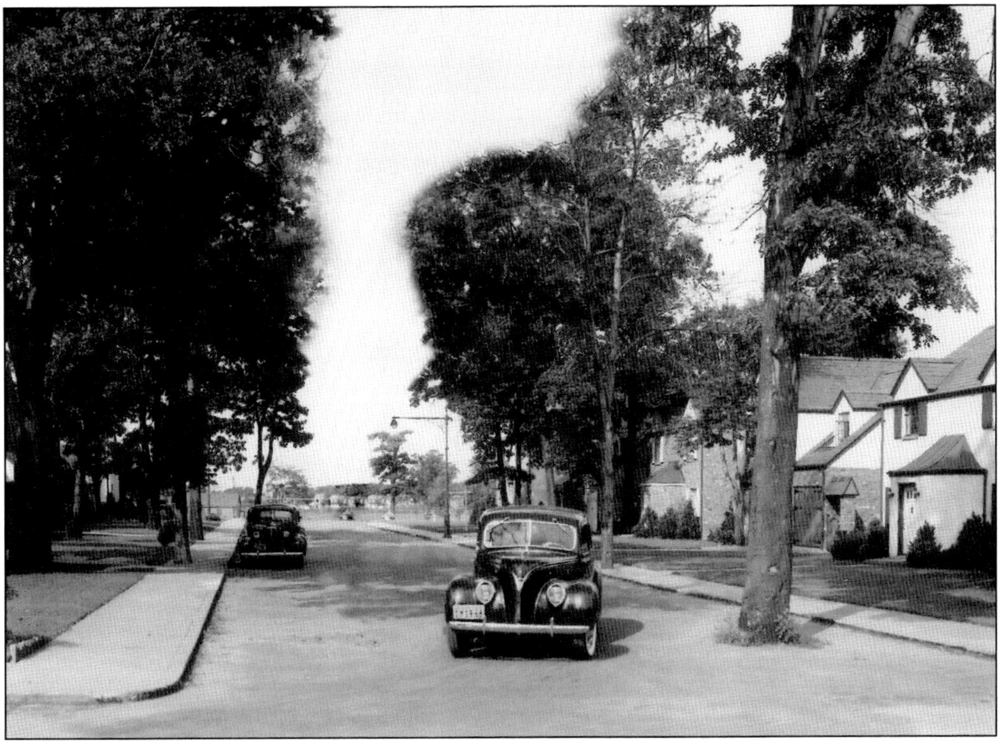

Addisleigh Park is an enclave in St. Albans (zip code 11412) developed in the late 1920s and early 1930s. It is famous for being the home of many sports stars and top entertainers in jazz and pop, all lured by the promise of seclusion, quietude, space, and beauty. Among its famous residents have been Count Basie, Lena Horne, Ella Fitzgerald, Illinois Jacquet, Jackie Robinson, James Brown, Joe Louis, Milt Hinton, Roy Campanella, Percy Sutton, and many others. (Q Gardens Gallery.)

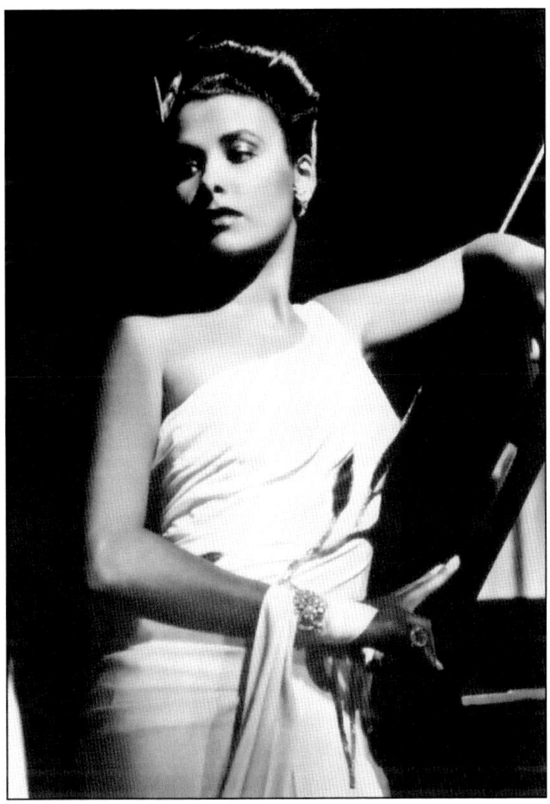

Lena Horne (1917–2010) broke new ground for black performers when she signed a long-term contract with major Hollywood studio MGM. Horne first achieved fame in the 1940s with film appearances in *Cabin in the Sky* and *Stormy Weather*, became a nightclub and recording star in the 1950s, and had a triumphant one-woman Broadway show in 1981. She was a singer, actress, civil rights activist, and dancer.

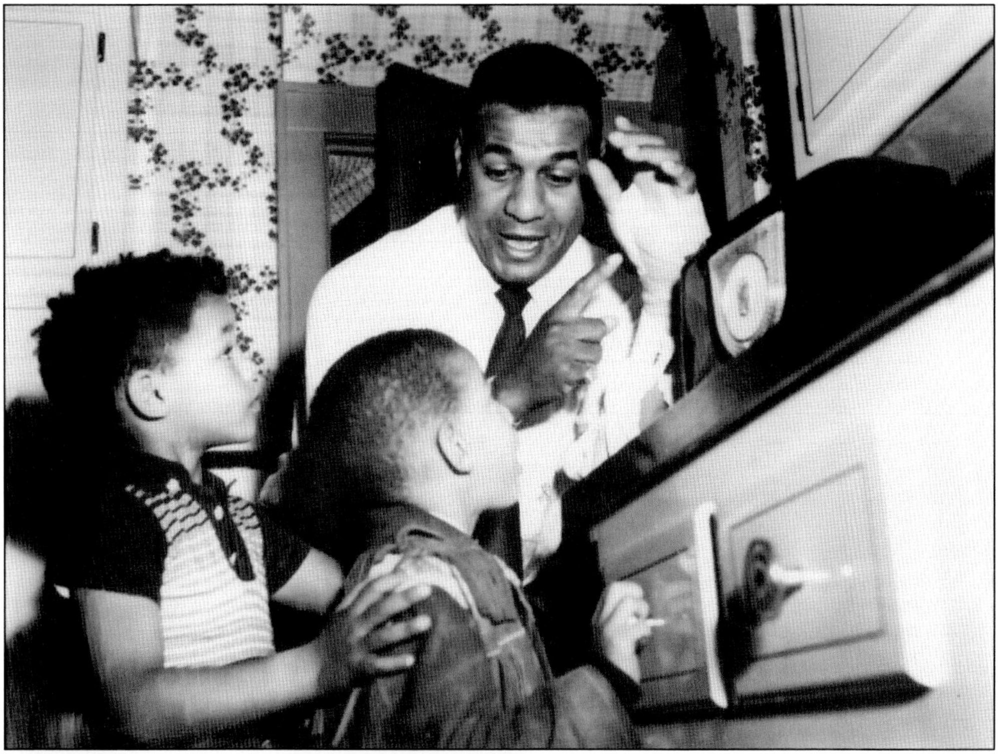

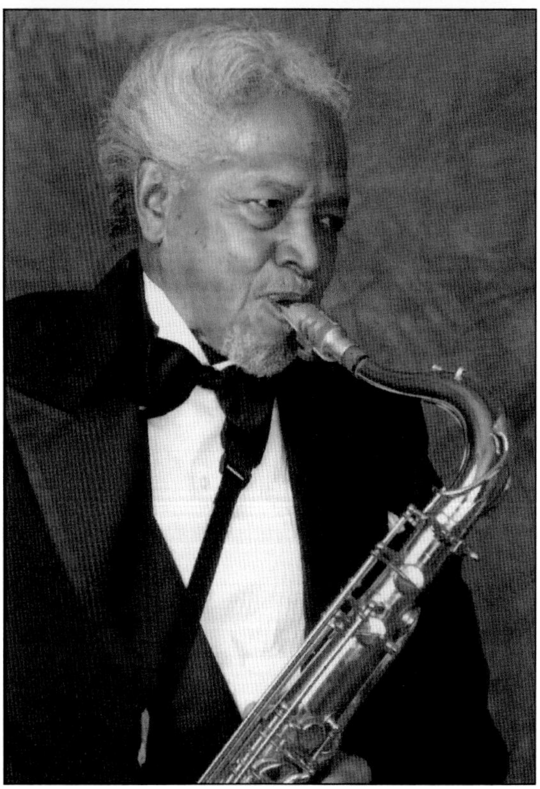

Roy Campanella (1921–1993) was a baseball player, primarily at the position of catcher in the Negro Leagues and Major League Baseball. Widely considered to have been one of the greatest catchers in the history of the game, Campanella played for the Brooklyn Dodgers during the 1940s and 1950s and was one of the pioneers in breaking the color barrier in the major leagues. His career was cut short in 1958 when he was paralyzed in an automobile accident.

Jean-Baptiste Illinois Jacquet, born in Louisiana in 1922, is heralded as one of the five greatest jazz saxophonists. At 19, he created an entirely new style and sound for the tenor saxophone with his solo on "Flying Home," recorded with Lionel Hampton. Two years later, Jacquet's solo, "Blues, Part II," recorded live, established a blueprint for the evolution of rhythm and blues and rock and roll. (Photograph by Jerry Lacey.)

Six

Jamaica's Vision
Looking to the Future

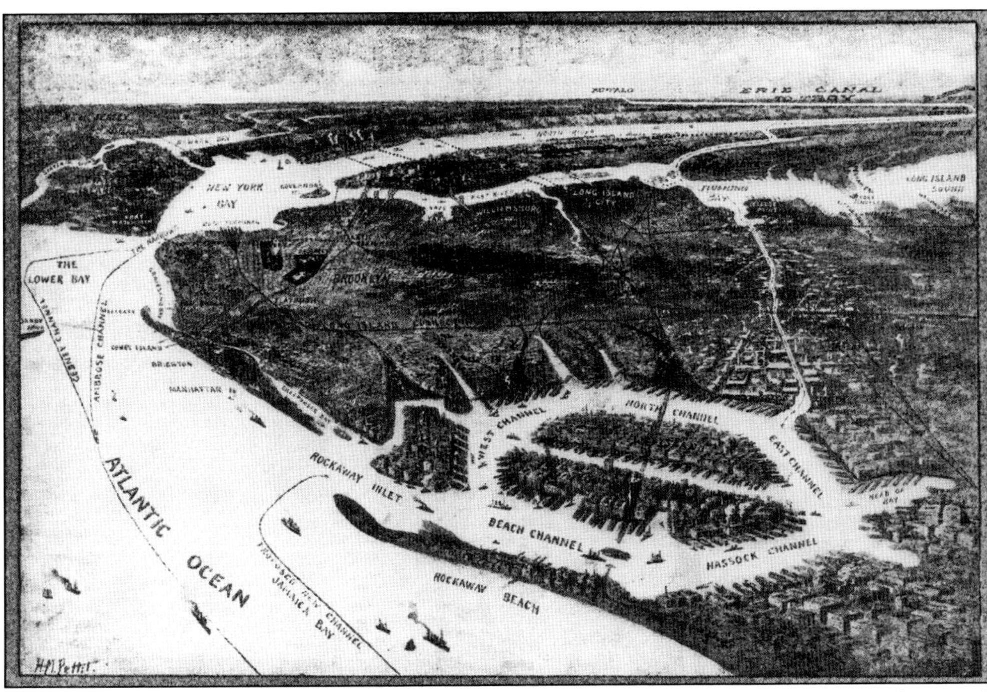

In 1910, there were dreams for Jamaica, such as building a seaport with a canal to the North Shore. Visions for a better tomorrow and a prosperous community are alive today under the Greater Jamaica Development Corporation (GJDC), one of New York's oldest not-for-profit local development corporations. Founded in 1967 by the Regional Plan Association, local business, and civic and community leaders, the GJDC has stressed economic development in pursuing its community-building mission.

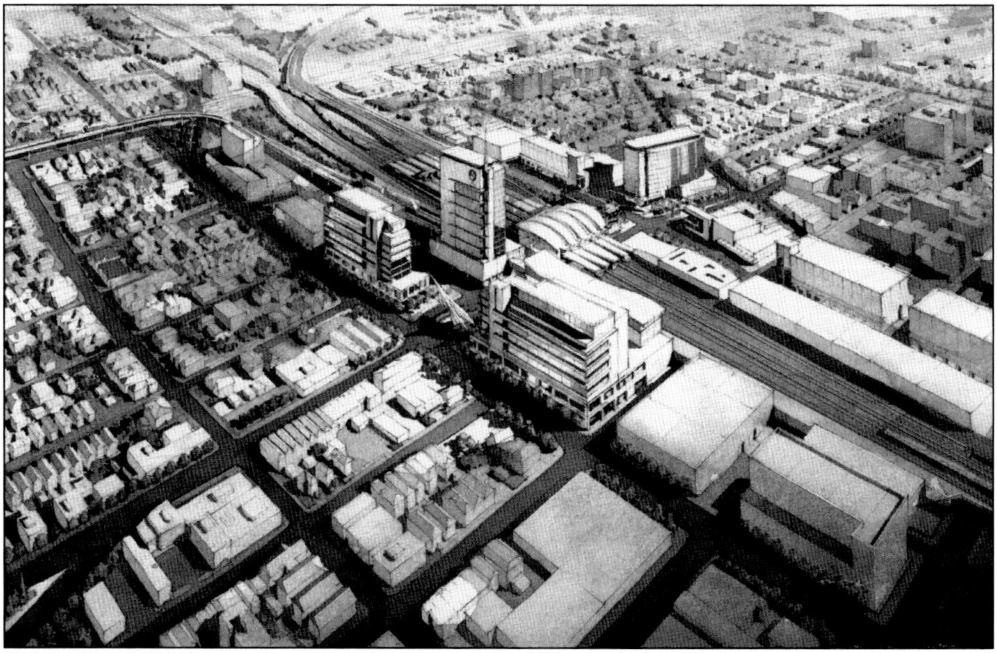

This is an early vision of downtown Jamaica as an international transportation hub supporting a nexus of retail, commercial, residential, civic, and airport-related activities connected to JFK International Airport and the rest of the New York metropolitan region via the AirTrain/LIRR Station complex. This view looks west, with Sutphin Boulevard crossing from the bottom left through the center of the image to the top right. Archer Avenue runs from the bottom right and intersects Sutphin Boulevard at the center of the image (making an X), with the Jamaica train station at left. (Greater Jamaica Development Corporation.)

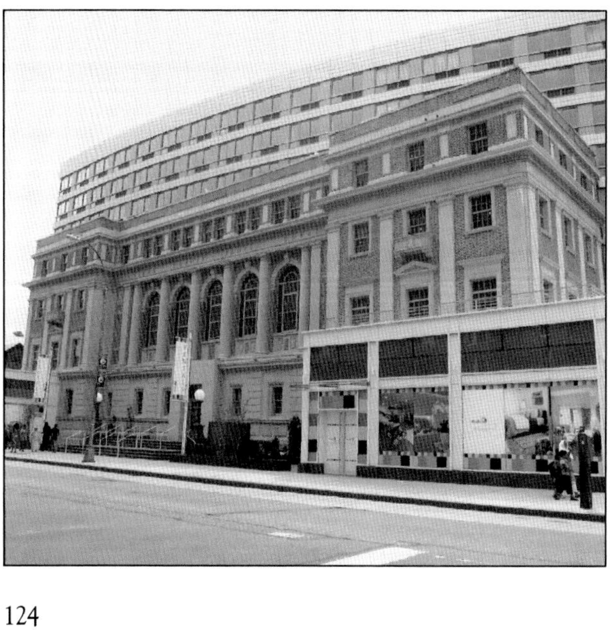

GJDC successfully advocated with the City of New York to adaptively reuse a historic structure in Jamaica—the former Jamaica Central Library (on page 71) that was later converted to the Queens Family Court building. In 2010, the Dermot Company, the developer selected by the city, completed the Moda, a 12-story development featuring integration of the original building's historic facade, affordable and market-rate housing, retail space, community facilities, public parking, and extensive amenities for residents. (Greater Jamaica Development Corporation.)

The landmark former First Reformed Church building (details on page 23) has been repurposed and transformed into a premier performing arts center. The City of New York, which owns the building, commissioned and managed a $22 million series of careful improvements. The newly renovated building features a 400-seat multipurpose performance space and state-of-the-art audio visual systems. The performing arts center can accommodate theater productions, music concerts, dance performances, and arts education. (Greater Jamaica Development Corporation.)

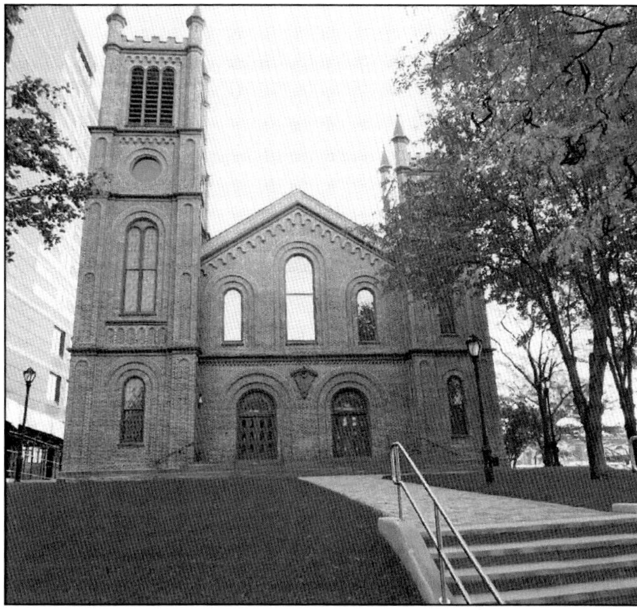

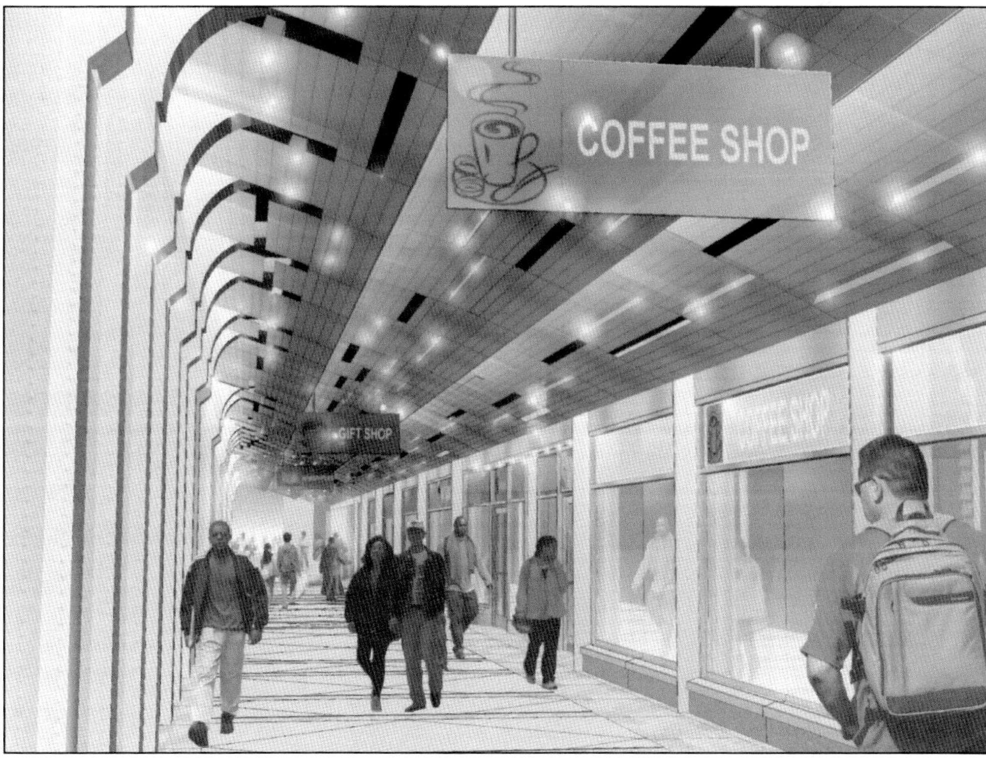

Greater Jamaica Development Corporation is managing a $12 million project to reclaim a series of loading docks and a railroad underpass located across from the AirTrain/Long Island Rail Road Jamaica Station complex on Sutphin Boulevard for productive use. This undertaking will transform the underpass into an attractive, pedestrian-friendly space with special lighting, new signage, improved access to trains and buses, and new retail space. The project will be completed in 2011. (Greater Jamaica Development Corporation.)

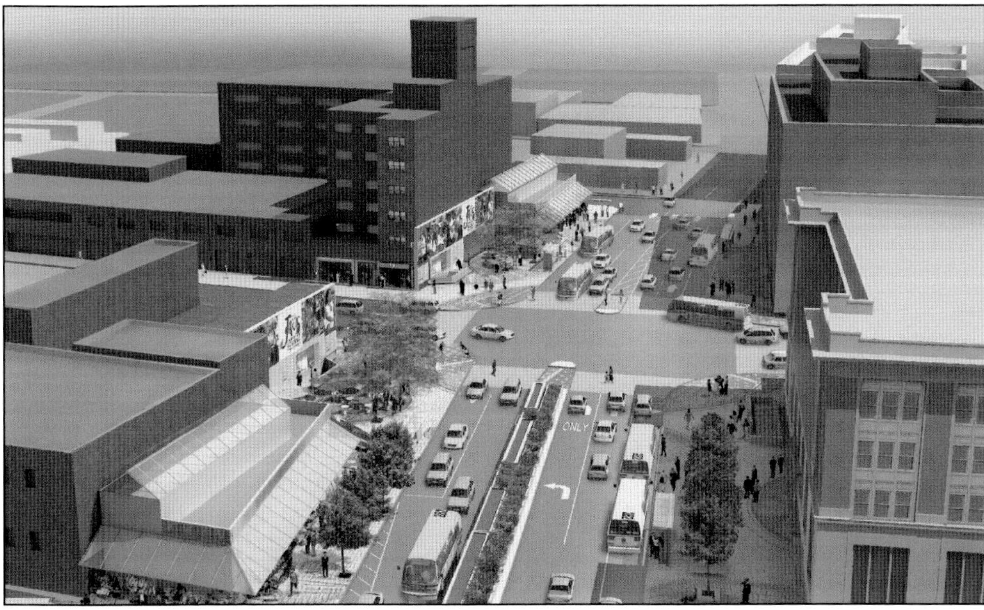

A series of public space and infrastructure improvements being managed by Greater Jamaica Development Corporation will transform Station Plaza (the area surrounding the AirTrain/Jamaica Station complex) into a welcoming and attractive gateway to Downtown Jamaica, with improved accessibility, safer intersections accommodating more pedestrians and new bus traffic, enhanced public plazas, new park and green open space, decorative landscaping, lighting, and new informative signage. Looking east on Archer Avenue, Sutphin Boulevard intersection is seen in the center. (Greater Jamaica Development Corporation.)

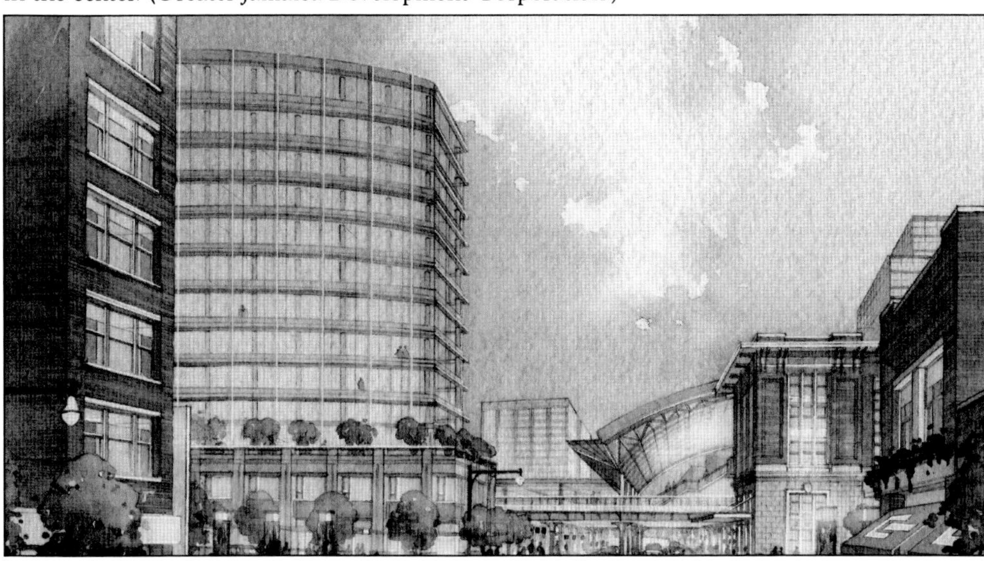

Reclaiming urban space and rebuilding infrastructure has catalyzed and supported the development of a vibrant, sustainable, and livable Downtown Jamaica featuring a wealth of retail and commercial activities, new affordable and market-rate housing, unmatched access to the New York metropolitan region and JFK International Airport, and new civic activities and communities that reflect the neighborhood's rich history and cultural diversity. This illustration shows Sutphin Boulevard, looking south from the Archer Avenue intersection. (Rendering by Thomas W. Schaller.)

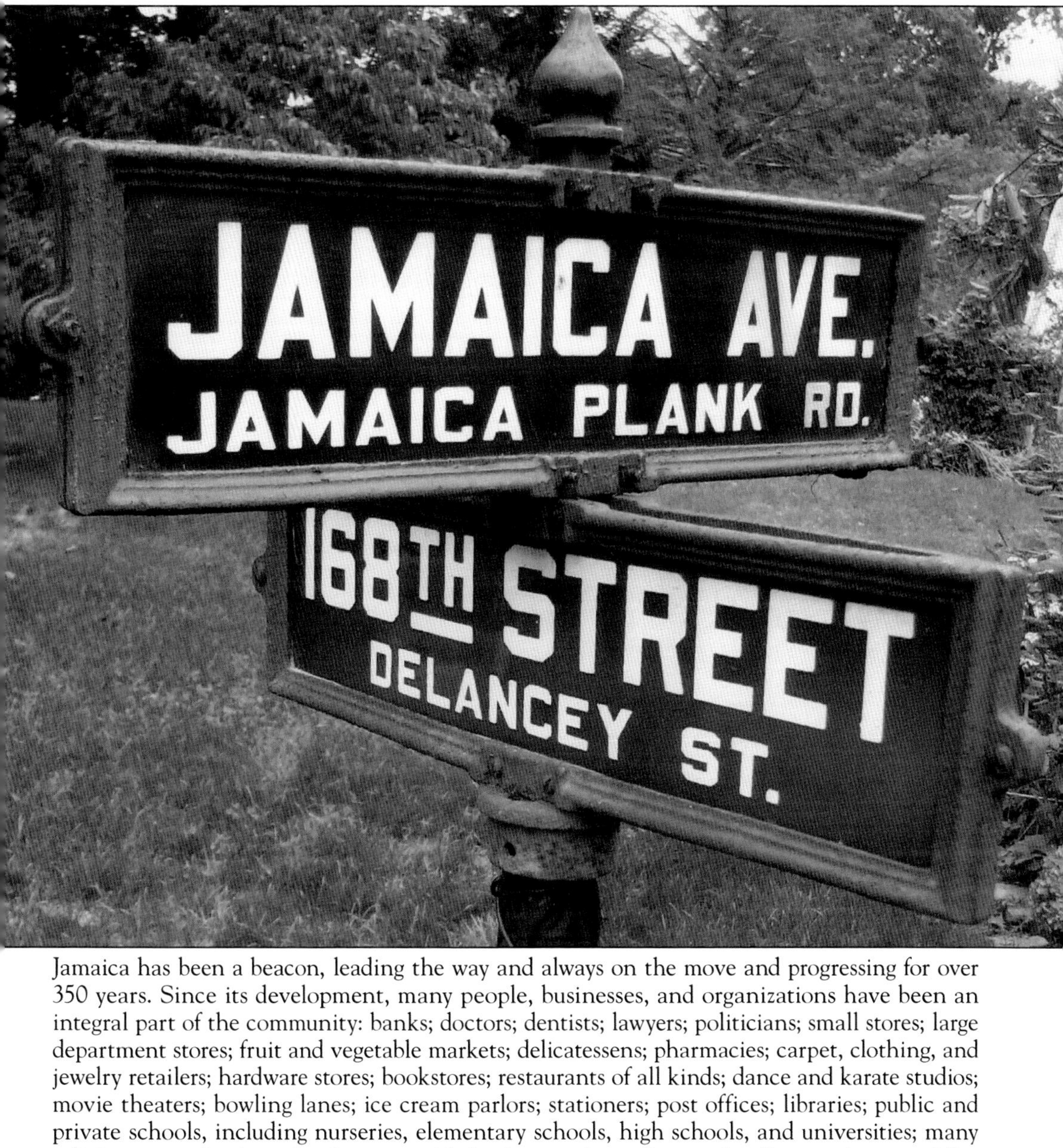

Jamaica has been a beacon, leading the way and always on the move and progressing for over 350 years. Since its development, many people, businesses, and organizations have been an integral part of the community: banks; doctors; dentists; lawyers; politicians; small stores; large department stores; fruit and vegetable markets; delicatessens; pharmacies; carpet, clothing, and jewelry retailers; hardware stores; bookstores; restaurants of all kinds; dance and karate studios; movie theaters; bowling lanes; ice cream parlors; stationers; post offices; libraries; public and private schools, including nurseries, elementary schools, high schools, and universities; many religious organizations that have provided solace and comfort; and police precincts and fire stations, whose personnel have continued to protect and serve. Last but not least are the citizens who call Jamaica home and who have created a vital, diverse, and harmonious community. They are all the caretakers of Jamaica.